Media and the Make-Believe Worlds of Children

When Harry Potter Meets Pokémon in Disneyland

LEA'S COMMUNICATION SERIES
Jennings Bryant/Dolf Zillmann, General Editors

Selected Titles in Media Education (Robert Kubey and Renee Hobbs, Advisory Editors) include:

Davies • Fake, Fact, and Fantasy: Children's Interpretation of Television Reality

Hart • Teaching the Media: International Perspectives

Livingstone and Bovill • Children and Their Changing Media Environment: A European Comparative Study

Tyner • Literacy in a Digital World: Teaching and Learning in the Age of Information

For a complete list of titles in LEA's Communication Series, please contact Lawrence Erlbaum Associates, Publishers at www.erlbaum.com

Media and the Make-Believe Worlds of Children

When Harry Potter Meets Pokémon in Disneyland

Maya Götz
Bavarian Broadcasting Corporation, Munich, Germany

Dafna Lemish
Tel Aviv University, Tel Aviv, Israel

Amy Aidman
University of Illinois, Urbana-Champaign

Heysung Moon
Yonsei University, Seoul, South Korea

LEA LAWRENCE ERLBAUM ASSOCIATES, PUBLISHERS
2005   Mahwah, New Jersey   London

HQ
784
.M3
M418
2005

Lawrence Erlbaum Associates, Inc., Publishers
10 Industrial Avenue
Mahwah, New Jersey 07430
www.erlbaum.com

Cover design by Kathryn Houghtaling Lacey

Library of Congress Cataloging-in-Publication Data

Media and the make-believe worlds of children : when Harry Potter meets Pokémon in Disneyland / Maya Götz ... [et al.].
    p. cm. — (LEA's communication series)
A study of 193 children in Germany, Israel, South Korea, and the USA.
Results of research workshops, lectures, and symposia presented in international conferences: the International Association for Mass Communication Research annual conference in Barcelona, July 2002; Children, Games, Toys, and Media, in London, August 2002; International Communication Association annual conference in San Diego, May 2003; and with the database finally analyzed into an "integrative book" in the summer of 2004.
    Includes bibliographical references and index.
ISBN 0-8058-5191-7 (cloth : alk. paper)
ISBN 0-8058-5192-5 (pbk. : alk. paper)
    1. Mass media and children—Cross-cultural studies—Congresses. 2. Fantasy in children—Cross-cultural studies—Congresses. 3. Self-perception in children—Cross-cultural studies—Congresses. 4. Role models—Cross-cultural studies—Congresses. 5. Imagination in children—Cross-cultural studies—Congresses. 6. Creative ability in children—Cross-cultural studies—Congresses. I. Title: Harry Potter meets Pokémon in Disneyland. II. Götz, Maya. III. International Communication Association. Conference (2002 : Barcelona, Spain) IV. International Communication Association. Conference (2002 : London, England) V. International Communication Association. Conference (2002 : San Diego, Calif.) VI. Series.

HQ784.M3M418 2005
302.23'083—dc22

    2004065605
    CIP

Books published by Lawrence Erlbaum Associates are printed on acid-free paper, and their bindings are chosen for strength and durability.

Printed in the United States of America
10 9 8 7 6 5 4 3 2 1

Contents

III CENTRAL THEMES: GENDER AND CULTURE

IV CONCLUSION

Preface

Almost anybody who spends time around children can attest to the fact that they incorporate their favorite media texts in their everyday lives. Children talk about media texts, dress up, and engage in fantasy play based on these texts, create imaginary companions from them, make related artwork, and exhibit other behaviors that show the importance the media play in their lives. We too, can recall our childhood experiences: Maya was inspired by Karl May's, *Winnetou*, in her fantasy of galloping a horse as the daughter of a Native American Chief; Dafna imagined a "*Secret Garden*" inhabited by fairytale dwarfs; Amy daydreamed about an "Old Witch Tree," with the supernatural power to grant wishes; and Hyesung fantasized about European forests she has seen in many Disney movies and fairytale books.

Research findings to date, however, mostly emphasize the negative potential that media, and television in particular, might play in the development and flourishing of children's imagination and creative abilities. We wanted to try to attain a broader understanding of these processes, not from a binary position of good or bad, but from children's points of view. What role do the media have in their make-believe worlds?

Rooted in the theoretical and methodological perspective of humanistic psychology and reception studies approaches, we wanted to allow children's authentic voices to be heard in their multiple complementary ways, and in a manner that would allow indirect investigation of the role of media in children's make-believe worlds. We also wanted to do so in a cross-cultural framework.

We therefore embarked on this very ambitious and painstaking research journey in Germany, Israel, South Korea, and the United States.

The first chapter of this book outlines the central debates and research findings in the area of children, fantasy worlds, and the media. These are grounded primarily in psychoanalytical and psychological cognitive developmental theories and studied through a host of experimental and field studies grounded in behaviorist research traditions. We present our critique and the theoretical foundations for our search for an alternative approach for studying the role of media in children's fantasyworlds.

Chapter 2 describes the method we designed for achieving this goal. As we, the researchers, experimented with "fantasy" process described in detail in the chapter, we became even more convinced of its utility. Generated through this process, the findings based on 193 children's fantasy stories are discussed in the following chapters. First, we provide a descriptive account of children's make-believe worlds (chap. 3) and the children's wishes for actions they would like to take in these worlds (chap. 4). We found that children compose very rich worlds and place themselves in them in ways that both empower and give them self-worth. These two chapters prepare us for the analysis of the media "traces" that we have found in children's make-believe worlds. We adopted the term, *traces*, to indicate signs of the presence of media texts in children's fantasyworlds without assigning them a particular value or psychological interpretation that other terms, like *media dependency*, for example, might carry. Chapter 5 highlights the centrality of media in children's make-believe worlds, but in contrast to previous research, it also emphasizes the multiple creative ways in which children use media as resources in their environment to express their own inner worlds.

Our analysis highlights two central comparative themes. Our discussion of gender differences (chap. 6) suggests the various ways in which the tension between, on the one hand, traditional gender portrayals that continue to dominate media texts and, on the other hand, children's wishes to act, are presented in their fantasies. We find that both girls and boys are restricted by media offerings. However, girls in particular go through painstaking efforts to mold media characters and narratives to fit their own desires and interests.

We tackle the second comparative theme; the complicated, heavily value-laden issue of cultural comparison in chapter 7. The four countries represented in this study share much in common; they are all very developed, thriving democracies with rich media offerings for children, both local and global. At the same time, each represents very different cultural, historical, religious, and political backgrounds. How do these similarities and differences fare in children's make-believe worlds? Although we found that children across the four countries share many of the same fantasies, regardless of their differing backgrounds, they also include many expressions of their local contexts in their fantasies. Here, too, the concept of traces proves to be valuable both theoretically as well as methodologically; we analyze cultural signs in children's make-believe worlds, rather than compare the four cultures to one another.

Cross-cultural sensitivity and awareness was a theme in the project's international research workshops (May 2001; September 2001; December 2001; March 2002; May 2002) and in a host of lectures and symposia conducted by the researchers in the four countries. Following the gathering and analysis in each country, Götz and Lemish took the lead in analyzing the entire database and writing the integrative book with the input of Aidman and Moon; presenting it at international conferences (International Association for Mass Communication Research annual conference in Barcelona, July 2002; Children, Games, Toys, and Media, in London, August 2002; International Communication Association annual conference in San Diego, May 2003); and finally summarizing the project in the summer of 2004.

Finally, as we unite our various findings in the conclusion chapter (chap. 8), we demonstrate the value of research projects such as this one in unveiling the complicated ways in which media are woven into the fabric of children's everyday lives, the creative and sophisticated uses they make of their contents, and the responsibility that producers of media texts for children have in offering them a wide array of role models and narratives to use in their fantasies.

Preparing this book took us personally across cultures, national borders, and methodological barriers. We were inspired and challenged in our work with one another (even though we did not even share a common language). We have grown intellectually and spiritually by the special privilege of visiting the fantasy worlds of so many creative children. This "Fanta Project," as we affectionately nicknamed it, would not have been possible without the sponsorship of the International Central Institute for Youth and Educational Television (IZI; Internaionales Zentralinstitut für das Jugend-und Bildungsfernsehen) of the Bavarian Broadcasting Corporation (Bayerischer Rundfunk) in Munich, Germany. We are deeply grateful for the support that made all of this a reality.

Many talented and enthusiastic assistants helped us in the various stages of the project: In Germany, Heike Becker, Karin Brunner, Miriam Brehm, Zoltan Heger, Susanne Reichenberger, and Ingrid Schrepf, among others; In Israel, Ola Qodha, Shiri Reznik, Vered Seidmann, and Michal Tirosh; In South Korea, Kyungyun Hwang, Geumsuk Oh, Eunjin Pyun, Eunmi Shin, and Youjung Yang; and, Georgette Comuntzis-Page in the United States. We thank them all deeply.

Several colleagues contributed insights to this project at various points in the process. In particular, we would like to thank David Buckingham, Ruth Etienne

Klemm, Lothar Mikos, Norbert Neuss, Norma Pecora, Ellen Seiter, Jeseph Tobin, and Reinhart Winter.

We are grateful to Robert Kubey, advisory editor for LEA's Communication Series, and Linda Bathgate, editor at Lawrence Erlbaum Associates for believing in the merit of this project and giving us direction; to Providence Rao, for guiding the book production professionally and efficiently; and Kathryn Scornavacca for her professional copy-editing.

Our loving families who stood by us as we were engaged in our own personal "Fanta" deserve our deepest gratitude. We spent many days away from them traveling all over the world to attend international workshops and conferences where we presented this work and incorporated colleagues' feedback. Special thanks go to our spouses, Ole Hofmann, Peter Lemish, Uriel Kitron, and Seontae Kim for their loving support, insights, and solid advice. Two of our partners were also professional colleagues in this project: we are deeply indebted to Ole Hofmann for his technological expertise and ingenuity and to Peter Lemish for his theoretical insights and editorial proficiency.

But most of all we thank the 193 children in Germany, Israel, South Korea, and the United States who shared with us their innermost dreams and wishes for a better world. This book is dedicated to making their wishes come true.

—Maya Götz
—Dafna Lemish
—Amy Aidman
—Heysung Moon

About the Authors

Maya Götz (PhD, University of Kassel, 1998) is Head of the International Center Institute for Youth and Educational Television (IZI) of the Bavarian Broadcasting Corporation, and lecturer at the University of Kassel and at the Munich Academy of Television and Film, Germany. Her research areas are children, youth, and television; and gender reception studies. Her publications include *Girls and Television: Media Appropriation in Female Adolescence* (Munich: KoPäd, 1999, in German); *Only Soap Bubbles? The Significance of Daily Soaps for the Everyday Life of Children and Adolescents* (Munich: KoPäd, 2002, in German); and many book chapters and articles, mostly in German.

> Maya's exciting make-believe world took her back to the age of eight in Germany, when she imagined herself to be the daughter of a Native American chief. She pictured herself as she galloped on a special horse through the plains of the Wild West, wisely protecting her tribe from attacks by cowboys. Her story revealed the role of films and phonograph records based on Karl May's character of Winnetou (but not the books themselves, which she thought at the time were boring ...).

Dafna Lemish (PhD, Ohio State University, 1982) is Associate Professor and Chair of the Department of Communication at Tel Aviv University, Israel. Her research, teaching, and activism focus on the role of media in children's lives and on gender and media representations and consumption. Her publications include *Growing Up With Television: The Little Screen in the Lives of Children and Youth* (Tel Aviv: Open University, 2003, in Hebrew); *Media Education Around the Globe: Policies and Practices* (edited with B. Tufte and T. Lavender, Hampton

Press, 2003); and many book chapters and articles in international academic journals, as well as media-literacy textbooks for the educational system in Israel.

> Dafna's beautiful "Secret Garden" was inhabited by many colorful and smiling little dwarfs, but surrounded by a thick wall and a heavy gate that always kept her outside and in search of a way into the garden. This make-believe world was reminiscent of the rare chrome pictures in an English book of The Grimm Brothers' Fairytales that she loved to look at as a little girl, brought to Israel from New York (although she couldn't read the text ....).

Amy Aidman (PhD, University of Illinois at Urbana-Champaign, 1993) is Assistant Dean in the College of Communications at the University of Illinois at Urbana-Champaign and has faculty appointments with the Institute of Communications Research and the Graduate School of Library and Information Science at the University of Illinois. She is the former Research Director for the Center for Media Education, a Washington, DC-based research and policy organization. Her scholarly activities center on the relationship between children and media, media literacy, and media policy and culture. Her writing includes articles and essays in the academic and mainstream press on these topics.

> Amy's fantasy took her back to her early childhood in Ohio, where she used to play in the woods next to her house. There she used her vivid imagination to contact the spirit of a tree known as the "Old Witch Tree" with a wish about her family's upcoming move to Miami. Her wish was to continue to be with the same extended family and friends, even though her nuclear family was moving. Her fantasy tells the story of envisioning fun on the beach in Miami with her family, but without losing the connection to loved ones in Ohio.

Hyesung Moon (PhD, University of Bielefeld, 1999) is Senior Research Fellow at the Institute for Educational Research, Yonsei University, Seoul, Korea. Her research areas are media education and analysis, and consumption of information technology. Her publications include *Between Confucianism and European Thinking: Children, Youth and Culture-Information Programs in Korea and Germany: An Educational and Social-Economic Analysis of the Media Culture in Asian and European Societies* (Hamburg: Kovac, 1999, in German); and articles on media education in Korean.

> Hyesung's make-believe world took her away from the big city of Seoul, where she was raised, to a wonderful European forest seen in many Disney films and fairytale books. There she was particularly happy—as she enjoyed being with the animals and listened to classical music in the background. However, she did not incorporate Cinderella and Snow White in her make-believe world, as they look so different from herself.

I

Studying Make-Believe Worlds

1

Children's Fantasy World and the Media: A Theoretical Introduction

"Television kills the imagination" is a common conclusion about the relationship between children and television. But does it? The questions raised in public discourse on the possible negative effects of media on the development of children are reviewed in this introductory chapter. We build on the many approaches to the concept of *fantasy* and proceed through various conceptualizations of children's fantasy world and its manifestations in psychological terms. The review and critique of research conducted on the relationships between media and children's fantasy world will lead us to offer our own alternative approach at the conclusion of the chapter.

Throughout history, questions and conjecture about fantasy and its significance for individuals and in society and culture have elicited scholarly and public debate. Fantasy is a powerful psychological process that enables human beings to create new ideas and concepts in their minds by building on existing ones. Aristotle saw in fantasy an element of order; Leonardo de Vinci emphasized its visionary capacities; Immanuel Kant attributed to it an ability to enlighten. In the age of Romanticism, fantasy became the creative principle of the whole universe. Percy Bysshe Shelley saw imagination as a capacity for seeing similarity in differences; and for John Dewey, it was making a conscious adjustment between the new and the old. For Theodor Adorno and for Ernst Bloch, fantasies are the bases for designing future utopias (Brann, 1991; Ränsch-Trill,

1996). Concurrently, the concern over the potentially harmful impacts of medi-ated texts on the imagination and creative processes, particularly with respect to children, also has roots in these early debates about fantasy. Plato, in ancient Greece, for example, perceived fantasy, images, and myths to be dangerously corruptive forces that shift the mind from conceptual thinking to the world of il-lusions. Print culture, now commonly considered to be valuable for the devel-opment of fantasy, was harshly attacked in the past for the same reason.

Although the range of information available through communication tech-nology and various media have expanded recently, concerns about children and imagination have remained very much the same. The impact of mediated mes-sages on children's imagination and fantasies is embedded in a discourse that can be characterized as "moral panic" about children's culture, in general, and their communication and leisure activities, in particular. With the introduction of each new medium, public response has ranged from major anxiety about po-tential negative effects on children to expressions of hope and visions about the promise for positive uses of new media (e.g., in regard to educational benefits, see Bianculli, 1992; Buckingham, 1993a; Livingstone, 2002; Wartella & Reeves, 1985). Thus, today's questions about the role of the Internet in the lives of children and youth are similar to those that were raised when comic books, film, radio, broadcast television, cable television, and computer games came into children's lives. Concern regarding the influences of content-related vio-lence, pornography, racism, sexism, and so forth, as well as everyday social and physical influences connected to living with mediated culture, are central to these debates. As Drotner (1992) observed, each moral panic tends to start from a position of "pessimistic elitism" and evolves to a stance of "optimistic pluralism." Such debates have spurred calls for technological and legal mea-sures of control (e.g., the V-Chip for controlling violence or "watershed" regula-tions regarding prime-time contents on television) as well as advocacy for media literacy (e.g., Potter, 2001; Tufte, Lavender, & Lemish, 2003) and "better" parenting (e.g., Price & Verhulst, 2002).

When television became a mass medium in the 1950s in the United States, it attracted a groundswell of public and research interest. People wanted to know if television was displacing other valued activities such as reading, doing homework, or spending time in physical play and sports. Research was based on the assumption that television absorbs a significant amount of children's time—time that is better used engaging in activities that spawn cognitive growth (reading, doing homework, creative activities), physical development (sports, outdoor activities), and social development (playing and interacting with peers). Over 40 years ago, Himmelweit, Oppenheim and Vince (1958), in England, and Schramm, Lyle, and Parker (1961), in the United States, set the stage for examining the meaning of the role of television in children's lives. Although the two research efforts were conducted independently, each reinforced the claim that television had indeed brought significant changes in children's schedules and the organization of their out-of-home activities. As Neuman (1991) suggested in retrospect, television seems to replace mainly activities that are functionally similar (e.g., reading comics) or unstructured ones (e.g., "hanging around").

The claim that television viewing is a passive experience for children—one that suppresses both cognition and imagination—has been a common thread in the public debate about the medium. Particularly popular were two books with provocative titles: Winn's, *The Plug-In Drug* (1977, 2002) and Mander's, *Four Arguments for the Elimination of Television* (1978). Lashing out against television, these books framed their arguments in terms of it being a hypnotic drug that should be banned. Both books were based on assumptions of children's lack of control over their viewing experiences and the numbing of creative cognitive processes. Television viewing was presented as an experience devoid of cognition and moral judgment. More specifically: "It is the erosion—or elimination—of the imagination that is perhaps the most worrying aspect of TV's hidden curriculum" (Nelson, 1988, cited in Messenger-Davies, 1989, p. 137). From this perspective, the child viewer is but a passive receptacle and the visual nature of television robs children of the opportunity to form images in their own minds as with reading books.

At the beginning of the third millennium, it is difficult to think about children's everyday lives (as well as our own) without the wide variety of media that have spread throughout the world and are continuing to be disseminated to the far reaches of the planet: television, computers, video-recording devices, video cameras, game-consoles, radio, disc and tape players, magazines, newspapers, books, movie theaters, cellular phones—and the list is constantly growing as new technologies are developed. The centrality of these media for understanding the construction of childhood and family, as well as for problematizing everyday life in late modernity is the focus of much of the current literature in this area (Livingstone, 2002; Livingstone & Bovill, 2001; Roberts & Foehr, 2004). Over the years, research has begun to investigate areas beyond media effects and to ask questions concerning the meaning and context of engagement with media.

When it comes to the discussion of the role of media in children's fantasy life, we find many case studies that offer rich descriptions that illustrate the potential connections between media texts and children's imagination and play: Embracing Ernie from *Sesame Street* as an imaginary companion in the United States (Taylor, 1999); playing *Batman* (Neuss, 1999), or *Dragon Ball Z* games in

Germany (Götz, 2003); imitating *Power Rangers* (Jones, 2003), or playing out the roles of friends in *Neighbors* in England (Messenger-Davies, 1989); aspiring to be like a member of the *Spice Girls* pop group (Lemish, 1998) or a *Pokémon Master* in Israel (Lemish & Bloch, 2004)—to name just a few. Clearly these everyday experiences suggest the existence of an intense relationship between media culture and children's fantasy world. Cumulatively, these studies lead to quite a different conclusion from the previous one.

As Huston et al. (1992) quoted from the American Psychological Association Task Force's report: "any casual observer of children is well aware that television characters and content serve as the basis for a great deal of imaginative play" (p. 90). Similarly, the Australian Senate Committee in 1978 reported:

> It was claimed that the escapist material mainly watched by children is stifling children's imagination and the development of their creative instincts. The committee was given numerous examples of how television characters and plots permeate through the daily lives of children. Their school compositions are based on television plots, their play is a re-enactment of television action scenes and their conversation centres on the programmes they watch. (cited in Hodge & Tripp, 1986, p. 100)

So what then, is the nature of the relationship between mediated texts and children's fantasy worlds? We first examine some central notions in the understanding of the world of fantasy in children's development, and then move to discuss what research can reveal about the relationship between media and children's fantasies.

CHILDREN'S FANTASY WORLD

The term *fantasy* originates from the Greek, *phantazesthai*, which means "to appear," "bring to light," or to "appear before the soul." *Phantasia* describes the ability to uncover something and to make it visible. The verb, *phantazesthai*, is specifically used for the having of memories, dreams, and hallucinations. "Phantasia-imagination" is the capacity for inner appearances, and for internal sense presentation, which resemble external perceptions (Brann, 1991, p. 21).

Fantasy is assumed to be a product of memory. That is, it is a free rearrangement of recollected or newly produced inner images of a vivid visual nature. Therefore fantasy, as used interchangeably with imagination, is commonly assumed to be based on the real world and uses it as a starting point from which to wonder. New visions and experiences come into being formed out of our impressions of reality. Imagination requires the ability to represent in one's mind, people, places, events, objects and the like through the working of abstract thought. In doing so, the person becomes a "creator," as the imagination is a prerequisite of creativity characterized by the involvement of new or unusual elements as well as their potential meaningfulness for others (Barron, 1969; D. G. Singer, 1993).

Various theoretical frames and conceptualizations of the human being have been proposed to explain the creation of fantasy processes (J. L. Singer, 1975). In Freudian psychoanalytic theory, for example, fantasies are viewed as being both primary thought processes that are attached to instincts and unconscious desires of the self, as well as secondary thought processes that are connected to consciousness (Freud, 1958; Pruyser, 1983). Most importantly, fantasies, as a form of private theater, fulfill important desires for the person as well as provide opportunities for personal growth. This psychological reality is just as important for Freud's analysis as the person's involvement in material, physical reality and is of great value in its own right, even when not linked to the real world. Therefore the common distinction made between fantasy and reality is not deemed important in Freud's view (Hipfel, 1997). Such processes are just as important for actual psychotherapy practices that follow Freudian theory, as fantasy play was used as a form of reducing internal drives—such as aggression in children, as well as in the development of the theory of catharsis (e.g., Feshbach, 1955). For example, Bruno Bettelheim (1976) analyzed the crucial role that fairy tales have in children's psychological development through the stories' symbolic representation of universal childhood anxieties and reassuring pleasures.

From a different theoretical perspective, according to Piaget's cognitive developmental psychology, fantasy is a construction of an inner reality adjusted to the needs of one's self. Inner representations are necessary in order to evoke perceptions and thought (Piaget & Inhelder, 1969) and therefore the cognitive process of fantasizing, or imagination, is the creation of symbols that differ from reality and vary from person to person (Piaget, 1969; Piaget & Inhelder, 1969). A large body of experimental psychology research has followed this line of argument in investigating the development of inner pictures and their relationship to cognitive development (summarized, e.g., in Singer, 1975, 1980). In the process of developing an identity, the child plays with these inner pictures as a way of processing experiences, struggling with challenges, and developing a self-image.

Piaget (1951) discussed the importance and similarity of these mechanisms in child development. Piaget understood the roles of imitation, symbolic play, and cognitive imagination as a means through which the child seeks to achieve an equilibrium between assimilation and accommodation. In this sense, fantasy activities serve as opportunities to work through symbolic conflicts and fears that result in production of images, stories, and so forth, that serve as symbolic compensation for emotional failures and/or unfulfilled desires (Piaget, 1951). During fantasy play, the child reproduces experiences in symbolic ways. According to Piaget, it functions to enable the assimilation of reality to the self, and therefore liberation from the necessity of accommodation (Piaget, 1969). Although imitation is perceived as "a continuation of accommodation for its own sake" (Piaget, 1969, p. 87), fantasy play is equated with assimilation. More specifically, "unlike objective thought, which seeks to adapt itself to the requirements of external reality, imaginative play is a symbolic transposition which subjects things to the child's activity, without rules or limitations. It is almost pure assimilation ... " (Piaget, 1969, p. 87).

Children's Articulations of Fantasy

Children's fantasy worlds are evident in a variety of forms and are influenced greatly by both developmental and environmental factors. Klinger (1971) argued that fantasies reflect the kind of topics that are of major concern to both the particular age group the child belongs to as well as the individual child's self-concept and personal goals. Fantasy play is a common avenue through which children act out their fantasies in what Cohen and MacKeith (1991) termed as the category of *simple creative behaviors* that can be either transmutatory, animistic, or appear as the inventing of people. These patterns of behavior are most common for children between the ages of 3 to 6, starting from about the age of 2 ½ years and reaching a peak at about 5 years of age (Fein, 1981; Klinger 1971; Piaget 1969; J. L. Singer & Switzer, 1980). Imaginary companions, particularly popular with 2-to 6-year-olds can have a role in their lives for a long time (Taylor, 1999). These humans, animals, or creatures exist only in the minds of their inventors and are known only to them and through them to their close associates. It is commonly assumed that children do not plan their imaginary companions or construct them consciously; rather, they just "find" them. They appear suddenly and without warning, as an idea or an image. This is especially the case with children who have vivid fantasies or who may be in cognitive or emotionally challenging situations (such as separation anxiety, envy over the birth of a new sibling, or other life-changing events).

Another type of imaginary activity can be observed when children personally act a part in a role play or other imaginary game or activity. They can either imagine being a machine, a living thing, or another person. However, they can also enact an incident. Cohen and MacKeith (1991) also distinguished between forms of imagined participation in the action of the stories of others. Here, children hear a story, read a story, or produce a play with a standard plot.

Imaginative play, acting "as if" in the make-believe world, can make a significant contribution to children's cognitive, social, and emotional development. Research evidence suggests that engaging in imaginative play in children is associated with increased abilities to concentrate, and with exhibiting empathy, happiness, self-assurance, and flexibility in unfamiliar situations. It also has been argued that imaginative play is positively related to creativity in the adult years (D. G. Singer & J. L. Singer, 1990).

Fantasy stories constitute another category suggested by Cohen and MacKeith (1991) as a typical part of children's fantasy repertoire. These can either be free-floating day-dreams during waking hours or before sleep, presleep serial stories, day-time structured stories, or even *paracosms*, which are imaginary worlds that last for a longer time in the child's life.

Related to fantasy play and the development of imagination, children's daydreaming behavior is the mental experience of fantasy in the waking state. The child's attention is directed inward, into his or her thoughts and images stored in memory (J. L. Singer, 1975). Thus, daydreams can be perceived as a form of internalized self-entertainment that employ pictures and internal monologues (D. G. Singer & J. L. Singer, 1990).

Psychological research understands *daydreams* or *waking fantasies*, as the imagining, inventing, and thinking up of unreal, feared, or desired situations. These can include a range of genuinely mentally challenging actions, such as anticipation of a problematic situation in everyday life. They can also include dreams that express great desires or fantastic adventures in which reality can be overcome in spite of limitations that would be at work in the real world. The various components of the fantasy, which are rooted in real experience, can be joined together to create new combinations and therefore make possible what is impossible. Much like dreams, daydreams, are wish fulfillment according to the Freudian perspective: "The motive forces of phantasies are unsatisfied wishes, and every single phantasy is the fulfilment of a wish, a correction of unsatisfying reality" (Freud, 1908/1995, p. 146).

The most significant difference between night dreams and daydreams, or waking fantasies, lies in the role of social interactions. The active "I" takes over in the narrative of the fantasy in a waking state and is vividly displayed, whether it is in a friendly or an aggressive role. Fantasies in the waking state also differ from night dreams in their characteristic positive emotional quality and typical positive endings (Strauch, 2004).

To date, it is clear that researchers have yet to find a direct way by which to approach children's inner pictures as well as the feelings and episodes embodied within them. We may see them engrossed in daydreaming and wish we could have a peek into their minds while they are experiencing their imagined worlds. However, children often articulate their fantasies in clearly observable ways: they talk, they play, they draw, they engage in private speech. Although children's fantasies never face us in a pure, unmediated form, they are "worked out" in the various ways of expression. Thus, as students of children's fantasies, we can attempt to observe, listen, and interpret them through a broad, varied, in-depth investigation of their many manifestations.

TELEVISION AND CHILDREN'S FANTASY WORLD

Research on the relationships between media and fantasy world have been conceptualized and investigated in the medium of television in general from two perspectives. One area of research involves the question of children's understandings of the fantasy-related characteristics of television. The other approach questions the effects of television viewing on children's fantasy worlds. We turn now to a brief summary of the state of research in these areas.

Understanding Fantasy on Television

The ability of young children to distinguish between reality and fantasy and the changes that occur in those perceptions over time have received attention in the field of developmental psychology, in particular with respect to television. Recent reviews of the literature on the development of the perceptions of young children of what is real on television suggest the need for a multidimensional conceptual approach because of the complexity of the issue involved (Chandler, 1997; Fitch, Huston, & Wright, 1993; Messenger-Davies, 1997).

Studies indicate that children use two principal types of criteria to make distinctions between fantasy and reality on television. Hodge and Tripp (1986) used the twin concepts of *external* versus *internal dimension*. By external dimension, they mean the reliance of children on their knowledge of the real world that results from their individual life experiences. The well known concepts used by Hawkins (1977) of television as a "magic window" to the world and of "social expectations" from it are but two examples of this type of external dimension.

Similarly, Dorr (1983) specified three levels of the external dimension. The first, typical of the thinking of very young viewers, refers to the concreteness of the television image. "One may say that something on television is real and mean it is exactly as it is without television" (p. 202). This level is also referred to by other researchers as "factuality" (Fitch et al., 1993). Dorr's other two levels accept the fabricated nature of the television world and judge each specific content according to the criteria of possibility or probability. Are events, characters, messages, and so forth, as presented on television, deemed possible in the real world; or are they deemed representative and thus probable in reality? For example, typical events in a soap-opera episode are possible in real life (e.g., interracial marriages, alcoholism, extra-marital affairs, abortions, the return of a lost son, etc.). However, the probability of all of them happening in one family in a short period of time is slim.

The second group of criteria for judging television reality has been defined by researchers as relating to the internal properties of the program, namely those related to the formal features of television. These are part of the syntax of television and often serve as markers to convey transitions in program content, within programs, and between television genres. According to a line of research developed at the Center for the Research on the Influences of Television on Children at the University of Kansas at the time and summarized by Fitch et al. (1993), formal features also serve as cues through which children learn to perceive the reality of television content and to classify programs. By kindergarten age, children begin to identify the grouping of television programs that are distinguished by the co-occurring features of form and content. For example, these features are already used by young viewers to define animation as unrealistic, whereas news is perceived by them to be realistic. Similarly, children learn to identify commercials as a distinct genre.

These two interacting dimensions—external and internal—can also be framed (applying definitions of Fitch et al.'s, 1993) as "real-world knowledge" versus "television-related knowledge." Both forms of knowledge are used by viewers, in varying degrees, to make sense of the reality of television and for genre classifications. For example, children's real-world experience teaches them that people are not capable of flying or winning fistfights with dozens of people at once. Their experience with television teaches them that animation indicates fiction whereas news formats suggest real-world stories. The demand to organize the world of television according to the integration of both these dimensions and to establish content and form expectations of different programs seems to be a central cognitive task undertaken by young viewers in particular.

Television and Children's Creativity, Imagination, and Play

The question of whether various media, particularly television, do indeed impact on children's creativity, imagination, and play—either positively or negatively—has been the focus of various studies throughout the years.

Relationships with Creativity and Imagination. Several early correlational as well as experimental studies found negative relationships between television viewing and children's scores on a variety of creative tasks such as thinking, problem solving, and writing abilities. Although individual studies may be challenged on conceptual or methodological grounds, the accumulative picture concurs with the popular belief that heavy television use, particularly of a violent nature, indeed impedes the development of children's creative abilities (for extensive reviews and critic, see, e.g., MacBeth, 1996; D. G. Singer, 1993; Valkenburg, 2001).

Among the more influential of these studies was Williams' (1986) comparative natural experiment conducted in a Canadian town she named Notel, as it had no television. Although similar in demographics and transportation connections to other small towns in the area, it differed by the fact that it was not able for a long time to receive the television signals due to its particular geographical location in a valley. Williams studied that town during the period prior to the introduction of television and the 2 years following its introduction. Further, she compared it to two demographically similar towns—Unitel (a town that had one television channel), and Multitel (a town with a few television stations). The comparison between children in the pre- and post-television period in Notel as well as the comparison to children in the two other communities revealed interesting findings. One of the most remarkable of them was the fact that the Notel children rated higher on tests of creativity in comparison with children in the two other towns, and these scores went down in the tests performed 2 years after the introduction of television. Although these findings, too, have been challenged and debated by other researchers, the study has continued to fuel and inspire a lively debate on the possibility that indeed a causal negative relationship does exist between television viewing and creativity and imagination.

Several researchers investigated how various media differ as stimuli of creativity and imagination. One area of research focused on whether a televised version of a story stimulates more or less creative ideas, story lines, and problem solving abilities than the same story told verbally (as in audio or print forms). A series of studies along these lines were conducted by Greenfield and colleagues, among others, comparing the influence of television with that of radio (Greenfield, Farrer, & Beagles-Roos, 1986; Greenfield & Beagles-Roos, 1988). These studies confirmed the hypothesis that processes of imagination (operationalized as any form of representational activity that creates new entities such as characters or events) were better stimulated by radio than by television. Rolandelli's (1989) review of these and other studies explained that the visual superiority effect of television is confounded by the advantages of the auditory-verbal track for comprehension. Once again, a host of related methodological and conceptual issues arise from these and other studies, as the reviews suggest (e.g., MacBeth, 1996; D. G. Singer, 1993).

Relationships with Fantasy Play.   The role of television as a stimulant of fantasy play is another area of research based on the hypothesis that television viewing may displace free play (Schramm et al., 1961). Singer and colleagues at Yale University conducted much of this research, with a specific concentration on the young children and imaginative play (see, for example, D. G. Singer, 1993; J. L. Singer & D. G. Singer, 1976, 1983). Their accumulated work, as well as that of other studies, suggests that ultimately, the types of content children watch is more important in determining outcomes of fantasy and imaginative play than the quantity of time spent viewing. One related finding is that fantasy violence in television content may inhibit or take the place of imaginative play, whereas certain educational prosocial programming may actually encourage it (such as *Mister Rogers' Neighborhood*).

These general conclusions were reinforced in van der Voort and Valkenburg's (1994) review of research on television's impact on children's fantasy play (interchangeably termed also *pretend, make-believe,* or *imaginative play*) defined as "play in which the child transcends the constraints of reality by acting 'as if'" (p. 27). Children pretend "that they are someone else, that an object represents something else and/or that the participants are in a different place and time" (van der Voort & Valkenburg, 1994, p. 27). Indeed, this study together with the accumulated evidence from studies carried out in North America as well as Europe support the conclusion that viewing violence and action on television decreases fantasy play in children who participated in experimental studies (to be distinguished from imitative violent behavior), while prosocial, nonviolent children's programs had generally no effect on such play. The overall conclusion from these accumulative studies is that television seems to be able to stimulate fantasy play only when it is specifically designed to do so (e.g., *Mister Rogers' Neighborhood*). However, nonexperimental studies suggest the possibility that television stimulates violent fantasy play (such as has been demonstrated in schools in Lemish (1997b) in regard to televised wrestling, or in Seiter's (1999) study of the *Power Rangers*).

Furthermore, based on experts' testimonies, Gunter and McAleer (1997) suggested that most commercial television encourages passive watching rather than active thinking and imagination, and rarely provides opportunities for young children to engage in creative imaginative play, presumed to be essential for their development. "Make-believe play is one of the most important ways in which preschool children learn about their environment. It can help children to develop a large vocabulary, it may play a role in development of sequencing or ordering of events, and it may foster concentration" (p. 171) they argue.

However, van der Voort and Valkenburg's (1994) review also suggests that while studies concerned with the introduction of television (such as Schramm et al., 1961, just discussed) document a decrease of playtime in general, there is no direct evidence that fantasy play decreases proportionately with it. Finally, although recognizing that children use television content in their fantasy play, their review suggests that many questions remain unanswered: for example, the frequency of television's contribution to fantasy play or whether induced play is more or less imaginative than a nontelevision related play. Overall, their conclusion supports Anderson and Collins (1988) who have said that it makes little sense to deliberate whether one kind of imaginative play is of higher quality and more desired than the other.

Relationships With Daydreaming   The Singers' work suggests that television's visually concrete presentational forms inhibit children's daydreaming in comparison to the abstract nature of words in print or spoken language. They assume that the ready-made fantasy world of television does not require a lot of mental effort and the fast pace of the programs does not leave room for daydreaming while watching (e.g., J. L. Singer, 1980; J. L. Singer & D. G. Singer, 1981; J. L. Singer, D. G. Singer, & Rapaczynski, 1984).

Complementary to this conclusion is the hypothesis that television may stimulate program-bound daydreaming; therefore the daydreaming of heavy viewers of violence, for example, will be preoccupied with aggressive themes and superheroes, closely related to their favorite television narratives (Huesmann & Eron, 1986; Valkenburg & van der Voort, 1994). Viewers of programs oriented toward prosocial behaviors such as cooperation, expression of empathy, delay of gratifications, ability to express feelings, and the like, have been found to incorporate such behaviors in their play (Gunter & McAller, 1997; Stein & Friedrich, 1972; van Evra, 1990), and therefore, the argument might follow, the same will happen in their daydreaming as well.

IN SEARCH FOR AN ALTERNATIVE: STUDYING CHILDREN'S "MAKE-BELIEVE WORLDS"

Imaginative activity is of special significance for children because it provides them with a way of appropriating the world. Using fantasy, children process experiences and develop their individual perceptions regarding the world as well as perspectives regarding their future. Through its connection to creativity, fantasy becomes an asset that needs to be enhanced and nourished in children. However, society at large seems to grant young children greater space and leeway in the display of fantasy than older ones, and views certain forms of its expression, such as aggressive forms, with caution (Fraiberg, 1959).

In summary, this brief overview of the accumulating body of knowledge largely suggests that overall negative effects of media on children's creativity, imagination, and fantasy play are stronger than its positive effects. However, it is important to point out that what is known in this area has emerged from the research tradition of media effects. These studies of children and media (for the most part, television) embrace developmental theories in cognitive psychology that center on the individual child. It is a research paradigm with roots in various stimulus–response models whose goal is to find correlations between television content and fantasy activity. The significance that media texts have for children's fantasy world can hardly be encapsulated in studies conducted through experimental designs or derived from correlational studies. Such studies mostly quantify fantasy activities which are defined in advance. Many questions can be raised regarding the type of activities selected for coding and the value judgments attached to them. Reservations can also be made regarding the suitability of the unnatural experimental setting for eliciting and observing fantasy related activities.

We suggest that in many respects these findings still leave us in the dark in terms of understanding the crucial role of media in children's everyday fantasy lives. Reception studies of children and their media (see, e.g., Buckingham, 1993a; Kinder, 1999; Mazzarella & Pecora, 1999; Tobin, 2000, to name just a few) give voice to children's experiences and meanings. In addition, anecdotal stories on experience with children's talk and play tell us there is more to the "story" (see, e.g., Jones', 2002 analysis of interviews with parents and specialists). The question remains as to whether something as complex as fantasy can be understood adequately without letting children themselves articulate it and taking seriously the natural social context in which fantasy occurs in their everyday life—including various forms of interpersonal interaction that occur naturally during play and daydreaming.

There are a number of ways that children can grant us an insight into their inner world of fantasies; for example, via their symbolic transmission into play, conversation, and artwork, such as drawing. Through such articulations, they actively construct their make-believe worlds. We choose the term *make-believe world* over *daydream* in a conscious effort to emphasize both the active and the positive nature of this imaginative construction. The theoretical perspective this study assumes is that children are active meaning-makers who make conscious choices when fantasizing (in contrast, e.g., to night dreaming). Furthermore, because they create make-believe worlds to suit their needs, interests, and desires, it allows them therefore to imagine possibilities that are beyond the realm of their real worlds.

This understanding is in line with the action-theoretical approach to the study of human life that holds at its core the perspective that all humans are action-oriented beings who engage in activities on the basis of their own needs, intentions, interests, and the like (Renckstorf, 1996). Further, the fundamental concept of human beings employed in this study is rooted in the rich traditions offered by phenomenology (e.g., Schütz, 1967), and sociology of knowledge (e.g., Berger & Luckmann, 1966), as well as the perspective shared by all streams of humanistic psychology, as described by Carl Rogers and others (Greening, 1984; Rogers, 1961, 1969a, 1969b; Rogers & Stevens, 1967). These approaches share the perspective that all people, including children, are presumed to act subjectively in meaningful ways based upon their own perspectives, worldviews, and self-image. This approach credits people with conscious awareness of their subjectivity and ability to take responsibility for their own ideas, feelings, and actions in the world. They are able to confront the challenges with which they are faced and solve problems. Human striving for individual development, self-fulfillment, and self-actualization leads to an ever-expanding autonomy that is balanced by a need for social relationships characterized by recognition, positive acceptance, confirmation, and esteem. The ongoing process of managing patterns of experiences with relationships, including those provided by media, is integrated into the concept of self, on which we focus in this study.

According to the humanistic perspective, children are often underestimated by experimental research that is psychologically oriented. In contrast, this study approaches children as socially competent people who actively make sense of the world around them. "Developmental growth," argues Wartella (2002), "is seen as more varied, less uniform and subject to influence by the objects and activities in children's lives" (p. 5). The current discourse on the constructed nature of childhood (Aries, 1962; James, Jenks & Prout, 1998; James & Prout, 1990; Jenks, 1996) and of the characteristics of the socially competent child, credits children with being autonomous individuals who actively participate in meaning-making processes, in much the same way as do adults in other stages of the life cycle.

Such approaches have been advanced in the study of children as media audiences and consumers by a host of researchers, ourselves included (e.g., Aidman, 1999; Buckingham, 1993a, 1993b, 1996, 2000; Buckingham & Bragg, 2004; Fisherkeller, 2002; Götz, 1999, 2003; Lemish, 1997a, 1997b; Lemish & Bloch, 2004; Tobin, 2000). Cumulatively, these studies have found that media are part of children's everyday life experiences and provide both a wide range of content as well as diverse forms of relationships that are integrated into their realities in a way that extends far beyond the moment of consumption. Media-related experiences, like all other sources of experience in the child's environ- ment, are integrated in the process of their developing selves, their relationships with their peers, family members, educators, and even researchers.

With this alternative conceptual framework in mind, we set out to study the role media have in children's active and positive constructions of make-believe worlds. We operationalized these make-believe worlds on the basis of their everyday understanding of their meanings, rather than psychological definitions of cognitive processes. We were interested in the child's experienced fantasies in a waking state, possibly ones that he or she has already experienced prior to the investigation. We labeled this make-believe experience the *make-believe world*—or in our team's working term—*Fanta*: a fantasy the child imagines and which is likely to recur during the day or at bedtime and which the child may even act out in imaginative play. Methodologically, the Fanta is the operationalization of the fantasy, as it clearly relates not to the entire make-believe world but to the restricted part that was expressed by the child in a particular research context and with the aid of specific research tools.

We set out to understand these make-believe worlds in children's everyday lives and to examine the nature of the relationships between children's media pleasures and their make-believe worlds. We adopted the theoretical notion of objectivation developed by Berger and Luckmann (1966) in their understanding of human reality as socially constructed. According to this perspective, "human expressivity is capable of objectivation, that is, it manifests itself in products of human activity that are available both to their producers and to other men as elements of a common world" (p. 49). The reality of children's everyday life is filled with objectivations of many kinds, including various forms of signification—such as their language, drawings, fantasy play, writing, and the like.

In order to aid our complicated analysis and to be able to make sense of the ways children articulate their inner worlds through their objectivations, we searched for a "sensitizing concept" (Blumer, 1964) advocated by grounded theory (Glaser & Strauss, 1967). The application of such concepts aids the analysis of empirical data material and the generation of grounded theoretical knowledge. To achieve this goal we borrowed the concept of *media traces* elaborated by Bachmair (1984, 1996) following the phenomenological perspective as our sensitizing concept. Media traces refer to the appropriation of media in children's objectivations, as a means of articulating their meaningful actions and experiences. Media traces include the indicators that point to the specific media text in explicit or implicit forms (such as naming it, describing an episode, adopting a character, using similar presentation style, and the like). Through the analysis of media traces in children's make-believe worlds, we attempted to reconstruct the meanings that these media have for children. In addition, we have expanded the use of media traces in our search for gender as well as cultural traces in our children's make-believe worlds, as is discussed in the following pages.

Our more specific research questions can thus be grouped in three comparative dimensions:

1. *Nature of make-believe worlds.* What do children's make-believe worlds look like? What do they consist of? Are there describable patterns emerging from children's make-believe worlds?
2. The child in the make-believe world. Where do children place themselves in (or outside) these worlds? What do they wish for themselves? What elements from their biographies do they bring with them to their make-believe worlds?
3. *Media in the make-believe world.* Do children incorporate media texts into their make-believe worlds? What elements of the texts do they import? In what ways do they make use of them? What meanings do children assign to the media in their make-believe worlds?

Two additional research questions cut across all three areas of inquiry:

1. *Gender differences.* What—if at all—are gender-related characteristics and differences in children's make-believe worlds, in the location of the self within them and in the role media play in them?
2. *Cultural differences.* What—if at all—are the culturally-related characteristics and differences in children's make-believe worlds, the location of the self within them and the role media play in them?

It is to the discussion of this ambitious and exciting study that we now turn. We first describe, in detail, the methodology employed in this study, as it pertains to the theoretical principles just outlined (chap. 2). We then attend to each of the five questions in separate chapters.

2

Studying Children's Make-Believe Worlds: Methods and Processes

The rationale, goals, and questions of this research call for a methodology that supports active involvement of participants. Such a study enables children to document and to reflect on their make-believe worlds, as well as to articulate their make-believe worlds in an environment that is comfortably structured and nonthreatening, and in a way that is age-appropriate. As we have argued before, experimentation and testing of subjects in a laboratory-type setting would not be conducive to eliciting children's elaboration on their fantasies.

Further, such a study requires a grounded theory approach (Glaser & Strauss, 1967) that frames *research* as an unfolding process—a process that involves reflection of the researchers themselves as part of the body of knowledge. Accordingly, no predetermined theoretical ideas or specific hypotheses were imposed upon the study in advance. Insights and understandings were discovered and developed inductively in the course of the investigation. This principle of openness and ongoing interpretation allowed the theoretical structures to emerge through intensive interaction with the children and in the interpretive-analysis process between the researchers.

As noted in chapter 1, the relationship between fantasy and media can be viewed from the perspective of inner psychological processes. As media researchers, we wanted to steer clear of a territory that is outside of our area of expertise and interest. Further, the research questions for this study are not geared to answer the question of "why," psychologically speaking (in terms of needs, personality, desires, experiences, etc.) the child imagines a particular fantasy story, but instead to examine the domain of "what" the children are imagining and where the differences and commonalities between them lie. Where it seemed necessary to touch upon inner motives, we consulted with child experts.

Describing and understanding *Fanta*—the child's make-believe world—was the goal of the study. During the research process, the goal was to attain a deep understanding of what we heard from the children, to find as well as to interpret the patterns in the fantasies, rather than to unveil psychological processes. The research design facilitated the children's expression of their fantasy worlds and enabled the researchers to "read" those worlds—in pictures and in written and spoken language. The research method and analytical processes applied in the study are elaborated in this chapter.

GETTING AT CHILDREN'S MAKE-BELIEVE WORLDS

We start by describing the target age group for this study, followed by the various research tools employed. These include a fantasy journey, a drawing and writing session, an in-depth interview with each child, and adult questionnaires.

Target Age Group

The children in the study ranged in age from 8 to 10 years old (more specifically, those who had already celebrated their eighth birthday up to those who had just celebrated their tenth). This particular age group was selected for a variety of reasons. Children of this age group, in middle childhood, are quite capable of expressing themselves both verbally and via illustration. Developmental theories assert that the 7- to 8-year-old period is one of significant changes in children's cognitive development. As they enter the period labeled by Piaget (Piaget & Inhelder, 1969) *concrete operations*, they develop the ability to solve concrete problems through mental representations. They are able to logically follow the steps in a process and to understand reversibility. Moving away from the egocentric thinking that positioned them at the center of the universe in early childhood, they are now better able to assume others' points of view. Less bound by centralized thinking, they can consider simultaneously different aspects of a situation. At this stage, their ability to engage in "perspective-taking" improves dramatically.

Having experienced several years of formal schooling, most children of this age group have developed rudimentary reading and writing skills and are gradually orienting themselves more toward their same-gender peer group. At home, they have started to acquire more independence from caregivers and have greater freedom of movement and increased control over their leisure activities. By this age, most children in the developed world have experience with a variety of media forms and contents. They are likely to have individual tastes in media that are often influenced by their social and cultural environments as well as by gender (Livingstone, 2002; Roberts & Foehr, 2004).

An integrative review of the literature on children and media (Gunter, & McAleer, 1997; D. G. Singer & J. L. Singer, 2001; van Evra, 1990) suggested that after the average age of 7, children have some of the crucial cognitive abilities that allow them to understand mediated contents (once again, mainly television). These abilities are now outlined.

- *Understanding storylines and narratives.* At this age they have the ability to reconstruct events, understand sequence, distinguish between central and incidental information, and connect causes to consequences.
- *Understanding characters.* Children of this age have acquired the ability to understand and describe characters not only by exterior appearance, but also personality traits, motivations, feelings, personal history, and social orientation, as well as the contexts in which they act and their interrelationships with others.
- *Understanding the interrelationships between mediated reality and reality.* Children of this age group have increased their ability to distinguish between reality and fantasy in media, however, primarily, they are still unaware of media's constructed and selective nature, its role in creating, representing, and omitting certain parts of reality, and of its contribution to and impact on the worldview of audiences.
- *Understanding audiovisual language.* By this age, children are developing the ability to identify and understand the codes and conventions of audiovisual expressions such as special effects, shooting angles, slow and fast motions, and other formal features of media.
- *Understanding production.* Children are on the way to understanding the idea that all media content, including realistic genres, are constructed as a result of human action and that mediated texts involve a team of professionals working behind the scenes.

At this age, however, most children do not understand media industries and are largely unaware of the complicated system of economic, social, political, legal, and human factors that influence media content. In summary, 8 to 10 years of age is an appropriate age to work with children who are at a communicative level at which they can express themselves clearly in relation to the tasks undertaken in this research. They are still eager to engage in fantasy activities, willing to cooperate with interested adults, and thus participate in the research enterprise.

The Fantasy Journey

In order to draw children into a state of mind that would help them enter their fantasy worlds, we devised a process of visualization using spoken imagery, relaxation, and music. In order to create a relaxing atmosphere, children were encouraged to rest comfortably on the available furniture and/or floors. Once settled, they were asked to close their eyes and to listen to a quiet monologue by the researcher. Unfamiliar, soothing music was selected and assembled especially for this project and was played under the researcher's voice. The music, which might be characterized as new-age instrumental, consisted of non-culture-specific melodic themes and nature sounds. A monologue was designed to be used by the field researchers that was drawn from similar texts that have been successfully used in earlier studies (specifically the one formalized by R. Horn & W. Horn, 1997, in Germany). It was translated into all four languages for use in the four countries. The opening narrative reads as follows:

> I am not sure you have had the same experience, but when I was a child of your age, I played certain things time and time again. I wanted to be someone really great, thought up stories and dreamt about them during the day and sometimes also during the night. Do you know what I mean? Do you also have something like this? Do you also dream about being someone special, in a special place and having lots of adventures? Do you like going to this special place in your fantasy, your favorite place, of which you have dreamt several times, and where you can be whatever you want to be?

Following this introduction, the fantasy journey shifted into the present tense in an effort to assist children in calling up their fantas—"*Imagine you are lying here … ".* Thoughts are making their way to you—" *… imagine … your thoughts are flying high, they fly higher and higher … nearly to the ceiling … then your thoughts are flying through the door… "* They fly through the land and finally reach the make-believe world—"*You look around … this is where you always wanted to be … what does it look like? … Are there people or animals? … plants or buildings?"*

After leading the children into their fantasy worlds via the narrative, the researchers were silent and allowed them about 5 minutes to continue in their make-believe worlds. The music continued to play in the background in order to retain the mood. Later, then, the children were gently guided out of the fantasy state and asked to make their way "home" in their thoughts—to come back to reality—"*It's time now to leave your make-believe world … you say good-bye and fly up into the sky again … ".* Finally, the guided journey was concluded—" *… you return back to [name of city] and into this [name of building/address] and into this room … and you can open your eyes now."*

Drawing and Writing About the Make-Believe World

Back in the "here and now," the children were given a large sheet of drawing paper and a variety of drawing instruments (e.g., pencils, crayons, markers) and asked to draw the make-believe worlds they envisioned on their journeys. They were encouraged to take as much time as necessary. In practice, the time taken for this drawing ranged from 10 minutes up to a full hour. When the drawings were complete, each child was given a piece of paper and asked to write a few sentences about the drawing.

Individual Interviews

As the individual children completed their drawings (according to their own pace), the field researchers conducted individual interviews in a more private area of the setting. The child and the interviewer looked at the drawing together and the interviewer read aloud the sentences the children had written. This rapport-establishing exchange set the ground for the guided interview that followed. The interview always began with positive reinforcement: *"So this is your drawing. It looks great/exciting/wonderful/interesting."* After these initial observations, a conversation was carried on about the drawing and the story behind it. The children were given the opportunity to introduce their drawings and the underlying stories from their own perspectives and in their own words. Questions asked by the researcher addressed several aspects of the make-believe world and the child's position within it:

- *The situation.* What is the situation displayed in the make-believe world? What are the various elements—objects, people, animals, and other elements that appear in it? Is there a related narrative embedded in it?
- *The child.* What is the child's individual position in or relation to the make-believe world? What is the child doing? What has he or she done before or will be doing after the frozen point in time in the drawing?
- *The meaning.* How does the child feel in the context of the fantasy situation? What does it mean for him or her?

Often, this line of exchange spontaneously elicited references to media that were then followed up. In cases where this did not occur, the child was asked at this point in the interview directly: *"Have you seen or heard something similar somewhere else, maybe on television, in a book, on the computer, or somewhere else?"* When the child pointed out a media connection she or he was questioned about it in detail. This discussion led naturally to a more general conversation about the child's media preferences and leisure time activities. Finally, each child was photographed (with parents' signed permission) holding up his or her drawing (except in the United States) and was presented with a token "thank you" gift.

The interview format attempted to create as authentic an exchange as possible between the individual child and the adult interviewer (the field researchers were females except for one male on each of the German and Korean teams). The communication was child-oriented and nondirective, trying to encourage the children to fully and honestly express themselves. Interviewers were careful to be respectful and to take the children most seriously, to be nonjudgmental, and to demonstrate congruence, acceptance, and empathy toward the children's messages. Following Rogers' (1969b) pedagogical approach, adopted here for research purposes, such are the preconditions for an atmosphere that allows children to open up and to participate in the process.

Congruence is understood in this study as the most fundamental—but most difficult to maintain—attitude. It presupposes that the interviewer does not present a professional face or façade, but attempts to be honest as well as to recognize and take seriously his or her own reactions and feelings. In doing so, the interviewer's personal and professional perspectives integrate to form a more holistic perspective and understanding of the situation and the meanings offered by the child. At the same time, the interviewer encounters children and their make-believe worlds as complete persons and does not impose a hierarchy of relationships. However, the nature of the communication between the adult researchers and the children studied differed greatly from case to case and from culture to culture in the degree of formality of the interaction, degree of children's talkativeness, reciprocity in the exchange, and the like.

Acceptance, in the form of unconditional positive feedback, means the ability to accept the child as he or she is and to react to the child in a respectful and positive way, trying to avoid as much as possible any prejudices and predetermined notions. In most cases, acceptance and maintenance of the child's positive participation in the activity was not problematic. However, in a very few instances, when the make-believe world communicated deviated from the range of normative, socially acceptable beliefs, values and behaviors—for example, an expression of especially violent wishes or racist comments—discomfort on the part of the researchers did occur and neutrality was difficult to maintain.

Empathic understanding, rather than evaluation or criticism, was the approach taken by researchers in an effort to understand the child's interpretation of experiences and emotions as accurately and sensitively as possible. The goal was to try to put themselves in the children's shoes and to see their experiences as though looking through their eyes. This does not necessitate giving up one's individual position or critical distance. However, it does entail a willingness to empathize and to try to take the child's perspective, even under conditions of disagreement.

In order to facilitate such a form of interaction with the child, field researchers adopted interviewing strategies suited to the situation, including (a) mirroring the child's responses back to the child in order to express respect and understanding and to stimulate continued conversation; (b) repeating the content as neutrally as possible to allow the child to reflect back on what was said; and (c) reiterating the child's perceived emotions in an attempt to deepen and further enhance explanations.

The individual interviews were tape-recorded and later transcribed verbatim. Additional information—such as general reactions to the interview, a sketch of the objects in the picture pointed out by the child, and other notes and insights—were documented by the field researchers to accompany the interview.

Parents' and Educators' Questionnaire

Parents (and educators in the German and South Korean cases; and camp counselors in the U.S. cases) were asked to fill in open-ended questionnaires for background information on the individual children. The adults were asked to describe the child in general terms, to specify the child's interests and media preferences, and to try and recall typical fantasy play by the child. Finally, information about the living conditions and family situation was included as well.

METHODOLOGICAL REFLECTIONS

Between Reviving and Evoking Fantasies

Through the visualized fantasy journey—drawing-interview process, the children were encouraged to imagine and communicate about their make-believe worlds. This was not a spontaneous or natural daydreaming situation, but rather one set up for the children. The time and place were determined for them. Further, children found themselves in the company of others and in settings that were not necessarily the ones they would have chosen for fantasy activities. Based on what children related to the researchers, as well as on how they talked about the experience, it was clear that in many cases, the procedure facilitated children's ability to enter their preexisting fantasies, whether or not they had been previously articulated. In other cases, new fantasies were evoked during the study period itself—fantasies that the child was imagining for the first time. In a small number of cases, however, the process failed to engage the children as desired. In these few instances, the children seemed to make something up during the interview or even to "copy" another child's drawing and/or make-believe story.

As noted, children reacted in a variety of ways to this opportunity. Many of them appeared to thoroughly enjoy the fantasy journey. A few became so deeply involved that it was a bit difficult for them to come back to "reality." Others were not deeply engaged and kept opening their eyes during the visualization process to check on what was going on around them. The children also used the invitation to draw, write, and talk about their make-believe world in different ways. Some of them wanted to draw in detail and spent much time and effort on their pictures. Others were delighted to have an interested empathic adult to talk to and they were eager to finish their drawings quickly and to get to the interview stage. Writing was the least attractive form of expression for most of the children, although the little they wrote was often impressive in that they were able to tell a great deal about their fantasies in a few words. Only a few wrote extensively about their make-believe worlds. Although all children participated in the study on a voluntarily basis, there were a few who were not motivated. Only a few seemed to have difficulty communicating through drawing, writing, or verbally.

The overall impression of the field researchers was that the participants enjoyed the experience. Some were even overtly grateful, as was Sarah (G, GR-5):[1]

> I have started it around my 8th birthday … and since then I have dreamt about this, but never drew it and never told anybody, because sometimes, when I sleep I cannot remember this dream so accurately … and I have never ever let it out, told anybody or anything. But now I can do it.

Studying Children's Drawings

In our attempt to consider children's perspective on the world we choose to rely to a large degree on their drawings. This nonverbal form of expression offers an approach that seems appropriate to study children's creative construction of reality. This is particularly the case in the study of something as complex as fantasy, where it is necessary to employ a research process that is not exclusively dependent on verbal language yet can also be made meaningful (Neuss, in press). Arguments for the use of drawings can be already found in Langer's writings (1942/1987) where she argues specifically against two assumptions of cognitive science: "Language is the only means to articulate thinking" and "everything which is not expressible thought, is emotion" (p. 93). Instead,

---

[1]Each child is assigned a letter indicating gender (B = boy, G = girl), abbreviation of country name (GR = Germany, IS = Israel, SK = South Korea, US = United States), and case number. Thus, Tessina is G, GR-3. Readers can consult the Child Index to find references to individual children throughout the book.

Langer emphasizes that "there are things which do not fit into the grammatical pattern of expression" and "have to be understood by a symbolic scheme different from discursive language" (p. 95). Drawings, in particular, integrate emotional elements more intensively and "inner pictures" are frequently easier to express through drawings because colors and forms evoke a more immediate effect than verbal language. This applies to the person drawing as well as during the act of drawing, and to the spectator when looking at the accomplished product. Visually formed experiences or fantasies that can be expressed inadequately verbally may find an appropriate medium for their expression through nonverbal forms, such as drawings. For example, one specific utterance such as "I dream of being a princess" provides only limited clues regarding the imagined appearance of this figure or the context of the dream, whereas in a drawing, those unexpressed details can come to life.

In our particular case, drawings as a means of investigation are credited with a number of attributes. The method is particularly relevant to this age group, as drawing is a crucial means by which children actively appropriate the world and through which nonverbal interpersonal communication and the reflection of an experience or a wish can take place. The act of *drawing* is a consciously manufactured temporary space for reflection where the access to inner pictures occurs without the pressure for narration. Although drawing has to be active and make decisions regarding the whole range of inner world of pictures, while drawing, the child chooses one picture and forms it according to his or her drawing competence. Thus, the fantasy or the wish undergoes a symbolic compression and accentuation in the drawing—*objectivation,* in the Berger and Luckmann's (1966) sense of becoming an object. The result is an articulation of a subjective content of the consciousness that becomes expressible for the child and interpretable for the researcher. Apart from its autonomous existence, the drawing also becomes a stimulus for the narration part of our process, as the child explains his or her drawing to an adult in an everyday, or research-related situation, and reveals parts of the nonvisible fantasy world to the listener.

The use of children's drawings in media-related reception research with children is rare, although it has been employed in related fields. For example, it has been used as an instrument for the assessment of inner images of social "others" in Israel (e.g., Teichman, 2001; Teichman & Zafrir, 2003) and of life in Africa for Japanese students (Maeda, 2000). Lealand & Zanker (2003) asked children to draw their real as well as their fantasy room. They interpreted the drawings as "a fluid text of children's peer group cultural aspirations" (p. 11) and used them to map flows of consumer culture and media use. In formative evaluation research, like the well-known studies of the *Sesame Street Workshop*, children's pictures were used to elicit supplemental feedback from children (Montasser, Cole, & Fuld,

2002). Tobin (2000), in studying children's interpretation of television violence, and Dyson (1997) in studying superheroes, gathered children's drawings and then used them to illuminate and illustrate some of their research findings.

In the current study, we use the drawings as a central instrument for understanding and interpreting the child's make-believe world because they provide an insider's view of the inner images of children's make-believe worlds as well as provide a basis for the interview. We realize, however that, not everything that is important for the child in the fantasy can be illustrated in a drawing, as children face the challenge of how to present their experiences or imaginations under the limitation of pragmatic conditions like drawing material, the two-dimensional nature of the sheet of paper, and its limited size. Moreover, the child has—due to age and stage of development—only limited abilities and techniques for graphic expression at his or her disposal. Drawings are therefore, presumably, a compromise that needs complementation and can only be more fully understood in direct communication with the child.

STUDYING THE MAKE-BELIEVE
WORLDS COMPARATIVELY

The cross-cultural aspect of this study was envisioned as a central dimension in our attempt to understand children's make-believe worlds. As with other comparative research (see discussion in Livingstone, 2003), the goals were to (a) understand children growing up in our own cultures through comparison with others; (b) to examine how transnational communication processes operate in different national contexts (such as popularity of particular texts); and (c) to build a more abstract, universally applicable theory of the role of media in children's make-believe worlds while recognizing and accounting for differences and diversity. Atkin, Greenberg, and Baldwin's (1991) work based on Bronfenbrenner's ecological typology points out the need to examine, among other things, the macrosystem of the child world that includes relations at the level of subculture or culture (e.g., socioeconomic status), along with belief systems or ideologies underlying such consistencies. Their study limits its definition of macrosystem to occupation, income, education, and ethnicity. It overlooks some of the more structural issues that differ across cultures—national identity, underlying social or political conflicts, national goals, and media systems (Lemish, 1997a).

Korzenny and Ting-Toomey (1992) suggested a list of variable clusters that should be considered in cross-cultural research. The first cluster that they label *antecedent variables* includes social, political, historical, cultural, and media contexts. When it comes to media systems, there is wide variation from nation to nation in the historical development; shape of the media industry; the ideology embraced; the governmental, societal, and cultural mechanisms of control; preferred types of programming; tension between global and local forms of entertainment; and unique functions for and uses by audiences. It follows that children's employment of media in their make-believe worlds is best analyzed as an interaction not only of individual, contextual, and social characteristics, as has been suggested before, but also of more general understanding of media as culturally situated. This study aims to contribute to the understanding of such influences through a comparison between children growing up in different cultural settings. In keeping with Kohn's (1989) second model of comparative cross-national research, the nation is perceived as the context of study (and not, e.g., the object of study, or the unit of analysis, as in other models). The purpose of the cross-cultural dimension of this project then was to study children's make-believe worlds across countries that are diverse, in relation to dimensions with relevance for understanding children's fantasies.

Cross-cultural comparisons such as this one are not free from either theoretical or empirical pitfalls, as discussed, among others, by Livingstone (2003). These issues are addressed later, in the discussion of the results of the comparative aspects of the study.

The Four Countries Studied

The four countries selected for this study were Germany, Israel, South Korea, and the United States, representing four very different regions of the world. The four are diverse in their ethnic, religious, and linguistic compositions. They have unique histories, traditions, and national goals, and are faced with fundamentally different perceptions of their role in their particular geographical region as well as in the world. Yet, at the same time, all four are vibrant democracies that place a high value on education and technological advancement and compete in the global market of goods and services. All are highly technological in orientation and have thriving media industries. They have a well-developed communications infrastructure, including local commercial and public television and radio stations, cable systems, satellite connections, Internet activities, a thriving print industry, and a flourishing market (local and imported) for products such as books and magazines, computer and video games, films, music compact discs, and tapes.

To briefly highlight the central characteristics of each of the four countries selected, we can summarize them (albeit in an oversimplistic way) in the following manner.

Germany. The Federal Republic of Germany, established in 1949, is a liberal Western democracy with a population of slightly more than 82 million inhabitants. The proportion of foreigners is 8.9%. The main religions are Roman Catholic and Protestant, each with adherents amounting to just under one third of the population. About 10% of the total population are members of other religions. Influenced by the critical discussion on the national Socialist past and the disastrous consequences of two world wars, of a political level, Germany devotes its efforts to antiextremism and an active role in the European community. The values of Western industrial nations are its guiding principle. The main industries are mechanical engineering, electrical equipment, and electronics. The Federal Republic ranks second after the United States in the list of the world's exporting and importing countries.

The most important event in recent history was the reunification of the country in 1990, which increased the area of the Federal Republic by one third. There are still grave differences between the former territories of the German Democratic Republic (East Germany) and the so-called "old" federal states. Apart from the various historical limitations, the economic power of the eastern federal states is just below two-thirds of the West German level.

Israel. The modern State of Israel, founded in 1948, on a territory and history of what was once a thriving Jewish kingdom some 3,000 years ago, and later occupied by many nations, consists of Jewish immigrants from all over the world. Twenty percent of the population of about 7 million are non-Jewish citizens of Muslim, Christian, and Druze faiths, who define themselves as part of the Arab world. The country's formative years were characterized by efforts at creating cultural integration and the development of a collective identity as well as by wars and security concerns. In the last 30 years, the nation has been divided by a major sociopolitical religious division over the Israeli–Palestinian conflict and the related issue of the Jewish and/or democratic character of the state.

Israeli society has a history of intensive diffusion of, even infatuation with, technological innovations, particularly in the realm of communication (such as purchase of video recorders and mobile phones; and subscription to cable and Internet; Caspi & Limor, 1999; Lemish & Cohen, in press). In addition, it is a society typified by close familiarity and cohesive social networks that are conducive to much interpersonal contact and communication (Herzog & Ben Rafael, 2001). As a whole, the country is oriented toward the Western world, with a strong American influence on both political and cultural life (Liebes, 2003). The English language is taught in elementary school as a first foreign language and is perceived as a central tool for education and social mobility.

South Korea. Established in 1948, South Korea is a democratic republic with a population of around 48 million inhabitants. Korea can look back over a long history. The first kingdom, Go-joseon, was founded as early as 2333 BC. As a consequence of the Cold War, the Korean peninsula has been divided since 1945 along the 38th parallel into the Republic of Korea (South Korea) and the Democratic People's Republic of Korea (North Korea). The main religions are Buddhism (26.3%), Protestant Christianity (18.6%), and Roman Catholic Christianity (7%). Buddhism and the basic tenets of the values and norms of Confucian ethics characterize the structure of the Korean family and everyday customs as well as the educational system to this day.

One of South Korea's main features is its remarkable economic growth. In the 1970s, industry was dominated by steel and chemical production. Throughout the 1980s, up to the beginning of the 1990s, the electrical industry (televisions, computers, audio equipment, etc.) and the automobile industry were the major export branches. Since the middle of the 1990s, the information technology and digital areas have been the country's major industry. South Korea ranks fourth in the world in interactive technologies (IT) production. For example, in 2000, 82.3% of households had access to the Internet; 71.4% of all households had a high-speed Digital Subscriber Line (DSL) connection.

The United States. The territory of the continental United States was originally populated by indigenous peoples, now known as Native Americans. Colonized by Europeans, starting with the discovery of this New World in 1492, the United States declared independence from England in 1776, after the American Revolution. The new government embodied democratic principles and was based on a spirit of republicanism. Today, the majority of the almost 300 million residents of the 50 states is White, however the United States is an increasingly diverse society, with Hispanics and African Americans accounting for large percentages of the total population, and Asians, Native Americans, Alaskan Natives, Native Hawaiians, and Pacific Islanders constituting other minority populations. There are a significant number of people who identify as being of more than one race/ethnicity. Almost 47 million speak a language other than English at home. Christianity is the main religion and there are numerous denominations, but the United States is officially a nondenominational country and historically, people have immigrated to the United States seeking freedom of religion. It is the third most populous country in the world and accounts for 5% of the global population.

Since the end of the Cold War, the United States has become the world's most powerful nation and plays a central role in influencing conflicts and partnerships among nations, as well as economic development around the world. It is a driving force of global capitalism. The media system is overwhelmingly commercial. A small public broadcasting network of television and radio stations was established after the commercial system was in place. A handful of large corporations own the bulk of media outlets and distribution channels, and tightly control content.

The Sample

The samples in the four countries took into consideration a variety of parameters for the purposes of the study. The scope of the investigation called for a small, in-depth, case-study type sample. Although achieved mostly through convenience sampling (in South Korea, in schools; and in the United States, mostly in summer day camps) and purposeful sampling (in Germany and Israel), particular effort was put into attempting to reach a similar proportion of boys and girls and in representing the various typical profile compositions of each country's population (in all but the U.S. sample).

In Germany, the investigation was carried out in urban and suburban areas, in the south (Munich) and eastern part (Dresden) and included children of lower as well as middle-class population. In Israel, Jewish children of both middle- and lower class from the central part of the country were included (mostly secular but also religious), as well as Arab children (both Moslem and Christian) in realistic proportion to their share in the population (20%). In South Korea, the investigation was carried out in Seoul and in rural areas with children of different demographics. In the United States, the study was conducted in a mid-sized university town in the midwest with primarily middle-class children (see Table 2.1).

The study was carried out in the four countries during the spring and summer of 2001. In Germany, children were studied in their after-school daycare centers. In Israel, this study was performed in the homes, where small groups of friends gathered. In South Korea, the study was conducted in classroom settings. In the United States, the study took place in a summer camp setting and home environment. The fantasy journey was conducted in small groups (mostly

TABLE 2.1

Sample

Country	Boys	Girls	Total
Germany	22	38	60
Israel	24	27	51
South Korea	22	25	47
USA	15	20	35
Total	83	110	193

the same gender in Germany and Israel, mixed gender in South Korea and United States). Clearly, the variance in the social as well as physical contexts of the study in the four countries needs to be taken into consideration when attempting to make sense of any comparative aspect of the analysis.

Finally, it is important to note the limitations of the scope of the sample. Similar to all in-depth, qualitative case studies, these are four rather small samples, nonrepresentative of the populations of children within the countries, as well as noncomparable across them. This does not allow one to draw any overall quantitative generalizations. Rather, the aim is to discover deep-rooted connections between media and children's fantasy worlds and to gain initial insights into the workings of cultural differences and similarities with respect to the topic.

ANALYZING THE MAKE-BELIEVE WORLDS

The analysis of qualitative data, based both on visual as well as verbal output, in a rather large and multicultural sample from different continents creates unique conceptual as well as practical opportunities and challenges. As Livingstone (2003) so vividly suggested, it involves not only hard work and financial resources, but also the emotional labor of overcoming cultural, linguistic, professional, and personal barriers. "Researchers find themselves comparing not only their findings but also their theories and concepts, methodological preferences, research ethics, writings styles, and publication strategies" (pp. 482–483). As she argues, these comparisons reveal differences, not only of personal preference, but also of social scientific discipline and of academic culture.

The four teams in our study were composed of the four authors, who served as team leaders and as the leading media and children experts, along with research assistants. The German team included five assistants (four females and one male) who were bachelor of arts graduates in Education or Psychology. The Israeli team included three female research assistants, all in the final year of bachelor of art studies in Communication and Psychology (one of whom was an Arab, who completed the work with the Arab sample in Arabic), as well as a research coordinator who was completing her master's degree in Cognitive Studies. In South Korea, the team included five assistants from the field of Education (one female PhD as well as four graduate students, two of whom were male). In the United States, the researcher had one assistant who is a professional researcher with a PhD in Communication.

The German team, who initiated and sponsored the project, was one step ahead in the data gathering and analysis, and set the stage for the work conducted by the other international partners. Each team conducted its own data gathering and analysis following intensive cross-cultural as well as national workshops. The basic theoretical position as well as the general guidelines for analysis were agreed on in advance and improved on during the process.

The analysis was completed in three complementary stages: (a) analysis of the individual make-believe world; (b) national-group analysis of the make-believe worlds; and (c) the cross-cultural analysis. It is important to note that the national and cross-cultural analyses were performed simultaneously, as they were dependent on each other.

Creating a Personal Portrait:
The Case of Tessina (G, GR-3)

Analysis of each individual case was based on the drawing, the child's written statement, and his or her interview transcript. There are numerous and diverse perspectives employed by psychologists, education scholars, and art historians in interpreting children's drawings. However, once again, it is important to emphasize, that because the focus is not on psychological processes, we diverted from methodologies used to analyze children's drawings in cognitive studies as well as from those used for therapeutic purposes (see, e.g., Cox, 1993; Golomb, 1992; Machover, 1949). Our study also deviates from typical human figure drawings studies (see, e.g., Teichmann, 2001; Teichmann & Zafrir, 2003) in which spontaneously produced images are scored according to set criteria and complemented by questionnaire items. Instead, the approach used is an integrated thematic analysis of the child's perspective. Additional information and perspectives on the child, gathered from educators and/or parents, was used as background material. A personal portrait of each individual child's make-believe world was reconstructed, as described in the example to follow.

Following Neuss's (in press) line of argumentation, children not only grow into a conventionalized system of symbolic meanings, but also assign their own subjective understanding of meaning and personal motives in nonconventional ways. Therefore it is not always possible to use "common sense" to derive meanings from elements drawn in their pictures. As a result, and in order to give the child the possibility of interpreting his or her own drawing, there is a need for a joint communicative interpretation process. Often the child's verbal output can highlight the subjective meaning through a process of naming and defining of both visible elements of the drawing and their relation to each other as well as of imagined (nonvisible) elements and relationships. Neuss' approach, then, calls for a methodology of qualitatively directed, communication centered research on children's drawings. Apart from access to the drawing itself, it is crucial to be familiar with the process and the action of drawing, the communication related to the drawing, and something about the child's environment in order to approach the meaning of the drawing from the child's perspective.

Drawings offer an aesthetic possibility of expression that differs from verbal language. However, the drawings are able to express only parts of the complex fantasies and thoughts of the self. In our view, the drawing is not the loyal "mirror of the soul" (Baumgardt, 1969/1985), where all you need to do is look into it and read its meaning, but rather a representation of mental processes. The viewing and interpretation of children's drawings—especially the nonlogical, unrealistic, and impossible aspects in them—are marked by ambiguities. This ambivalence of interpretation we accept as a principal constructive character of human consciousness. Interpretation and ambiguity are thus accepted not as deficiencies, but as existential elements of human identity and communication.

However, this does not necessarily mean an interpretative arbitrariness, as meaning is extracted based on the empirical material, with reference to contextual data in the drawing, as well as the child's explanation. In order to deal carefully with potential ambiguities and to avoid imposing a theory-guided interpretation on children's drawings, we also adopted the standards of qualitative methodology where, apart from the description of the object of investigation, the understanding of the way meaning was produced as outlined here in detail. The development of analysis of one particular German girl we called Tessina is provided in order to demonstrate the process. Note that all names were changed in order to protect the children's privacy.

Description of the Child. As a first step, a one- to two-page long summary about each child, including basic demographic information and media preferences, was written up by one of the team members and presented to the research team during a working meeting. The summary for Tessina is as follows: Tessina is a 9-year-old girl who attends third grade in an elementary school. Her father works in a travel agency and her mother is in the process of being professionally retrained. When she was 3 years old, her family moved from Kazakhstan to Germany for political reasons. Since moving to Germany, she changed her residence several times from a village, to a small town, later on to a farm, and at the time of the study, to an urban area not far from Munich. She does not have any siblings, but names her next-door friend as *"something like a sister."*

Tessina's mother describes her as *"lively, bubbling, eager to talk, good-natured, very animal-loving, intelligent, sensitive, sweet, sloppy."* Her special abilities are that she is *"talented in acting, painting, and ability to adjust to change. She is creative, quick to understand, and untidy."* Her caregiver, who has known her since she started school 3 years earlier, describes her as lively, independent in her homework, and very adaptable to the group. Tessina made some good friends in her childcare center. Her caregiver describes Tessina's special abilities in the following manner: *"Tessina is able to play with her friends for a long period of time and is full of fantasy. She is artistically talented and often likes to make beautiful paintings. Tessina likes to be involved in role-playing in both the doll corner as well as in the construction area with dinosaur characters and building blocks. She can play with her friends for hours. She rarely plays on her own. She adjusts to others and takes on changing roles in play."*

Analysis of the Drawing. The research team meetings began with free association about the child's picture, with each participant expressing her or his perception of the picture (see Drawing 2.1) and the meanings associated with it (with respect to color, shapes, content, emotions triggered, etc.).

The team member in charge of Tessina provided the summary of the description of her drawing. Here is an excerpt from it:

> The colored picture fills the entire sheet of paper. The right upper half of the picture is occupied by a clear drawing of a front of a castle. It has two towers, rounded at the top, on the left and right sides. Below each tower there are two blue windows with bars. In the middle of the castle, there is a huge, round, brown gate. The castle is painted grey and is situated on a crescent-shaped island in the middle of a blue ocean. The castle throws a wide black shadow on the sand-colored yellow island. Left of the castle there

Drawing 2.1. Tessina (G, GR-3) "Seashells at Night."

is a palm tree and a bit further out front, there is another unidentifiable plant. Close to the water, underneath the palm-tree, there is a crab painted in red. In the middle of the island, toward the water, there is a plant and two animals, identified by Tessina as a turtle and a sea-horse.

The picture (like the written sentences) was viewed as an articulation of a daydream, and thus interpreting it required a position of openness to all possible meanings and interpretations. Wherever possible, in-depth psychological interpretation was deliberately avoided—even when it may have seemed obvious. Such, for example, was the case of Shuval (B, IS-12) whose dentist mother restricted his intake of sweets, while his make-believe world, entitled "Chocolate Tree," was all about their consumption. Instead of attempting a psychological approach, we followed interpretations offered by the children themselves, and tried to make sense of them. In accordance with this approach, the next step of analysis was to attend carefully to the child's explanation and discuss the child's description of the make-believe world with the help of the interviews transcripts.

Wishes to Act. Special attention was given to the child's expressions of possible desires to act in the make-believe world. This was accomplished through interpretations of the drawings, interview narratives, and/or written text. In Tessina's case, for example, it was concluded that her wishes indicated a desire to experience herself as special, to be protected, and to protect endangered animals. The focus was not on asking "why?" this is the case, but rather "what" was the wish to act, and "how" it was expressed by the child. In some cases, as in Tessina's, the wishes seemed quite explicit and clear and were easily connected to a child's other interests and media experiences. In other cases, the research team admitted to being unclear about those connections.

Tessina is clearly interested in animals, in particular, in endangered species and projects her experiences and emotions onto the endangered animals depicted in the documentary series she views on television. In her make-believe world, she creates a place where animals, herself included, are safely protected. Stories of the paradise—named Seychelles—an actual place visited by her mother, is used as a background for a fantasy about such a sense of security. She banishes threat and conflict by structuring the rules around access and visiting hours to the island in a way that allows entrance to animals during the night and to people during the day. Tessina is a part of both worlds of humans and animals and lives in peace and harmony with them without being put in a position to experience power, aggression, or fear in either role. She fantasizes a place characterized by harmony, where bad things are not allowed to happen and all special creatures (like herself) find refuge behind secure walls and a large, protective gate.

Media Traces. At an advanced stage of the reconstruction–interpretation process, specific attention was given to pinpointing media traces. There were several levels of analysis. The first level delineated explicit media traces, that is, those media sources indicated clearly and unambiguously by the child in the interview.

Tessina answers the question if she has ever seen or heard something like what is depicted in her fantasy, by relating that she has heard about it from her mother " ... *also from television, because of the animals!*" She watches many animal programs regularly, but cannot name a specific title. She talks about scenes in animal documentaries, where animals like elephants, dolphins, and whales are hunted or threatened. In some cases, as in Tessina's, the media reference points to an entire genre; Tessina explicitly mentions television documentaries as the source of this knowledge, but she is unable to name a specific program. In other cases, however, the child identified a more definite source, such as a movie or even a specific episode. The media trace was identified and reconstructed through a three-step process. First, the media trace was identified in the empirical data (e.g., an element in the drawing, a comment by the child); subsequently the quoted media trace was acquired (e.g., by obtaining access to the particular movie, book, or computer game, and/or by accessing information about them); and, finally, the narrative content of the original media text was compared with the child's media trace in the make-believe world (see Bachmair 1993). In this way, it was possible to find out what the child had (or had not) taken from the media and the symbolic meaning the child assigned to the media text adopted and integrated in the make-believe world.

Miniature Stories. In order to prepare for second level analyses and to further advance the study, we developed a procedure for creating a brief condensed narrative that summarizes the essence of the make-believe world. These short narratives are based on all empirical data available and are presented in a coherent and accessible text. The stories are told in a first person style, from the child's perspective, sticking as closely as possible to the original interview and emphasizing the crucial elements as understood by the researchers. Although the stories are written in the first person, these are not verbatim transcripts written or spoken by the children, but were constructed from careful examination of and contemplation of the materials gathered.

These texts were critical as a mechanism for streamlining the process of analysis. These miniature stories were integral to the next two stages of analysis and were better suited to this type of study than other forms of extraction (like various forms of coding). They also allowed us to overcome the barriers created by the need to translate transcripts from four different languages and to communicate among ourselves in languages that were not our own. In doing so, we felt that we were moving away from the original meanings of the make-believe worlds and from an ability to represent them appropriately. Only the researchers in the native language were best able to grasp the accurate meaning suggested by the child and to present it in a condensed form. All miniature stories were translated into two languages—English (the common language of the German, Israeli, and American teams) and German (the common language of the German and South Korean teams), and were therefore accessible to all researchers.

Tessina's miniature story thus became the following:

> It is night in the Seashells. My mom told me that this is a paradise for endangered animals. When night falls, all endangered animals come to my island, to my castle. Here they are safe from poachers. Everybody has his own separate room: the crab, the dolphins and also the elephant, who has a gigantic room, of course. Naturally, the whale's pool is even larger. And they can all come and go as they please. There are also humans in my dream, but they only come for a visit during the day, when the animals are not there. As soon as the sun sets, the humans leave the island and the animals come to me. Then it is night in the Seashells, a paradise.

Group Analysis of the Make-Believe Worlds

Based upon the reconstructions of the individual cases, the next steps were directed at structuring and ordering the empirical material in order to be able to create categories and generate some understandings of the phenomena at hand. Categorization was designed to provide further insight into the four major research questions:

- The make-believe worlds;
- The child in the make-believe world;
- Biographical traces in the make-believe world;
- Media traces in the make-believe world.

The process of *thematization*, which is the goal of an analysis such as this, uses grounded theory methodology (Strauss & Corbin, 1994), that involves breaking down and reducing the data into smaller, meaningful concepts that were labeled and stored. Each transcript was coded, assigning data-text incidents to the emerging categories independently (Lindlof & Taylor, 2002).

Thus, for example, "harmony with nature," "harmony with animals," "peaceful feelings," and "calm," became "The World of Harmony;" while "fighting," "facing threat," "facing danger," and "being in conflict," became "The World of Conflict and Threat." Both "The World of Harmony" and "The World of Conflict and Threat" later became subcategories of the first research question about the nature of the make-believe worlds.

The categories that developed within the teams were discussed, evaluated, and negotiated once and again during face-to-face cross-national workshops with the researchers as well as through ongoing exchanges by phone and e-mail. Several categories proved to be redundant, unclear, or esoteric. Some categories with different names turned out to refer to the same concept. Following clarifications and decisions, team members returned to sorting their miniature stories over and over again, for each of the four major research questions. As the process continued, the categories began to crystallize around specific parameters and the definitions were clarified in ways that made sense. Team members practiced evaluating the miniature stories of the other teams as well, in order to reach consensus as well as to check for intercoder agreement and reliability (not in the statistical sense). This process of sharing interpretations and comparing between and among cases helped to fine-tune the categorization scheme where types were created by grouping single cases according to their similarities and differences (Lindlof & Taylor, 2002).

Cross-Cultural Analysis

Cross-cultural analysis constituted an integral part of the analysis from the very beginning. During the first joint workshop in Munich, in May 2001, the researchers participated in the "fantasy journey" visualization procedure. During the workshops and meetings that followed in the next 3 years of the project, as experiences of the different members were presented and discussed, theoretical positions argued, individual cases analyzed, and preliminary similarities and differences pointed out, the cultural grounding of our empirical data became more evident. At the same time, we were repeatedly struck by the commonalities of children's make-believe worlds in what seemed to be universal human themes, as well as global media influences. Walking the thin line between the desire to find the "universal" human child that we can all identify with, and the urge to point out the unique qualities and contributions of our various cultures in the making of children's fantasy world became a major challenge of this joint work.

II

Research Findings:
The Worlds, the Children, and the Media

3

The Worlds of Make Believe

The worlds imagined by children create a framework or context in which they can act out their fantasies. The backdrop of the imagined world can be compared with the sets and the props for a theatrical production. Like settings for a drama, they create a mood and an appropriate arena for enacting the dream scenario. In our study, for example, we learned about worlds that are characterized by idyllic natural settings, populated by real, imagined, and extinct animals, many of whom can communicate with people. Great battles and kingdoms were imagined along with a panoply of natural and supernatural powers and magic, from becoming invisible to being able to fly. The children traveled on rocket ships and hot air balloons to lands far away in time and/or space in their fantasies. They created a range of inventions and machines designed to produce all kinds of phenomena. There were adventures, fun, and dangers to overcome.

In order to better understand the range of worlds children envisioned in their fantasies, we studied the drawings and their corresponding stories and found patterns in the representations of worlds. Recurring themes and elements in the sample led us to conceptualize nine broad "world" categories. Although the 193 children lived in various parts of the globe—with very different cultures, traditions, and media offerings—it was possible to group their fantasy worlds into the following nine types based on the data: harmony and peace; conflict and threat; amusement; foreign land; supernatural power; travel; sensual pleasure; royalty; and technology (see Table 3.1).

Although the number of cases in some of the categories is not necessarily impressive, the nature of our study prioritizes highlighting themes rather than

TABLE 3.1

Children's Make-Believe Worlds

Worlds	No. (%)	Distinctive Features
Harmony and peace	73 (38)	Worlds where nature, animals, and people live in peace and tranquility.
Conflict and threat	28 (15)	Worlds where great challenges have to be overcome in hazardous situations.
Amusement	23 (12)	Worlds offering excitement and action as well as small adventures, but not involving personal risk.
Foreign Land	19 (10)	Worlds characterized mainly by the exotic and by difference.
Supernatural	14 (7)	Worlds that focus on the unexplainable and magical.
Travel	10 (5)	Worlds focusing on being in transit, not on the final destination.
Sensual Pleasure	10 (5)	Worlds of pleasures derived from eating or other delights to the senses.
Royalty	9 (5)	Worlds in which people are born as rulers who care for others but also have to occasionally defend their sovereignty.
Technology	7 (4)	Worlds focused on futuristic technology and machinery.
Total	193	

mapping their frequencies in any representative way. In addition, for the sake of analysis, we chose to place each case in only one of the "worlds" categories according to where the researchers agreed it fit most clearly; however we recognized that many of the samples had elements of more than one of these worlds. Beyond describing the backdrop for the children's fantasy in terms of these worlds, there were common features found in the children's fantasies and drawings (geographical, animal, natural, supernatural, etc).

A somewhat similar form of analysis was conducted by Cohen and Mackeith (1991), who produced a collection of children's fantasies based on remembered stories gathered from adults in the late 1970s in England. They conducted an analysis of the worlds and came up with parameters of "paracosmic imaginings" that had key commonalities:

First, children must be able to distinguish between what they have imagined and what is real. Second, interest in the fantasy world must last for months or years; they weren't interested in passing worlds. Third, children had to be proud of the world and consistent about it …. Lastly, children had to feel that the world mattered to them. (p. 14)

Cohen and Mackeith (1991) grouped the worlds according to the following themes: animals and toys; imagined countries; schools; technology (in particular, railway systems); theater; and miscellaneous. A number of these paracosms continued over a period of years and involved extremely complex and detailed thinking and planning. In some cases, entire governments, infrastructure and systems, documentation, highly developed personalities, and/or languages were created.

Some of the invented stories collected in the present study fall more closely under the definition of *free-floating daydreams*, as they may have been less controlled, more ephemeral (see "Invented Stories," in Cohen & Mackeith, 1991, p. 108). However, even with more than 50 years between the children who produced them, there are some similarities between the two sets of fantasy worlds. For example, in this study, some children set their fantasies on islands; many involved animals; distant lands and travel were integral to a number of the worlds.

The methodology for the present study, as already discussed, is quite different, because we asked children to spontaneously imagine the world of their daydreams and to subsequently draw and talk about these places. We were also hoping to elicit worlds akin to paracosms, but cannot attest to finding that our children used them in their imaginings consistently over a long period of time. However, it is clear to us that children knew their worlds were not real and that they presented them with pride and identified with these products of their imaginations. And, in some instances, they were clearly paracosms in the Cohen and Mackeith sense. Our main emphasis though, was in trying to reconstruct children's ways of giving meaning to the scenarios, objects, and characters in the worlds they created, rather than on our own interpretations of them.

This chapter highlights the common aspects of the worlds of present-day children—the nine types of worlds and the features that characterize them. Accordingly, the following is a presentation of the fantasy settings the children imagined and to which they related, with examples given to illustrate the patterns.

THE WORLD OF HARMONY AND PEACE

Many children imagined worlds in which utter harmony with nature, animals, and humans prevailed. Seventy-three of the cases fit best into this category—that is more than one third of all cases. This most popular world is represented by scenarios of peace and tranquillity, where nature is lush and beautiful and the children are free to explore and enjoy themselves. In many instances, the children envision their loved ones—family and friends there with them. However, in some cases, the child is the only human present. A connectedness to nature, animals, and at times, other people characterizes this world. In addition, dangers are absent or neutralized.

Rona (G, IS-11) portrays her own paradise. This make-believe world epitomizes a state of peace and harmony with nature an animals, set in a biblical context—the Garden of Eden. She lives here with her family and friends openly in a natural setting where there is a complete absence of danger. In her Garden of Eden, one can eat the apples with no ill effects. The creatures coexist; a shark is mentioned, but it is not talked about in a threatening way. Rona's world does not include commerce—no shops—everything is free for the taking. By eliminating the need to buy and sell, she imagines a world of total freedom where all can enjoy the bounty of the earth. The children, adults, and animals are free to play and move about as they please while observing the good things nature has to offer. It is a world where there is space and time to watch the flowers bloom and trees grow. Obligations like attending school do not exist in this world. Every day is a holiday. Rona occupies herself by looking after animals and flowers—her contribution to paradise (see Drawing 3.1).

The idea of a paradise is common in these fantasies. Tessina (G, GR-3) creates her own nocturnal paradise in "Seashells at Night." She bases her fantasy on a real geographical archipelago in the Indian Ocean, which she learned

Drawing 3.1. Rona (G, IS-11) "Paradise."

about from her mother. Tessina's fantasy depicts a safe haven for endangered animals, where each animal has a place to live and humans are a benign presence in the daytime, and absent at night, except for Tessina herself. She assigns herself the role of protector of the animals. Judging from her picture, this is a world where you can see the stars at night and pollution is not an issue.

Seo'young (G, SK-32) of Korea also creates a world in which nature and animals abide in a beautiful and plentiful land. In "A Journey to My Fantasyland," Seo'young is the only person who inhabits her world, but there are lots of happy animals. She imagines herself having wings with which she can fly into a rainbow to play with the animals. There they all have everything they need. They do not have to work for it because nature—in this case the rainbow—provides it all.

> I am in my fantasyland. There I have wings like a bird and fly with big thrusts of my wings. Here is a rice field and a watermelon field and wonderful flowers, blowing even at yellow trees. Underneath one of the yellow trees a teddy bear sleeps safe and sound. And, after all, lots and lots of animals live here. A deer drinks water out of a well, a bunny plays on a slide, a bird built a pink nest on a tree where she also laid her eggs. And if she needs food, then she looks for it in the rainbow.

> I'm flying towards the rainbow. In the sunshine it's shining in seven colors. Under the rainbow I can do whatever I want and find anything I need and in the rainbow itself I play together with the birds and animals. The animals are happy to see me. There are no other people.

Seo'young's world is a kind of a "forbidden forest," similar in her words, to the *Harry Potter* books, where only people, like herself, who are close to the animals are allowed. However, although the *Harry Potter*'s forest is very dark and mysterious, hers is colorful and full of light.

Like Seo'young, Carrie (G, US-10) is the only human to inhabit her land. Also, she too, is conscious of keeping the animals happy and unafraid. Dolphins and unicorns live here, but dangerous animals are banned or neutralized. The alligators there only eat fish for the food they need and they do not bite. Carrie is conscious of creating a safe, sunny preserve for the animals.

Often, in these type of worlds, children develop a sense of open space and vast landscapes. But the world of harmony and peace is also experienced in some of the children's stories indoors, within a familial type of community, as is the case of Hagit (G, IS-17), who wants to live in the home of a family of colorful mice.

These stories are characterized by a certain serenity of surroundings, a sense of personal security and tranquility, while blending into nature and being at one with nature and animals. Several patterns appear in them more frequently than others: There are gardens that form a refuge from the surrounding world; villages; countrysides; farms and riding stables; seas and beaches; jungles and exotic resorts; and a few "heavens" in the spiritual sense. These worlds are also characterized by extensive drawings of vegetation—trees, flowers, grass—as well as wild animals. Frequently, there is an aesthetic framing of these scenes by drawing clouds on top. The elements of these worlds seem to fit together to create both an aura of wholesomeness and an atmosphere of utopian perfection.

THE WORLD OF CONFLICT AND THREAT

Not all of the children fantasized such peaceful worlds. Many imagined worlds of strife and conflict, where they could engage in fighting, and sometimes violent struggles. After worlds of harmony, the next largest number of cases fell under the category of *conflict and threat*—28 of the cases. In these worlds, the scene is one of fighting or impending battle. It is not uncommon for media settings to make up the backdrop for some of these worlds. These are worlds in which kingdoms have to be protected, as dinosaurs and other powerful beings threaten the peace. As will be discussed in reference to gender (see chap. 6), mainly boys' fantasies fell into this group. These children use their allies, weapons, magical powers, personal cunning, and special abilities to rescue themselves and their loved ones. They conquer their foes, assume special positions, and provide order in their fantasized worlds.

In his make-believe-world, "Under the Sea," 8-year-old Yun'sang (B, SK-6) sets out for the bottom of the sea to watch a fight with a leopard who threatens all the other sea life. Yun'sang is on the side of the good sea creatures. He is a part of the battlefield in his make-believe world, although he cannot be seen in the drawing.

> Every day I do magic with a tiger to get into my dreamland. When I call, he takes me there, and when I want to get back, he takes me home again. My dreamland is the land of submarine sea. Here everything is peaceful until the cheetah appears. The whale makes a sound, which the cheetah doesn't understand, and this is how all the fish get alarmed. Then I start to fight. I'm supporting the whale and when it gets dangerous I'm hiding in his tummy. Inside of it, it is dark and very narrow. In the fight, a whale died and a shark was wounded. I have given the whale a funeral and healed the other animals and given them comfort. Here in the submarine world there are also invisible animals like lions and flying horses, fighting for us, too. And on the surface ships are sailing with red flags. Ten fishermen per boat normally want to catch the fish and eat them, but because of the fight they turned away and went far away. Now they can come back and maybe catch the cheetah and maybe also some fish—but the cheetah dies in the end in any case.

This scenario takes place in a natural setting with animals. Everything starts out peacefully, yet the central theme is one of fighting. Yun'sang himself is allied with a whale in fighting against a cheetah. One unusual aspect of this fantasy is that one of the casualties is a "good guy" (a whale) and the child has to deal with that death by imagining his funeral. Although this world is a war zone,

Yun'sang's role in it is that of a paramedic caring for the dead and wounded (such a distinction between the nature of the make-believe world and the child's particular role in it is developed further in chap. 4).

Lucas (B, GR-2) imagines himself being captured by an unfriendly Pokémon. His drawing shows how he is rescued by another Pokémon. In this case, it is the media character who saves Lucas, the prey, in this fantasy. He plays with the excitement of being caught and then freed as part of the daring adventures that he enjoys in *Pokémon* land (see Drawing 3.2).

Joe (B, US-13) imagines himself to be a red dragon who is the underdog in the beginning of his imagined battle. Finding himself attacked by a spear-throwing, arrow-shooting mob, he uses his wits to get out of a tight spot. The rationale for the attack is that people simply do not like red dragons. The fantasy world centers on the chase and Joe's attempt to fight back and to hide. Joe escapes and the mob is killed by a kind of avalanche within a volcano.

In the world of conflict, the children incorporate and use fear and the adrenalin it produces to endow their fantasies with emotional realism. In talking about these worlds, children were sometimes almost breathless from relating what they had imagined. These worlds are occupied by imaginary creatures (dinosaurs, dragons, Pokémon, often located in game-settings or sports arenas

Drawing 3.2. Lucas (B, GR-2) "Poliwrath versus Chix."

(rather then in nature with animals and plants), in the form of a special task or match. The children in these worlds are often assisted by use of different weapons and accessories.

THE WORLD OF AMUSEMENT

Cases in which children imagined a more raucous kind of fun, exciting action, and a carnival-like atmosphere—the kind that comes from theme parks and other sites of amusement—were placed into the *world of amusement* category. Most of the creators of these 23 cases were boys. If there were conflicts or dangers, it was to augment the excitement and fun. These include fantasies with children experiencing thrilling times in settings they often explicitly refer to as amusement parks.

For example, Ben's (B, US-1) imaginary amusement park provides physical fun for his friends and as a special bonus, it has the capability to turn visitors into any animal and then they can enter the special animal amusement park. Only Ben and his friends can see this complex. It is simply invisible to everyone else (see Drawing 3.3):

Drawing 3.3. Ben (B, US-1) "Amusement Park."

My favorite place is an imaginary amusement park—a really big one. There is a candy tree there, a clubhouse, and an animal amusement park. You can do loads of things there, like swing from a treehouse, land on a trampoline, and then jump into the pool. I am running over an obstacle course—swinging from a rope onto a trampoline and landing in the pool. Several of my friends are there with me in the treehouse and one of them is in the candy-cane tree. The people can go into the animal converter, and once they have been converted into animals, they can visit the animal amusement park. There are lots of animals there and they can have rides on many different types of merry-go-rounds. This amusement park is in my backyard and it is invisible. Only kids that are my friends can see it. Others just walk through it. The animal amusement park is floating.

Pierre (B, GR-41) visits Disneyland Paris in his fantasy and imagines how exciting one particular ride will be. He describes a roller coaster-like ride and his emotions of fear and being thrilled. This amusement park is so exciting that Pierre pictures himself with his mouth wide open in awe. The amusement park that Myong'hun (B, SK-33) imagines has lots of rides, a circus, and food. It is also characterized by a very long waiting line, in which one might get bored, because the wait to get in seems very long. Toni (G, IS-38) sets up her world of amusement in her house of dreams within a neighborhood of fun. There are all kinds of fun things to do in the house—different slides, climbing structures, a swimming pool. Her cat is pictured prominently as joining in on part of the fun. She imagines being with her friends and family in this world.

These worlds of amusement are largely characterized by a sense of physical, kinesthetic fun. All kinds of rides and fast-moving activities are portrayed, including jumping on trampolines, swinging, sliding, or involvement in sports like basketball or soccer. The worlds of amusement recur in several patterns: amusement parks, sports arenas, special lands (e.g., *Pokémon*), performance stages, or game settings. They include both humans as well as imaginary creatures aided by accessories. In many ways, these worlds are akin to worlds of conflict in the sense of excitement and thrill they produce. However, they diverge from each other in that the worlds of amusement do not pose danger nor do they include fighting of any sort. Together, the worlds of conflict and those of amusement create the second largest cluster of worlds created by the children.

THE WORLD OF A FOREIGN LAND

Nineteen of the make-believe worlds fell into the category of *foreign land;* the land of the "other" if you will. Children's fantasies of foreign lands are characterized by exotic geography, animal life, buildings, and the differences of the people. From Mexico to Cyprus and beyond, children imagine themselves all over the world and, in some cases, in places that exist only in their own imaginations. Islands, deserts, beaches, and mountains are dreamt about as a part of these idyllic foreign lands. Betty, (G, US-5) for example, is going to a beach in California on her scooter. She describes the sand, the turquoise color of the water, the sun and sky as well as the shells, crabs, and sea creatures.

A magic flying carpet takes Hannah (G, GR-33) to a foreign land where there are snakes and turban-wearing snake charmers, swamps, crocodiles, oases, and cacti. This is a place where she feels familiar with the people and their ways because she makes long imaginary visits there. She knows the place and the locals so well in her fantasy that she imagines herself being allowed to give guided jeep tours through the jungle.

> I am on my dream island. I flew there on my flying carpet. I have been there many times and I stay between three days and two months. That's irregular. On this island there is a village and people who already know me and so do the snakes. They are happy when I come and keep me company on my way into the village. There the snake-charmer is happy, and gets his flute out and the snakes dance to his music. I always live together with a woman in her house. I have my own room there and always get a lot to eat.

> And there is another part of the island. There you can rent a jeep and go on a guided tour. And because I was on so many guided tours, I'm allowed to work there myself. In the jungle you have to be very careful. There are lots and lots of swamps and crocodiles. There is also an oasis on the island. I go to get water there. And there are cacti there. I'm wearing a turban. Because of this everybody knows that I belong to them.

Hannah, who is from the eastern part of Germany, is influenced by *The Tales of 1001 Nights* and imagines a foreign land, Arabian style, which is obviously very different from her own surroundings (see Drawing 3.4).

Drawing 3.4. Hannah (G, GR-33) "On My Dreamland."

Maroum (B, IS-10) who is an Israeli Arab boy, presents an image of Switzerland that is a tranquil natural setting with mountains, sea, fruit trees, fish, sun, and blue sky. Interestingly, he does not project himself into the fantasy. He imagines the Swiss flag waving in the breeze and nature running its seasonal course. He reported that he learned about Switzerland from his father.

Kathy's (G, US-17) fantasy is based on a real experience she had when in India with her family and they drove through the mountains. She dreams of hiking to the mountaintops at sunset, and enjoying the mountain's purple, snow-capped beauty. This is a world of birds flying in the wind, lovely shapes in the clouds, and the shimmering colors of a golden sunset.

Whether they learned of these foreign lands through personal experience, stories related from others, or the media, it is clear that children imagine far-away places in the real world and have very clear ideas about how they look and how it would feel to be there. Their story settings are mostly nature scenarios with beaches, seas, and islands, landscapes such as deserts, and foreign villages. A special effort is made to draw the sky above them. The pull of the exotic comes through clearly in the worlds of foreign lands that the children imagine.

WORLD OF SUPERNATURAL POWER

The popular trend in current children's culture of supernatural themes in books, movies, and television programs was also evident in our study. Fourteen of the cases fell into the category of supernatural power, although certainly many more fantasies had elements of such abilities. These worlds are populated by fairies, witches, and wizards, aliens, dragons, and many other kinds of animals and fantasy creatures. Children are especially involved with the magical and superhuman abilities they and others possess in these places.

Milena (G, GR-39) dreams of a magic land with animals who speak, fairies (all female), and sweets galore. In her fantasy, Milena is a fairy and can fly like a bird and can "naturally" do magic. It is a land of fun and all you do are the things that please you the most. Marsha (G, US-16), invents a land that resonates with her feelings about herself as a kind of magical, witch-like girl. In her imaginary world it is always night and all of the people are witches and wizards. As with many of the fantasies, there are animals and the witches can converse with them. The nocturnal world she imagines is a mysterious and enchanted setting for conjuring up her swirling spells.

This is a land of witches and wizards. It is where I hang out with my friends. My friend, Sara, is with me in the picture. It is always night there and it looks like a painting with a black sky with stars, lots of trees, a lake with reflections, and a full moon. It is a really beautiful place—a tropical place where extinct animals live and there are other new types of animals that no one knows about. There's a fox-cat that comes with me. This is where I use my magical powers. I'm putting the magic into the pool of power. The spells I am using make the water and fish become colorful. It's rare that I use my magical powers. I've been thinking about this place ever since I was little. I was born on Halloween and I have always felt that I am kind of a witch (maybe not really, but I kind of feel like I am one). When I come here, I become the witch that I feel that I am. I like doing magical stuff and flying on a broom. I have always liked the night and black, too. Also, witches and wizards have a special connection with animals and can talk with them, and I like that.

Marsha deeply identifies with the idea of witches and magical powers—as she explains, with a Halloween birthday she plays with the idea of herself as a witch. This is an instance of a clearly recurring world—a place she has dreamed and thought about for years.

Ohad (B, IS-34) imagines an intercelestial world inhabited by aliens. He appears as a microbe who can fly around quickly and multiply at will. Part of his fantasy is to avoid getting eaten by the aliens. The aliens take many forms and some are more advanced than people of our world—both in their abilities and in their technology. Ohad's interest in unidentified foreign objects (UFOs) comes through in the world he creates, as he can be witness to all sorts of strange creatures and events. Various cartoons and movies (E.T.) infiltrate his imagining about aliens and their surroundings, as discussed in chapter 5, on media traces.

Sven (B, GR-21) flies on a fantasy dragon—one who can freeze objects at will—to a land where animals find refuge. Along with the flying dragon, one can find talking flowers, bombs that communicate with each other, and Pokémon, who can digest exploding bombs without harm. Sometimes the special creatures also appear in real-live settings, as is the case with the talking star fish at Karen's (G, US-26) grandmother's house.

The worlds of supernatural are thus magical in nature. They are occupied by fairies, witches, mermaids, unicorns, Pokémon, Digimon, and aliens. Some of them live and exert their power in the "real" world as well, however real-life creatures are rare in these worlds.

WORLD OF TRAVEL

Travel also figures in children's imaginations as they imagine traveling to all kinds of faraway geographical areas, countries, time periods, and beyond this world into space. Modes and vehicles of travel vary widely including horses, big birds, balloons, and rocket ships. The central theme is to be on a journey to somewhere else. Ten cases fell into this category.

Charlotte (G, GR-12) imagines herself on a gleaming white horse, fulfilling her greatest wish to make a journey to Spain. Her fantasy is a kind of a pilgrimage for her as she wants to help the poor people there:

I'm riding on an entirely white horse. It's very hot. I'm on my own, a princess with a crown and veil. Normally I live in my castle in Arabia. But now I departed on a long and arduous voyage to Spain to help poor people there. My horse picks a flower and carries it in its mouth for me. My parents rule in another country, in England. My sister rules Russia. My greatest wish is to travel to Spain.

Charlotte's story focuses on the horse ride in the desert, and in the interview she details the experience of being thirsty on the way.

Doron (B, IS-7) projects his thoughts into a fictional past to envision travel by horse and carriage down a path—to a jungle and to a basketball court. Although Doron says he himself is not in the carriage, he experiences the excitement of the adventures and venues in his mind.

Dam'dok (B, SK-40) takes to the skies with his family via multicolored balloons in all kinds of interesting shapes. This world of travel allows for a distant perspective on the earth and all the activities of the people and animals—down to the insects. Looking beyond earth, he can see out into the solar system. The family members each grasp their own balloon—making for a unique mode of travel.

Rocket travel through time is the world Kevin (B, US-27) dreams up in his fantasy. This world combines the themes of patriotism and U.S. space exploration. The space shuttle is specifically named as the method of travel and a time warp technology is invented to facilitate the travel through time and space which, according to Kevin, feels like it takes much longer than it actually does.

Worlds of travel provide the framework for being on the move. Whether it is by an airplane, rocket ship, balloon, a big friendly bird or even the traditional horse, these children dreamed about being "on the road" and the journey seemed to be as important as the destination. Sometimes children take with them a best friend or family members on their journey and thus people appear in these worlds more than in most of the other worlds. Houses and mountains also seem to occupy many of the worlds of travel.

THE WORLD OF SENSUAL PLEASURE

This type of world enables children to enjoy sensual gratification. In these fantasies, children frequently emphasized the many "good things" in life, with all kinds of wonders to delight the senses. Naturally there are plenty of sweet treats for them to eat: plantations of chocolate trees and trees with sticks of rock candy hanging down, butterscotch walls, and streets and trees made of gingerbread. Wonderful rainbows materialize before the children's eyes. Birds sing and cheer up sad children; soft flowerbeds invite them to sit nearby and to make themselves comfortable. Ten of the cases were classified as such worlds of sensual enjoyment.

The make-believe world of Katrin (G, GR-7) depicts a land where it is possible to eat candy nonstop without putting on weight. This is a kind of "finger-licking good" utopia. In Katrin's land, the buildings and people are made of gingerbread, it rains candy, and the candy supply never runs out. She takes pleasure, not only in being surrounded by sweets, but by being able to indulge to no ill effect.

The theme of sweets is also embraced by Shuval (B, IS-12), whose mother is a dentist. He imagines a chocolate paradise. There is a city with orchards made qualities of all brands, types, and of chocolate. The method for picking the chocolate from the trees is explained. There are even chocolate dogs who can be eaten if they bother you.

> This is a city of chocolate trees. There are regular trees as well, but most are orchards of chocolate trees. There are all kinds of chocolates here, one of them is still very small, one very big, and one a bit rotten, because it was out here for too long … that's why the cow on the wrapping is upside down. There are also chocolates that are hanging on a string. One can throw a tiny stone at it and the string will tear and the chocolate will fall down. Chocolates fly around in this city to all kinds of places. The ladders are made of real hard chocolates for people to climb on. The boy is my friend Matan, who happened to be on the tree. I am not there, because I am eating chocolates until my mother tells me to stop … I don't want to have cavities in my teeth. There is also a butterfly of chocolate that came to eat, animals of chocolates, lots of things. There are dogs that, if they make you nervous, you can eat them and that's it.

In Shuval's drawing, he points out the "rotten" chocolate (the one with the cow-logo of a well-known chocolate company turned upside down), reassuring himself and the audience that only food that is fit to be eaten is consumed in his world of sensual pleasure (see Drawing 3.5).

Beyond pleasing the palate, some children just wanted to imagine a place to feel good and relaxed in a general sense. For instance, the dream world of Seyong (B, SK-18) is a place "behind the sky" where he goes to relax. There is no pressure there, only little dogs to play with. He goes with his friends or alone, and he is transported there via his thoughts. Through a whirl of concentric circles, he crosses into his tranquil world on the other side of the sky. Part of the pleasure he takes in this world appears to be visual, as in his interview, he provides an extensive description of the colors.

Crystal (G, US-23) exercises a number of her senses for her own enjoyment in her fantasy—one that also involves the pleasure of relaxation. She rests on a bed of comfortable flowers and enjoys the natural beauty around, including a rose that goes through a metamorphosis to become a rainbow. The end result of all of the pleasant experiences is a world in which she can relax and enjoy herself.

Worlds that fostered sensual pleasure and enjoyment were these children's idea of a good time. They included mostly sweets and ice cream, sometimes in the form of edible houses and trees but also a few aesthetic pleasures for auditory and visual enjoyment. There is very little of nature and animals in these scenes—it is mainly a human-occupied world.

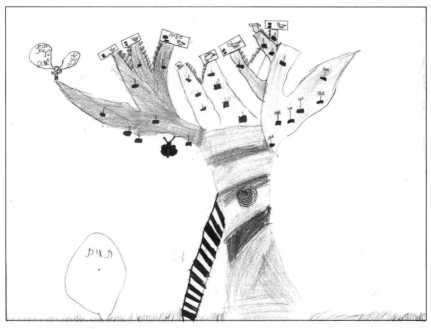

Drawing 3.5. Shuval (B, IS-12) "Chocolate Tree."

THE WORLD OF ROYALTY

Some children imagined worlds in which they had the power to decide every-thing and to be the ultimate rulers. These worlds include an aspect of royalty in which the child is a special figure in the kingdom—one with special powers or the ability to rule. The child is the focus of attention and the hero in his or her own kingdom. Although we had relatively few cases in this category—nine cases (none in Israel), the particular desire to be part of a royal world or to ob-serve one seems worth noting.

Sarah (G, GR-5) imagines an icy kingdom where, as queen, she is in charge of making sure that everything is run smoothly: Sick or injured animals are tended to, celebrations are planned, and the people are taken care of so that everyone can have a good life, Sarah included. She enjoys the sparkling snow and ice as well as riding on her flying horse. She is a benevolent ruler, a nurturer of the ani-mals and citizens, and one who takes time out for herself to enjoy her empire. She conveniently situates her parents in a neighboring land so that she can rule her own territory.

"Lions' Lair" is the domain that Teri (G, US-6) imagines. This is a place where lions rule and Teri, as Strike—the youngest member of the royal family, plays an important role in making sure that the evil lions are not allowed to take over. The royal family lives in the castle, but if you are not a part of the land of the Lions' Lair, the castle will not be visible to you. Strike is the central character in this land. She is a leader, along with her father, and she is the fastest runner, but she can also get into mischief.

> Lions' Lair is my imaginary place. There are adventures, fears, and dangerous people. When I arrive there the lions greet me in the castle. I am a part of the royal family and I am always getting into trouble and I always start the adventures. My name is Strike. I'm the best hunter and the fastest runner. I can make sure grass does not move when I'm sneaking around. The castle is my home. If you aren't a part of the lions' lair and you go by it, then you'll see nothing. When you get far away you will see the lions' lair disappear.

> There's this bad lion there. His name is Powell and there's a Chosen One that no one really knows about. Only the Chosen One knows that they are the Chosen One. And if Powell finds out who that is, the Chosen One will be in deep trouble. You see, when I turn into a lion I *am* the Chosen One. I'm the youngest one in the pack, and I'm always behind everyone making trouble and stuff. Since I am so fast, I am supposed to be watching the end of the pack to look out for danger. The leader is my father, the King. Sometimes I go too far and my father gets worried. He sends people to watch after me and when I come home I get yelled at. My father is always overprotecting me when I can do things by myself. I can only take on Powell with my powers and whenever I'm near him I can't use my powers. I can disappear. I can run really fast like a cheetah. And I can also have pretend horns on and I can butt him. And I can fly. I move so fast that Powell can't see me. I can't go anywhere near Powell when I'm invisible or else he can see me, because he's got powers, too. He can see me right through my invisibility. Powell can turn people into ice and he can fly, too. His tail is like a hard rock on the end, so if he wants to hit someone he can just flip his tail. Powell wants to capture the King and put him in his tower, so that Powell can find the Chosen One.

Clearly, being "The Chosen One" is a very important aspect of Teri's elaborate story. Born to a royal family, she has special abilities as her birthright and is involved not only in ruling but playing a role in the continuation of the reign of her family. Her special position permits her to do things that would have been otherwise unacceptable and also assures her the protection of others who honor her royal status (see Drawing 3.6).

In their own kingdoms, these children build the houses or palaces of their dreams and create lands that they reside in and rule over. They take personal ownership over their kingdoms and their inhabitants. Sometimes, however, they only observe the kingdom from the outside, as does Jun'sik (B, SK-29) who overlooks a castle inhabited by a king with some knights equipped with armor, bows, and swords.

The worlds of royalty contain explicit references to kings, queens, princes, and kingdoms and showcase their special places of residence (e.g., castles) and special protective equipment.

Drawing 3.6. Teri (G, US-6) "Lion's Lair."

THE WORLD OF TECHNOLOGY

Finally, seven of the children endowed their fantasy worlds with high-tech inventions that could help them overcome the limits of the "normal" world. These kinds of devices, similar to supernatural powers, were found in many of the worlds, but they figured in some cases to such a degree that they seemed to be the world's defining characteristic, as in the cases now discussed.

All but one of the children who imagined worlds that foreground technology were boys. Space travel, futuristic visions, and invention-based solutions to solving crimes, overcoming the enemy through technology, and making various endeavors possible characterize these worlds. In these fantasies, the children pay particular attention to creating technologies and they provide details to explain what these inventions do and how they work.

Christian (B, GR-28) has an adventure on the planet Pluto in which technology plays a dominant role. He not only has a fast riding "Pluto scooter," but he finds a "paralyzer" with which you can paralyze objects and people. In his story, the paralyzer helps him get away from some gangsters who were trying to harass and kidnap him.

A machine that creates suns is Gal's fantasy (B, IS-3). He imagines a contraption that manufactures suns and brings them together to make a dynamic rainbow.

> I draw how suns are being created ... This is the sun, and this creates the sun, and after it creates the suns a special sun comes out. These gray clouds and brown triangle—that's where they bring all the suns and together they create the rainbow. This is a kind of a special rainbow that is small at the beginning, and then it grows and then it becomes small again. And the orange is the gate to this area, you can see the fence that separates the suns from the rainbows. The light rays pass in and out, and then everything is whiter and full of color. I saw it as if I am in something huge that you can't come out of, as if I couldn't move. Like something prevented me from passing by and getting closer to this closed-in area. I saw all of this in a dream ... I imagined it.

Via the drawing and the interview, a complex technology and process as well as the possibilities this machine offers are explained. Particular attention is given to the role of light rays and color and Gal demonstrates his fascination with details.

Boram (G, SK-13) imagines a spaceship that looks like a human that will take her and a friend up into the quiet darkness of space to see aliens and to explore. She calls it a "superman rocket" and describes how a bell triggers its launch. She describes the purple fireballs that show that the rocket is operating. As mentioned earlier, this is the only female case in the technology category.

Chad (B, US-32) has devised a way to create water that flows down a waterfall and simultaneously works a dam that provides water for animals down below. He uses a numerical rating "514B" to rate the level of difficulty in climbing the surrounding mountains and imagines a secret elevator for taking him and his friends behind the waterfall.

These cases show evidence of a preoccupation with futuristic machinery and large scale technologies that might, if desired, even help one to rule the universe (e.g., create waterfalls and suns). Special flying cars and rockets, huge space ships, and sophisticated radar and robots are among the technologies that figured in these worlds.

CONCLUSION

It is clear from these examples that when given the chance to let their imaginations run freely, the children in these four countries projected themselves into the world of their dreams where, for example, the sun usually shines and the good triumphs over the evil; where one can fly or do magic; and enjoy the good things in life—both real and imagined. Overall, regardless of the children's country, worlds of either harmony with nature and animals or worlds of conflict and threats as well as amusement are the major contexts for their fantasies. Such contexts account for two-thirds of all the cases. Even though we can identify patterns in the types of worlds the children created, there is also a broad diversity in the features of those worlds and in what occurs in them.

Children often include biographical references in their make-believe worlds, that is, there are many traces of the integration of real-life experiences into their fantasies. They imagine their friends joining them in their fantasy world. Juliane (G, GR-58) and her friend Lea, for example, are traveling to the ponyland; Marsha (G, US-16) turns into a witch and, joined by her friends, takes a ride on a broom through the world of witches and magicians. Ravit (G, IS-36) takes only her female friends on the fantasy tour; and Seyong (B, SK-18) likes to be with girls when staying in his make-believe world in heaven, but does not admit his parents because they evoke too much pressure. In 20% of the children's make-believe worlds, they are joined by their real everyday-life friends (although they only draw 10% of them in the pictures).

In some cases, the parents and other adult relatives are mentioned (about 17%) or drawn (very few) by the children. For example, Felix (B, GR-15), his father and his sister are drawn lying on a sandy beach beneath the palm trees; Ellie's parents (G, US-18) live on the ground floor of a house situated in her fantasy world; Noa (G, IS-14) spends the time at the sea alone with her deceased mother; and Dam'dok (B, SK-40) is joined by his father and his brother on a journey through the universe. Sometimes, real-life pets are brought along by the children to their fantasy worlds such as Sabine's (G, GR-46) dog, who flies with her to Paris.

Apart from persons or animals, the children also include real locations that are part of their everyday lives in their make-believe worlds. Lior (G, IS-16) describes a big basketball gym that is close to home where she performs jazz dances with her dance ensemble. Anna-Maria's (G, GR-25) fantasy world, on the other hand, refers to the faraway land of Gran Canaria Island, where she had previously been on a holiday. She is seen lying on a deck-chair on the beach looking toward the sea, just as she has done in the past. In her imagination trip, Kathy (G, US-17) climbs mountains she had seen in India on a recent trip with her family.

In analyzing the kinds of worlds the children imagined, it is evident that they brought information from a wide range of sources—whether from formal or informal information, mediated or nonmediated sources. They mix and match the pieces and interweave them according to their own individual desires and dreams, in ways that produce deeply compelling and often detailed worlds for playing out their fantasies. For the sake of analysis, we have separated the description of the worlds from the actual activities enacted and desires expressed in the worlds. The next chapter delves more deeply into what the children actually do and how they project themselves into the contexts they have dreamed.

4

The Child in the Make-Believe World

Chapter 3 presented an examination of children's make-believe worlds. Fantasy scenarios or activities that children imagine for themselves are closely associated with the nature of the dream worlds. This chapter offers an analysis of how children envision themselves in their fantasy worlds and how they live out their wishes to act in them. The analysis enables us to answer questions such as: Into what roles do children project themselves and who accompanies them? How are everyday experiences used and represented? Are there patterns in the kinds of discrete activities that are imagined?

One obvious aspect of the child in the make-believe world is the position he or she chooses to assign themselves and others in this world. In many of the stories, the children are the central characters. In close to half of the cases, they occupy that role alone; in close to one third of the cases, they appear together with real others and much less often with a fantasy character. They position themselves as onlookers in only a few stories, while in about a tenth of the stories the children do not appear at all (see Table 4.1).

Via fantasy, children are free to play out roles and actions that are out of reach in real life. In a number of stories, the children take on roles that are far removed from their everyday identities. For instance, children may find themselves in the role of "the hero," "the man ready for a fight," "the young star," or "the queen," to name a few. In some cases, their fantasy identities are central and encapsulate the meaning of the whole story. However, in many other cases,

TABLE 4.1

Children's Positions in Their Make-Believe Worlds

	Child Alone	Child With a Real Person	Child With a Fantasy Character	Child Not Present	Child as an Outside Viewer
Girls (n = 110)	48 (44%)	35 (32%)	14 (13%)	8 (7%)	5 (4.5%)
Boys (n = 83)	34 (41%)	22 (26.5%)	7 (8%)	14 (17%)	6 (7%)
Total (n = 193)	82	57	21	22	11

the fantasy role is limited in scope and is simply a mechanism for developing a more complicated persona and narrative.

In all cases, however, regardless of the child's position within it, the make-believe world opens up possibilities for acting and experiencing. Even if the children are not visible at the center of their drawings, they are still active in imagining, drawing, and telling about them.

TYPES OF ACTIVITY IN THE MAKE-BELIEVE WORLD

So what is it that children actually do in their imaginary worlds? What are their wishes in terms of the kinds of activities, interactions, and outcomes they themselves reveal within their fantasies? The wishes to act are expressed in various ways and at different points of entry along the way in the process of imagining and expressing their stories. For example, children's activities can be central to the fantasy narrative, as in the case of a child imagining herself or himself as a queen or princess in a country, or as a treasure hunter who has to overcome obstacles. Alternatively, their wishes for action may come into play at the level of creating and shaping the story. Even when the children do not explicitly place themselves in their world and related stories or even when they see themselves as onlookers, the fantasizing itself is connected to certain forms of experiencing and the possibilities of taking action. Another way in which some children expressed their wishes to act was by "acting out" for the interviewer as their audience in the interview situation. Some children appeared to invest a great deal of effort "performing" their fantasy for the interviewer, as did Vanessa (G, GR-45), who pretended during the interview that her fantasy really happened to her.

The wishes to act that run through these stories can be grouped thematically based on the qualitative clustering procedure already described (see chap. 2). The analysis of the "worlds" was based on detailed depictions and descriptions of the surroundings and objects, and drew heavily on visual analysis of the drawing. In contrast, the thematic grouping process of the wish to act was accomplished via an interpretative reconstructive process. This analysis was based, in large part, on what children related during the interviews. Each type of wish to act that was identified through this process of analysis of the case studies has distinguishing features which are now detailed. Some of the wishes relate to an inner state of mind. For example, the wish to be in harmony is directed inward; it is a wish to be in a particular mental and emotional state. Other forms of affect require outer influences for realization; for instance, the recognition by others, as in the case of the wishes to be special.

The "distribution" of the wish to act and its distinctive features are summarized in Table 4.2. However, it should be clear that children's make-believe worlds often embraced more than one desire. For the sake of presenting the wishes in a coherent way, we elected to place each story under one dominant wish that we considered to be overriding.

Clearly the wishes to act are related to the various types of worlds presented in chapter 3. In many cases, children act out their wishes in worlds whose very

TABLE 4.2

The Wishes to Act in the Make-Believe World

Wish to Act	Number of Children for Whom it is a Central Wish (%)	Distinctive Features
Experiencing well-being	56 (28%)	Experiencing a feeling of well-being; internal serenity; unity with nature and humankind. This form of acting is directed inward to being in an emotional state.
Experiencing thrill	48 (25%)	Experiencing or watching fights; exploring new things; experiencing/seeing physical excitement, successfully mastering special tasks; going on adventures.
Bonding with others	36 (19%)	Shared interests with peers; intimate relationship of two persons; close association with animals, organized companionship, and close family relations.
Displaying one's specialness	22 (11%)	Staging oneself as special; receiving attention and recognition of others, sometimes with the help of accessories.
Protecting/being protected	17 (9%)	Pushing away an acute threat; preparing/obtaining a place of refuge; being helpful to others or being helped by others.
Acting independently	14 (7%)	The "I can-do it myself" attitude; self-determined control of the situation.

nature and structure includes such desires. The type of world and the wish over-lap—wishes for a feeling of well-being with the worlds of harmony, and wishes for thrills in the worlds of conflict and threat or amusement. However, this is not always the case, as these types of wishes to act were also found throughout the range of worlds. In addition, the wishes to act have several gendered character-istics that are discussed in chapter 6.

EXPERIENCING A FEELING OF WELL-BEING

Experiencing a harmonious feeling of well-being as the central feature of the make-believe world is the largest cluster of wishes and most often appears in the world of harmony and peace, but not always. For 55 children, mostly girls, this was the overriding wish for action in their fantasy. Rhonda (G, US-24) provides such an example when she fantasizes herself in the land of "waterfall and rain-bow" in a jungle, which is a world of harmony and peace:

> I went to the world of my dreams. This is a world I have visited many times. There was a waterfall. It was so pretty. Suddenly a rainbow popped up. There were all different kinds of animals and birds. And I was living in the jungle—in a cave. And I had a lot of pets. You don't see me in the picture because I was in the jungle, picking berries to eat. Some of my friends and family were there. We had traveled across the ocean to get there in a boat built of sticks and weeds. The animals there were friendly and could talk like people. There were beavers, birds, bears, wild cats, wild dogs, lions, tigers, all kinds of things. We talked about things like friendship. We talked about how we got here. We talked about how they got there. My parents were out getting some water and my friends were out playing, and I was picking berries then. The animals were sleeping. It felt really good and it felt very quiet. It was not loud—almost never loud. It was just like a break from the real world. The fantasy ended with me going into the cave and falling asleep and then going back into real life.

Rhonda draws and describes a world in which everything is harmonious. Her picture consists of rounded areas that match one another and aestheti-cally express a peaceful way of living together. The sudden appearance of the rainbow highlights the beauty in the wonderful world that they are already enjoying so much. Within this world, intense and intimate communication by Rhonda and the other living beings is central. She wants to discuss peace-ful topics like "friendship" and to think about existential questions. For Rhonda, her own experience of harmony with others is central. She explic-itly says, *"I felt very good and completely peaceful here."* Her daydream is a "break from the real world." It enables her to act in complete harmony with others. Rhonda falls into a blissful sleep at the end of her fantasy. This is a peaceful mechanism for transporting her back into reality at the end of the fantasy journey.

In some cases, the children describe their fantasy experience explicitly, as did Son'he (G, SK-39), who stresses several times in her interview *"I'm incredibly happy here."* (see Drawing 4.1).

> I flew to the dreamland on the clouds. It was wonderful. It was like cloud park. It was very clean there. It is the first time I have experienced such a wonderful land … Whenever I think of it, or when I'm angry, I come here to feel better. When I'm happy I also come here. Then I feel even better.

Other children position themselves outside the scene in their drawings. In this position, they can observe themselves and others, such as Hannah (G, IS-24), who describes her feelings while looking at the landscape: *"I feel good."* The beautiful and harmonious experience is for the children central to their daydream. It is a non-specific feeling, not necessarily spectacular in kind, just "feeling good," but it is nevertheless dominant, in terms of frequency. The world they imagine offers them the necessary aesthetic framework in which to act and experience this emotional state of well-being.

EXPERIENCING THRILL

The fantasies of 48 children, mostly boys, are based on a wish to experience thrill. These fantasies of thrill involve stories that allow children to encounter

Drawing 4.1. Son'he (G, SK-39) "The Fantasyland."

adventures, wage battles, and/or make thrilling discoveries. They can involve keeping danger at bay and overcoming obstacles through transformation to other more powerful forms of being, or with the help of a powerful ally. This wish for action is often located in the world of conflict and threat and in the world of amusement, but not always. Thus, violent fights often figure in these fantasies and are characteristic of this cluster.

The wish for action is portrayed not only in the children's stories, but figure as well in their drawing styles. Lines are used as artistic means of indicating action and motion. Painting an object several times indicates its movement, as the path of the ball into the soccer net in Raviv's drawing (B, IS-18).

Some of these stories involve an attack on the child's fantasy self. For example Gregor (B, GR-9) is electrified by a Pokémon with special powers. Sometimes, as in Jed's case (B, US-35), the threat is to the child and others. Jed imagines himself as a *Dragon Ball Z* fighter on the counteroffensive against Cell, the evil enemy who threatens the earth. In some cases, however, children expressing this wish for excitement do not imagine themselves as playing a fighting role. More frequently (noticeably in the Korean sample) they position themselves as observers of the threat. For example, Gui'hyung (B, SK-4) describes the fighting in his make-believe world of dinosaurs. He himself is not part of the fighting, but experiences the thrill through his ability to create the scene.

In addition to fighting, the fantasies that express wishes for thrill have other distinctive features. A frequent variant of the "thrill experience" is the fantasy that involves exploration or discovery. In spaceships, airplanes, or on wings of their own, children enter an alien, unknown country. On the journey, extremely tense situations are imagined and when the destination is reached, new places are discovered and explored. In the stories, which again are more likely to be those of boys, pleasure is expressed in anticipation of the exciting and unknown things to be explored in these alien places. Micha (B, GR-60), for example, talks about his desire to travel to the land of the dinosaurs and how exciting it will be. A big dinosaur came up to him roaring and stamping *"nastily."* Micha was *"a bit"* frightened so he flew back again.

Standing up to a challenge or holding one's own against the odds in the make-believe adventures is a fantasy of thrill some children relished. David (B, IS-4) describes his adventure in "Treasure Island" this way:

> I left home and walked to the Sea of Galilee with a map, but I got lost. This is an island divided into two parts and here is a bridge. I came by kayak and built my own tent. In it I have weapons, clothes, food, and things that help me on my journey. Here is a hammock between two coconut trees. There is a tribe of cannibals there. There are snakes and elephants, lions, crocodiles, and I go through many adventures, such as fighting the cannibal. He followed me, jumped on me, tied me up, put me in the pot, but I got

out and shot him in the leg. Later I go through rivers filled with crocodiles. I am chased by a nervous rare white elephant with very big ivory tusks. I fight a lion, cross the shaky bridge and get to the cave with the gold. I search for the treasure, find it in the box, return all the way back to the tent, fold it, take everything with me, and return with the kayak. I also feel happy, because I found the gold.

David's drawing of Treasure Island from a bird's-eye perspective is the same as that of a computer game. However, he allows himself complete freedom of imagination while building on the original narrative. He even chooses to place his adventure in his own country's largest lake—the Sea of Galilee. He finds himself in an exciting world in which he is attacked by cannibals and white elephants. He skillfully copes with the threats and shows himself to be courageous, self-reliant, and lucky. He is active, seeks his own way and manages to accomplish his mission. Although there is a threat to his life, it can be overcome through his own efforts.

This moment of averting a threat comes up in several fantasies. Christian (B, GR-28), for example, relates an exciting fantasy in the planet of Pluto, where he, as an inventor, wards off the threat of meteorites. In an attack by gangsters, he manages to avert the danger with the help of his friends and his own invention. In this way he faces challenges from the world around him by taking vigorous action.

The feeling aroused by these fantasies, along with the thrill they produce, is described by the children in very positive terms. Pierre (B, GR-41) tells us that in his make-believe world in Disneyland, Paris, he feels extremely good when experiencing a scary ride. He enthusiastically reports on the ghost train: *"You jolt along and it gives me the creeps and it's fun."* Pierre's sense of fun is tied up with the thrill and the fear of going on the ghost train. Clearly this is a kind of enjoyment experienced by many people around the world who enjoy the frightening sensation of amusement-park rides.

BEING CONNECTED

Another cluster of typical wishes involves bonding with others. The others can be people or animals. The act of "being in a relationship" is the central wish in these fantasies. The children talk about close partnerships and friendships in groups or dyads. This wish to act was central in 36 of the make-believe worlds and was identified in fantasies of boys and girls with about the same frequency.

The wish to be part of a select peer group was a dominant theme in these fantasies. For example, Byong'je (B, SK-2) reports how he and his friends, Young'jun and Hyong'uk, are planning to visit a recreational park. However, in his picture and in his story, the primary interest is not the experiences in the park per se, but rather organizing the outing and going to the park with friends. Common mutual interests, such as sports, frequently figure in the make-believe worlds. In this vein, Jong'yun (B, SK-31) plays football with six friends and with Solaman (a media figure). Narmeen (G, IS-49) plays basketball with her twin sister and best friend. The stories of this type are usually not very long, since presumably everything necessary has been said in the description of the setting and nothing more needs explaining.

A number of children who expressed the wish to be part of a select peer grouping articulated their ideas using similar conventions in their drawings. For example, it was common for the children to depict the stature and facial expressions of the various group members in a similar manner. However, by changing the clothes so that they are different colors the friends are characterized as individuals and their facial expressions indicate enjoyment of sharing the experience together. For example, the three friends in the picture by Seo, have the same clothing but each wears a different color pullover (light blue, dark blue, yellow) and pants (blue, red, yellow). Similarly, Narmeen colors the upper parts of the three girls in a variety of colors (yellow, brown, blue). Even if this may appear insignificant at first glance, it does mean that while drawing, the child had to change the crayon, a deliberate and thus significant action. This becomes particularly meaningful when comparing other drawings, where children either colored all the characters in the same way or alternatively, completely different from one another. How peers are arranged in the drawing reveals further typical features. The friends are geometrically placed in relation to one another, reflecting the mutuality of the relationship: a group of three usually forms a triangle and a group of four is placed in a square formation.

Dyads and the desire for an intimate relationship between two characters, figure prominently in these fantasies. In dyad stories, the children are concerned with acting and creating together as a paired unit. Such is the case of Isabell (G, GR-52) who lives with her best girlfriend in their own Kingdom (see Drawing 4.2):

> My friend and I invented a secret land. Only the two of us know of it and we are the queens there. Because otherwise, if I was the queen, it would not be not fair to my friend. And if she was the queen, it's not fair to me. So we thought we'd rather both be queens. Our castle is close to an island in Greece and on our island nobody gets killed. And, there is also no robbery. No bad guys are allowed. At the border we have special secret agents who are taking care that no bad people come in. In the center of the island there is our castle made of blue diamonds. One part of it is mine, the other belongs to my friend, and we share the middle part. In the evening, when the sun goes down, I do a piano concert and my friend plays the flute. What I like most of all is when the whole land comes to listen to us. Our land is called "Is-Theres", like us: Isabel and Theresa.

In this make-believe world, which Isabell and her friend have created and inhabit in their imaginary play over quite a long period of time, equality between two girls is clearly vital as is the secret nature of their island. They share their

Drawing 4.2. Isabell (G, GR-52) "Is-Theres at Night."

palace on equal terms, eliminate crime together, occupy their evenings with a joint concert, and name this island using a combination of their names. Isabell derives her power and pleasure from the idea of having this private place with her friend in which the two of them rule as queens.

Dyads, in some cases, involve an intimate relationship with a sibling or other family member. Dana (G, IS-42), for example, creates a fantasy in which she and her brother raise fish and seahorses together and play on the dock in a world that reminds her of *The Little Mermaid*. The wish for an intimate relationship becomes quite clear in Noa's (G, IS-14) story, in which she expresses a desire for a reunion with her deceased mother: *"Only me and my mother are there,"* she says. She states that she intentionally leaves her father and brother out of this make-believe world, because she is in a close relationship with them in everyday life. The intimate relationship of the mother and daughter is expressed very clearly in her drawing: the two figures stand close together, side by side, at the right-hand bottom corner of the picture, while in the rest of the picture the minimalist drawing of "air lines" and a sandy ground indicate a deserted seashore. The picture is all about Noa and her mother, not about what is all around them.

Animals, real or imagined, also figure in a number of these fantasies of intimate relationships. Angelo (B, GR-42) dreams of flying on his winged-horse,

Pegasus, into a country populated by many animals. On his flights across the country, he occasionally takes other animals with him, such as a mouse or a leopard, which he snuggles up with whenever he is tired. This sensual component of bonding—the physical touch—is articulated by the children only in stories about animals and creatures, in contrast to those involving other people. At this age, children may be too shy to express a need for human touch—either seeing it as too "childish" for their age, too shameful, or perhaps even sexual.

You'jin (G, SK-11) imagines the efforts toward forming a trusting relationship where both sides first have to overcome their own fears: *"When I was here for the first time I was frightened, because the wild animals roared so loud that I hid behind a big flower. But the animals became friendly when I visited them more often and then even the little animals made friends with me."*

In a very similar way, Bilgrim (G, GR-38) also imagines an underwater world in which the smaller fish are afraid of her at first. But after some time, this shyness goes away and they swim together in the sea. It seems that these children are trying to form and to develop relationships with other living beings. Bonding with animals and helping animals overcome their shyness with people is important to these children.

Another way in which children express their wish for relationships and connection is by creating communities for living together and knowing each other. So'yun (G, SK-28) paints a town where the houses are connected by passages. Each of these houses looks unique. She herself wanders through the corridors with her friends and meets the nice people and animals living in this town. Tom (B, IS-27) also imagines he is in a community consisting of many houses arranged aligned in a row. Elli (G, US-18) dreams up a world in which there are different houses; a home for animals; a nature information center; but also, for example, a playground, swimming pool, and a lake. *"I have a lot of friends in my world,"* she says. *"All live together and look after each other."* There is even a cloud through which other friends can be linked to her. The elements of her fantasy (the nature center), playground, pool, lake are taken from the real world of the daycamp in which she and her buddies spend their summer. So her fantasy is a way of allowing her and her group of friends to remain together and to extend the bond and the fun they have in the daycamp to their home lives.

Aesthetically these desires to act are characterized by drawing a network composed of different parts, each signifying unique existence. Thus Elli paints the houses in various colors and designs. Son'yun invents make-believe houses, such as the drop-of-water house, the sunflower house, the beer house, or a house with a laughing face. The individual elements of the community symbolically express individuality. This becomes very clear in the case of Tom (B, IS-27), who, for example, paints a community of 22 small houses in a row, all with the same square shape, red roof, yellow walls and blue circle in the middle. His own house, however, third in the line, is unique and original in appearance: it is three times larger, much more cheerful and colorful (with vivid purple, red, yellow, green, and blue colors) and unusually shaped.

In this pattern of stories, children's actions are quite limited in that they may just drift along in their make-believe country and enjoy their relationships with others. In some cases, the children themselves are not even pictured in the drawings. In these cases, it is more the idea of being together and having relationships in supporting communities than the individual child's active role in the fantasy.

BEING SPECIAL

Another typical wish to act centers on the state of being special. In 22 of the cases this wish was central. Possession of abilities that set the child apart from and above the crowd are important in these fantasies. For example, Oz (B, IS-45) imagines himself taking part in the World Cup soccer match in England in his "Mondial" make-believe world (see Drawing 4.3):

> This match is taking place in England. It's the world championship and it has to have a stadium that doesn't belong to Maccabi Tel Aviv or to Real Madrid, so it will be fair.

Drawing 4.3. Oz (B, IS-45) "Mondial."

There is a sign and a table with the trophy that says that Maccabi Tel Aviv is world champion. I am here in yellow. I am 25 [years-old], number 9, because it is my lucky number and I am also number 9 in class. I kick the final penalty kick for Maccabi Tel Aviv ... the ball turns around until it reaches the net ... and the goalie is crying because his team has lost ... he is wearing blue and his name is Cassias, and he is a good goalie ... Everybody was praying that I would kick the penalty kick ... and there was lots of pressure ... but when I made it I took off my shirt and threw it to the fans, ran to the audience, and hugged my parents and friends and teammates, and cried with excitement .... everybody was there except people I don't like .... and outside of the field there were Pokémon too, all of them, and 101 more, and I would have liked to be Ash.

Oz imagines a scene in which his free kick scores the goal that decides the World Cup. The others placed their hopes on him and he does not disappoint them. In the interview, he vividly describes his triumph and how all those around him are screaming with enthusiasm. What in the case of Oz is formulated quite clearly and outspokenly is rather less obvious in other cases, as with Dor (B, IS-13), who also imagines himself as soccer star. In his picture he places himself at the very top, just below the airplane announcing the victory of the soccer team. It is therefore not so much he himself alone who is in the prominent position, but the interplay between him and his admired idol. While he states *I am the best in my soccer team*—he also writes the name of this player behind his own and lets him hold his favorite animal. In this way, a form of identification in which Dor imagines himself in the position of the soccer star becomes obvious.

These cases involve children being special by being in the spotlight. It is through the appreciation of others, who are likely to be a part of a mass audience, that this specialness is articulated. Tali (G, IS-6) imagines herself with her favorite star, Natali Orero, in the limelight of the stage. The people shout admiringly, *"Applause for Tali,"* when she appears onstage. In this fantasy, admiration and acknowledgment are central. Max (B, GR-20) also shows himself to be special in his daydream when he stands as the competent captain on the bridge of the MS Europa and commands a whole ship. Similarly, Jack (B, US-25) wins in the show, *Who Wants to Be a Millionaire,* and both the studio audience and the television audience play a role in his feelings of excitement and happiness. Being a winner on the show is more about being in the spotlight than it is about winning the million dollars.

Being special in the children's make-believe worlds can derive from some extraordinary abilities that they have acquired or inherited. Teri (G, US-6) imagines herself as the secret successor to the kingdom. She is the chosen one and endowed with special talents, such as becoming invisible. In Marsha's (G, US-16) world of magic, the emphasis is also on her uniqueness and special abilities. She imagines herself as a witch with magical powers. However, she does not require a leading position or the acclaim of others. In Marsha's real life, she thinks of herself as having always been a bit like a witch. She uses this self-perception in the make-believe world by imagining herself as a classic Halloween witch and creating a world of witches and wizards.

In other similar examples, Saya (G, GR-4) takes advantage of her natural long dark hair to interpret herself as a special person—a Native American who lives with animals. Tanja (G, GR-53) expresses her specialness by wearing a magnificent dress and feeling like a princess.

In these make-believe worlds it is not necessary to have one's achievements acknowledged by others in order to experience one's own specialness. In Tanja's or Saya's make-believe worlds, for example, other people are not allowed in at all. These children (mostly girls) draw themselves as being integrated into the environment, and not as the main focus of attention, and yet clearly characterize themselves as being special by detailed drawing of themselves.

PROTECTING AND BEING PROTECTED

Protection is another theme running through the wishes of the children. To protect or be protected is the explicit wish of 18 cases. One way this is expressed is through the action of warding off immediate threats. In Udi's (B, IS-1) world, for example, witches and wizards from a world that he calls Evilina threaten his country, Magicia. His family members, who possess powerful forces of their own, receive support from the *Pokémon* planet. Together they succeed in protecting the country. Jody (G, US-15) is worried that animals become extinct and becomes a protector from attackers who threaten them. She draws herself in the center of the picture in a "ready-to-act" protecting position. She takes the role of a fierce, but protective, saber-toothed Arctic tiger.

In make-believe worlds like this one, the child's role as protector is an important part of the narrative, even when it is not explicitly stated. Similarly, in Jeremy's (B, US-20) fantasy, he relates how he experiences a challenging adventure when he has to free a princess and protect her from great harm. In some stories, there is a complementary relationship between protecting and being protected. For instance, Robby (B, GR-43) reports on his imaginary companion, a dragon who protects him and takes revenge for him, but who also needs Robby's protection. He and his dragon appear at the center of the picture wearing matching clothes.

In some of these stories, an imaginary place of refuge is an important element. For example, Tessina (G, GR-3) takes endangered animals into her island. In her castle, with its thick walls, she creates safe areas for them to escape from those who would prey on them. In order to provide the animals with additional protection, she also introduces a basic rule: Humans who potentially threaten the animals are not allowed to stay on the island at night.

Peter (B, GR-10) has similar daydreams. He wants to buy a nature reserve where the ecological balance can thrive undisturbed. Those protected spaces are imagined, not only for the benefit of others, but sometimes for the children themselves as well.

ACTING INDEPENDENTLY

The wish to act independently is found in 14 of the children's stories. A strong desire to act and to prove themselves based on their own merits, strengths, and will characterizes these stories. For example, Raz (B, IS-33) imagines how he survives in a jungle on an island. He relates: *"I am on the island and it's really difficult to survive there."* In his narrative, he puts special emphasis on his self-sufficiency. He recognizes the problems ahead and equips himself with the things he needs to survive on the island. His own competence and ability to cope with the difficulties faced is for him, as for others whose desires are similar, a defining aspect of the fantasy.

Similarly, Charlotte (G, GR-12) imagines herself on a strenuous journey that she takes with her horse every year to travel from Arabia to Spain in order to help the people there. She is motivated by her desire to help out and protect the inhabitants from hunger. But what is of central importance to Charlotte is her choice to do this on her own.

Interestingly, this wish to act is often expressed in connection with the child's actual everyday world. Annelie (G, GR-36), for example, imagines that she is again on holiday in Lanzarote, but this time she is skilled enough to go swimming alone, something her parents prevented her from doing the previous time. Shuval (B, IS-12) imagines a chocolate tree from which he can eat as much as he wants whenever he wants—something he is forbidden to do in real life by his dentist mother. Dominique (G, GR-40) wishes she could fly so that she can go back and forth on her own between her home and a garden plot that her family tends. In these stories, the children put the emphasis on acting according to their own wills. The children want to organize, take on responsibility, blaze their own trails, and shape their own environments. To do so, they imagine a world around them where others do not tell them what to do or interfere with their desires to act on their own.

The children picture themselves and the situations in which they can act independently in the drawings. Sarah (G, GR-5) is a typical example of this desire for independent action. She imagines herself as an ice princess inside an ice castle (see Drawing 4.4):

> I am an ice princess and I have an ice castle. Everything around me is glittering and sparkling. I'm not cold, since I was born here and I am used to the cold. I have a flying

Drawing 4.4. Sarah (G, GR-5) "Inside the Ice Castle."

horse (you can see it at the edge of my picture, when it's entering) ... This is very important, because I need to check if everything is okay. Sometimes an animal is sick and I help out. The rabbit, for example, cut its paw and I treated it, so that it can run around again freely. In this land I am the queen. My parents live in a neighboring land, but I'm ruling on my own. And I care about everybody in my country, so that they can have a great life—and me too. We set up great celebrations, where everybody who has time can come. I organize them and sometimes I even show up myself, if I find time. But most of all I enjoy flying with my horse.

Sarah decides for herself how she organizes her own special world, just like girl characters in the books she likes to read.

BIOGRAPHICAL TRACES
IN CHILDREN'S WISHES TO ACT

Concrete references to real life can be the takeoff point for children's wishes for themselves in their imagined world. In all four countries, we found similar patterns in which real-life experiences were expanded upon in fantasy. For instance, children's narratives may provide further developments of a special interest, build on a story told by a significant other, expand on a positive experience or correct a negative one.

Further Development of a Special Interest.   In their everyday lives, children develop special interests that contribute to identity formation. They enjoy such interests, cultivate them, identify with them, and are defined themselves by others through them. In their fantasies, children sometimes place their interests right at the center of their world and make them their main motif. Max (B, GR-20), who loves ships and is a real expert on this topic, learned everything he knows about ships from books and from television programs. In his make-believe world, he is the captain of the MS Europe and demonstrates his detailed knowledge of the command bridge. After a short stop at Bergen, where he meets with the crown prince, the ship steams along to New York. Similarly, Gal (B, IS-3), who is very interested in astronomy, constructs a special machine that creates suns that form a special colorful rainbow. David (B, US-31) loves dinosaurs and is an avid viewer of television and movies on them. He imagines being a very big dinosaur and being able to run very fast. When engaged in their fantasy, these boys expand their special interests in their make-believe worlds in a way that goes far beyond the limits of their everyday lives.

Further Development of a Story Being Told by a Significant Other.   Some children's takeoff points are stories or narratives that have been shared with them by other people who play an important role in their lives, such as family members. In their imagination, they expand these stories to fit their needs. In doing so they integrate someone else's positive experience as a starting point for their own individual fantasy, repeating yet building upon it and thus making it their own.

Tessina (G, GR-3) dreams of a place she calls the Seashells, a renaming of the Seychelles, with which she is semantically more familiar. There she imagines a paradise for endangered animals with a white sandy beach and deep blue sea. In addition to the biographical experience, as related to her enthusiastically by her mother, Tessina is creating a world according to her own inner images and corresponding experiences. She incorporates a European castle familiar to her from her home region of Bavaria. Mary's (G, US-9) make-believe world shows a beach in California with yellow sand and palm trees that she has seen in some of her mother's photographs. What especially pleases her are the numerous shells and starfish in the ocean. Maroum (B, IS-10) has heard about Switzerland from his father. He imagines a quiet, green land, with blue skies, fruit trees, and a shining sun. His own version of Switzerland includes a huge ocean full of playful fish.

Sometimes the stories told by significant others are not about concrete places or experiences but are spiritual in nature. Yun'jong (G, SK-24) and her family live a very Christian-oriented life. In her make-believe world Yun'jong draws upon this family background and elaborates on it, as she imagines herself meeting Jesus in heaven.

In these cases, stories told by others are the starting point for children's fantasies. Their imaginary stories build upon what they have been told and incorporate key elements: the photograph of the beach, the shell brought along, or even the flag of a foreign country.

Further Development of a Positive Experience. In some stories told by the children, it became obvious that the story was based on a positive, happy event. In their fantasy they want not only to relive it, but to make it even better. Mira (G, GR-31), for example, had once been on holiday at the North Sea with her parents and wants to go there once more. In her make-believe world, she is at the familiar beach, but she expands on this experience and imagines a treasure island and a related adventure. Myong'hun (B, SK-33) wants to relive an amazing experience he had at an amusement park. His thrill from the actual experience is relived in his imagination: *"My mouth is open wide, because I'm so surprised and overwhelmed by this land."* While in real life people have to wait in lines for a very long time, in his make-believe world, the waiting turns into a fun experience: *"And if somebody is hungry, you can eat imaginary bread. And, if somebody gets bored, the circus comes and does everything you wish."* In addition, in this dream park, one is allowed to take as many products and toys from the park as one wishes without having to purchase them. Not only are the fun parts as great as he remembers, but in fantasy, he can eliminate the parts of the experience that he did not enjoy.

These examples indicate that children wish to relive a wonderful experience in the realm of fantasy and to improve or expand upon the situations in order to fulfil their fantasy wishes.

Correction of Negative Experiences. Children also have negative experiences that make them unhappy in their everyday lives. Some children describe such negative experiences, but correct them and turn them into something positive in their fantasies. Sabine's (G, GR-46) parents have recently divorced and her family has difficulties due to this decision. In her make-believe world, she is trying to change the situation. She explains how after a fight took place in her family, she fantasizes about flying to Paris with her dog. *"I fly to Paris, since I have had a fight with my family. First I went to bed and cried and my dog comforted me. The others just went to Paris. Now I fly there."* She is the youngest of the three siblings and was made to go to bed early. But in her dream city of Paris, where her family members are all scattered, she is able to meet them all and bring them together again *"and fortunately no one argues any more and I'm so happy."* In her story, they spent a wonderful week together after which they all returned home to Germany, have barbecues and celebrate, and never have to argue again. Betty (G, US-5) rides on her scooter to a beach in California in her make-believe world. In reality, a planned trip to California was canceled. Noa (G, IS-14) wants to be with her mother, who passed away 4 years ago. In her fantasy, she expresses her desire to be together with her mother—just the two of them alone, together, on a beach where Noa once celebrated her birthday with both parents. Similarly, Young'son (G, SK-12) expresses the wish to walk on a cloud because she believes her deceased grandmother is there.

In these cases, the children recall their negative experiences, like family conflict, death of a family member, or a thwarted wish, and try to turn these negative experiences into something positive. Real-world experiences find their way into children's make-believe worlds and can become the starting point of a story. Regardless of the source of information—be it their own experience or something related to them by others—children change them in their make-believe worlds to fulfill their wishes.

CONCLUSION

In many of the make-believe worlds, children are imagining themselves as active. They allow themselves to be carried away by the atmosphere, to enjoy excitement or harmony, to feel close to one another, to feel protected, or to protect others. They demonstrate their own specialness and independence. Some wishes to act are expressed clearly in various forms of behaviors as in the case of most of the wishes for excitement and thrill. But not all the actions are observable behaviors.

Overall, the children in this study are in search of actions that empower them. They actively develop elements drawn from their real lives in their make-believe worlds. They are mostly wishing for positive things—for themselves and for others—and avoiding dealing with negative or aggressive desires that they most probably have. Although this may be explained by conforming to the norms and expectations of the social context of interacting with an unknown adult in research, it is also much in line with the literature documenting the positive nature of daydreaming, in contrast with subconscious night dreaming, where many repressed thoughts and drives surface, as discussed in the theoretical introduction.

5

Media Traces in Children's Make-Believe Worlds

The question of the relationship between the media and children's make-believe worlds is central to this study. Is it the case, as is often proposed, that the media destroy children's imaginations and fantasy worlds (Mander, 1978; Winn, 1977)? Do their aspirations, dreams, and wishes for themselves and the world around them totally overlap with and derive from values and messages they are exposed to via mediated content? Or, do they actively use media content to create their own meanings? With such questions in mind, we analyzed the media traces found in children's make-believe worlds. We were interested in understanding how children use "raw content material" that originates in their media-related experiences in their fantasy world of make-believe.

EXPLICIT AND IMPLICIT MEDIA TRACES

One can make the argument that everything in children's make-believe worlds, if not taken from their direct experience of the "real" world, is somehow related to the media, at least on a subconscious level. For example, a child's drawing of a knight or a spaceship is most likely related to an experience they have had through a mediated source—be it a book, a television program, a school poster, or a museum exhibit. In the interest of a more meaningful way to analyze media's role in children's fantasies, we focused our attention on those references in the child's make-believe world that we ascertained had direct connections to the media. We distinguish between those traces that can be thought of as "explicit;" that is, when the child specifically named the source, for example, the name of book, TV program or the like, and those that are implicit, that is, when it was very clear from the interview or written story that the child was making a connection to the media in explaining the make-believe world and/or the drawing itself (see Table 5.1).

Rather than viewing all media traces as equal, we suggest that media traces figure in children's fantasies along a continuum. At one extreme, the make-believe world is completely located within a medium-related experience (e.g., the land of *Jurassic Park* or *Pokémon*). At the other extreme are cases in which we could not identify any direct media traces, explicit or implicit (e.g., an aesthetic design or a reconstruction of a real-life experience that does not appear to carry with it any resemblance or trace of anything mediated). The latter was, indeed, the case in about 25% of boys' and 40% of the girls' stories.

The importance of this finding can not be overstated; although growing up in a media-saturated world in all four cultures in the study, a significant proportion of the children did not use media as stimulators of their make-believe worlds. Even if we consider our methodological reservation (i.e., that it is possible that children's employment of media-related content and style escaped the researchers' eyes in some—even many—instances), clearly the child had to process it in such a creative way that it was undetectable.

It is also important to note that all media formats can provide a source of inspiration for the children's fantasies. In our study, there were references to television programs, movies, videotapes, computer games, books, and other print material. Clearly, all mediated materials are potential fodder for children's make-believe worlds. However, according to our findings, visual media—TV, videotapes, and films, and the combination of visual media with books, seem to have the most central role in children's stories.

This may be partially accounted for by the fact that the visualization exercise used in the study is primarily a visual task, as the drawing is its final product. In addition, the children were asked to describe verbally what they

TABLE 5.1

Media Traces in the Make-Believe Worlds

Media Traces	Number (%) of Total 193 cases
Media traces total	122 (63%)
Explicit traces	97 (80% of total traces)
Implicit traces	25 (20% of total traces)
No media traces	71 (37%)

visualized in their dreamland. Perhaps this created a context in which it was natural to import images from media. But this in itself does not supply a completely satisfactory explanation because children were also given the opportunity to articulate their inner world in words—verbally in the interviews, and to a lesser degree, in writing. Despite the growth and dissemination of new communication technologies, other current research, such as the cross-cultural European study of children's media environment in 12 countries (Livingstone & Bovill, 2001), provided evidence supporting the continued dominant role of television in children's lives.

Children's content interests often carry across different media, and it is hard to detect the exact source. For example, the presence of Pokémon-related themes in the child's story originated in a children's media environment characterized by cross-marketing via multiple outlets, which included television programs, videotapes, movies, computer games, books, merchandizing, advertising and the like. So when Audrey (G, US-28) talks about Pokémon land and says, *"I always like to imagine that I am a Pokémon,"* her statement is not necessarily connected to a particular medium, but to the whole range of those outlets that carry the Pokémon world to her. We have no way of knowing if she is a fan of the television series, the trading cards, the videos, the movies—or if she likes the whole package.

Occasionally, we faced media traces that we were unable to link directly to a specific text. For example, dinosaur-land scenes, popular with the American and South Korean children, are clearly media-dependent; no child has ever seen a live dinosaur. Their perceptions of what they looked like, how they behaved, what the landscape around them was like, and so forth—are all dependent on mediated sources. However, determining which media text was behind a specific drawing is a different story. Was it the new release of the third *Jurassic Park* movie? Was it a videotape of the first movie? Was it a book? A poster presented in class? A visit to the museum? A combination of several texts? Sometimes it is impossible to tell. This is much in line with an argument put forward by Lemish, Liebes, and Seidmann (2001). According to that argument, children tend to follow content interests across diverse media forms rather than becoming medium-specific dependent. A synergy of media interests creates a media environment for the child, as, for example, is the soccer environment of the boy who plays FIFA (Fédération Internationale de Football Association) computer games, watches soccer matches on television, reads the sports pages in the daily paper, and hangs a poster of his favorite player above his bed.

Market forces intentionally fuel and exploit this desire to experience different characters and themes in a variety of formats by offering a diverse thematic environment of media products and merchandise—be it *Pokémon*, *Harry Potter*, or *Star Wars*. Market forces were indeed apparent in our study. For example, the transition detected in Eastern Germany from a *Pokémon* to a *Digimon* environment occurred with changes in broadcasting schedules; the presence of *Shrek* in the American children's stories emerged with the coming out of the movie and supportive merchandise. At the same time, these market influences were only part of the picture. Intertextuality was also formed subjectively by the individual children's creative ability to tie together a special theme from various sources. In doing so, they were proactive in picking out that which intrigues and engages them, as well as what has special meaning to them—be it dinosaurs, horses, magic, supernatural forces, outer space, and so on.

So what do children take from media content and use in their make-believe worlds? To answer this question, we developed a grounded analysis of the drawings and transcripts of interviews through use of multiple stages of categorization. Pooling the categories created in the separate national analyses and refining them through collaborative efforts of secondary analysis resulted in six empirical clusters: *settings*—with a subcategory of *objects; characters*—with a subcategory of *costumes; narratives*—with a subcategory of *formal knowledge.* These categories respond closely to the three central elements of all stories: Setting, People, and Narrative (Vande Berg & Wenner, 1991). Finally, an additional seventh category of analysis that cuts across all of the other ones is that of *media aesthetics:* traces in children's drawings of styles of visual codes and conventions (e.g., the drawing of movement, verbal output, figures, etc). These categories need to be looked upon as an organizational scheme imposed for the sake of analysis rather than "pure" conceptually distinct phenomena, as children themselves often combine the categories in their make-believe worlds.

SETTINGS

The first category refers to situations in which a story is located in a media-related setting—that is a place, environment, or context. In our analysis, setting includes a range of media-related traces. Some fantasies practically imitate or stay close to the original media settings, whereas in others, media settings are adapted and/or adopted in varying degrees.

An example of full employment of setting is Jack (B, US-25), who locates his make-believe world within the popular quiz show, *Who Wants to be a Millionaire?* In the interview, he declares, "*I was the best millionaire in my dreamland.*" His drawing places him in the middle of the stage, with studio lights shining on him from all directions, and green American dollars flying around. In the interview he tells his story (see Drawing 5.1):

> I was on stage in the theater and I was the best millionaire in my dreamland. There were fireworks exploding all over. There were fizzy firecrackers going off all around and

Drawing 5.1. Jack (B, US-25) "The Best Millionaire."

a couple of thousand people were in the audience. Everybody was clapping for me, there were lights and cameras and dollars flying throughout the theater. A million dollars were coming out of little slots in the theater … the spotlights were on me in the center of the stage and I was wearing a black top hat. I was really happy and very, very excited. I felt like I was blessed with the million dollars and I felt like I was part of a good family. This dream came from a show I watch 'Who Wants to be a Millionaire?'. I saw it yesterday, and then today it just popped into my dream.

The source of Jack's dream is obvious. *Who Wants to be a Millionaire?* is a popular television quiz show all over the world. The candidate has to answer several questions by picking the right answer from four optional ones. The winner who passes through all levels correctly wins $1 million dollars. This is done in the presence of a studio audience of several dozen people (not thousands). In the U.S. version, big colored pieces of confetti (not $1 million green American dollars) descend from the ceiling. There are no fireworks, either. Jack, however, adopted the setting regarding the celebration of the winner drawing all the audience's attention. Jack incorporates the implicit ideology that *"Everyone can be a millionaire and be at the center of it all."* However, he also improves the most significant moments for him and intensifies the scene according to his own wish to be special and successful. The improvements include the way he chooses to symbolize spotlights as well as the fireworks on the stage around him. At the same time, some characteristics of the show, such as the guessing process or the candidate's possible failure, do not exist in his dream world of amusement and in his wish to be special.

Thus, adopting an entire setting by no means implies an automatic limitation on the range of story possibilities. Narrative is not necessarily constrained by the original media setting. In some fantasies, it is more difficult to trace them back to a specific media setting, as for example, in "Gingerbread Land" pictured by Katrin (G, GR-7):

> In Gingerbread Land, everything is made out of gingerbread—the houses, the castle, and also the people. Sweets rain down from the cloud. Any sweet you can imagine. You only have to wish for it. The sun fills them up again, so that it never runs out of sweets. In Gingerbread Land you can also nibble at everything. Not at people, but at the houses. Then they have holes. You fill it with more gingerbread and stick it on with sugar glazing. This is so much fun, because afterwards you can lick your fingers. The streets in Gingerbread Land are made in the same way: You spread out gingerbread and then it rains sugar glazing and then the street is done. In Gingerbread Land, everything is peaceful, except if somebody's chasing a sweet cloud trying to rope it, because he wants everything for himself. Then he needs to go to the dungeon (below the castle), for two days or so, and then he is set free again. In my Gingerbread Land, only sweets are eaten and you never get fat.

In her interview, Katrin revealed that this make-believe world was rooted in the story of *Hänsel and Gretel* that she has seen on video at home. However, the most inspiring scene was an incidental one in *Bumpety Boo*, an animated television series. She has drawn the smiley face of Bumpety Boo on the castle. The media source Katrin employs is a TV cartoon, which describes the adventures of a boy named Ken, his dog, and a speaking car named Bumpety Boo. An evil sorcerer, Professor Honkytonk, who plays an antagonistic role, wants the car for himself. In each episode he tries to fool the three friends but finally fails. In the course of the interview, it is revealed that a castle was included in an episode aired in Germany several weeks prior to the study. In this specific episode, Ken, Mopsy the dog, and Bumpety Boo win the biscuit-made castle in a quiz show and start nibbling it. As a result, the castle walls cave in; however, they manage to escape—much to the dismay of the sorcerer who falls into a well from which he cannot free himself.

This is just a very short segment lasting only about 2 minutes of the entire 8½-minute-long episode. Apparently it left a strong impression on Katrin. Certain features are very similar to the cartoon castle: Katrin's castle resembles the biscuit castle in shape and color. Ken and Bumpety nibble on the banister and also on the windows and walls; so, too, in Katrin's fantasy world, everything can be eaten. However, Katrin changes other features of the setting or adds something to it.

First of all, Katrin does not imagine a single crunchy castle built from biscuit dough, but an entire land of gingerbread. The houses and streets in her land are edible, but have to be filled anew. She gives a detailed description of how enjoyable it is to place the sugar glazing on the walls. This means that in Katrin's make-believe world, the houses cannot collapse as the castle did in *Bumpety Boo*. Similarly, she employs a mechanism guaranteeing that they never run out of sweets: the sun fills them up again. Katrin also leaves out the existence of an evil character. Her land is peaceful, but sometimes includes an unethical person who desires all the sweets for himself or herself. This person will be punished and put into the dungeon under the castle, from which he or she will soon be reintegrated into society. She develops a counter world in which such mischief as Professor Honkytonk does not exist. Finally, she changes a basic feature of the setting. In her world, you cannot grow fat, so one can eat, but not be "punished" for it. We can conclude that Katrin pictures an entire world with its own inner logic based on a sequence of only 2 minutes.

A further example in which a child clearly employs a media setting in his make-believe world is Gui'hyong's (B, SK-4) "The Age of Dinosaur." His drawing portrays a detailed and accurate scene of the dinosaur era, including various kinds of species, skeletons and smoky volcanoes—akin to depictions in the movie *Jurassic Park*, a reference he makes directly when telling his own story. This is how he describes his experience (see Drawing 5.2):

> I have been to my dream world often, and there were many dinosaurs. When I was four years old, I shook hands with them and we made friends. But the dinosaurs got more and more massive and this is why I watch the land only via telescope. When they see me now, they open their mouths wide and want to bite me. But some of them are vegetarians. I see Daddy dinosaur with his little baby and the Dad is eating a dinosaur that already died. In my world, most of the dinosaurs die a natural death and won't be killed by people, like in the movie I saw. In my world they don't become extinct, anyway … in my dream world, I can fly whenever I want and when I see dinosaurs, I really feel good.

Gui'hyong takes the *Jurassic Park* setting as a whole. He describes himself as part of this world since making several visits to it at age 4. At that time the dinosaurs were friendly toward him, but that has changed now. Gui'hyong takes the element of change in the dinosaurs' behavior from the original plot line and incorporates it into his fantasy world. Compared to all three movies of *Jurassic Park*, the dinosaur land seems to be a very pleasant place to be—at least on the surface.

In *Jurassic Park 1*, the dinosaur world becomes a leisure park for the whole family. The main characters drive through the park in an electronic vehicle. It is

Drawing 5.2. Gui'hyong (B, SK-4) "The Age of Dinosaurs."

when they pass by several secure enclosures that they encounter the dinosaurs for the first time. They care for an injured gentle dinosaur of the species of Herbivorous Triceratops and pet it on its face. Later on, the enjoyable, peace-loving and harmless atmosphere gives way to life-threatening scenarios.

The basic plotline is consistent throughout the whole trilogy: a peaceful world turns into a life-threatening trap. Gui'hyong adopts this basic motif, but neglects another very significant message conveyed by the movie—the fact that humans never think about the consequences of their actions when they play God and meddle with nature. Gui'hyong's fantasy does not carry any specific message. The dinosaurs in his land have become aggressive and want to bite him with their huge mouths. It is as simple as that. This is why he has created in his story a "removed place" to safely observe his land and the spellbinding dinosaur scenes through a telescope. Additionally, the dinosaurs in Gui'hyong's world are not killed by humans as in the movie. They do not even eat each other. In his story, they simply die a natural death and are not an extinct species.

Media Objects in the Settings

A specific aspect of setting is children's adoption of media-related objects. Occasionally, children choose to incorporate in their drawing just one particular object, decontextualized from the original setting and placed in their own setting.

For example, Gyu'sang (B, SK-34) borrows a green car in his drawing of "A Strange Village" from a popular computer game. Narmeen (G, IS-49) places a bench in her drawing of a basketball game with friends in their village's basketball court. When asked in the interview about this bench (which stands out as very atypical of her environment) she says that it is taken out of her favorite animated Arab television series, *Arthur,* seen via satellite broadcast. In the series, the central boy character likes to sit with his little monkey friend on his shoulder on a similar bench in the park. There they spend time bonding and relaxing. She specifically states that she wishes that her own basketball court had such a bench, so she herself could sit down to relax and to think about things. She takes nothing else of the *Arthur* setting, characters or plot—merely the little bench.

Summary

Children adopt a setting from a medium forming a world in which they develop their make-believe world. They extract one single scenario from the original media text that is special to them. Often this becomes the original plotline. Other details are left completely aside, or a counterplot is built on them. In Jurassic Park, the dinosaurs live on their own and are not killed by humans. In Gingerbread Land, not everything is destroyed and it can be repaired. The persons who committed some misdeeds are put in prison for a few days until they behave pro-socially again. Children, too, change the original media setting to a great extent. Although in the original text, the setting serves as the location for the entire narrative, the children picture the settings according to their own inner logic, which is used to organize how they wish to act and what they want to experience.

CHARACTERS

Children also employ characters abstracted from media content in their make-believe worlds in a variety of ways. They might adopt a character's personality as a whole, or incorporate specific traits such as abilities, appearance, names, or costumes. As with settings, sometimes the similarity to the original character is quite apparent from first sight of the child's picture. However, sometimes the character can be completely absent from the drawing. Only through the child's retelling of the story does the character's presence become known.

Media texts are populated with a variety of characters—real (popular culture celebrities, sports heroes, politicians, etc., as well as trained animals); realistic (fictional human characters played by actors and actresses); and imaginary (animated figures, puppets, outer-space creatures, prehistorical animals, etc.). All are potential material for abstraction in children's stories. A child may adopt a single character or choose two or more. The fact that children develop emotional relationships with media characters is well documented in the professional literature and is understood as a mediating process between consuming media content and socialization processes (Hoffner, 1996; Hoffner & Cantor, 1991). There are a variety of ways in which children employ media characters in their make-believe worlds. In our study, we found two basic types of relationships with characters. The first is the *identification type*—when children imagine that they are the characters themselves. The second is the *parasocial relationship type* (Horton & Wohl, 1956)—when children appear themselves in their make-believe worlds and are engaged in a relationship with the media characters.

Identification

This form of relationship is understood as a process through which the viewer shares the perspective of a media character. Identifying with a character in this way allows the child to participate in the character's experiences to a certain degree. This process is defined as an expression of the child's wish to be like or to behave like the character that is the subject of identification. In our study, some of the children took on the identity of media characters and by doing so were able to project themselves into a character in a variety of ways. For instance, they portrayed themselves as engaged in the character's adventures, dressed-up in their clothing, and adopted their characters' personality characteristics.

As Peter Pan, Martin (B, US-22) relived the adventure story of *Hook* based on the fantasy film by that name:

> I am Peter Pan in my dreamland. I am going to fight Captain Hook. There is a tree house with a ladder that goes up to it. That's where Peter Pan and the Lost Boys live. I am flying. Captain Hook is in the ship at sea. I didn't really think of it as my fantasy, but I just sort of thought of *Hook*, my favorite movie, so I drew it. I knew I was going to win against Captain Hook and I felt good. I have been practicing for a couple of days—playing basketball. Peter Pan flies to put the ball in the basket. That is in the movie. Hook gives him 4 days to practice for the fight, so he can save the children ....

Martin sticks closely to the original characters, setting, and plotline of his favorite movie and plays the role of the main character. He leaves out several events and characters of the movie and adopts only the cornerstones, which he is able to reproduce in full detail but adding a hat on Peter Pan's head in contrast to his appearance in the movie, a detail that seems meaningful to him. Rarely are the borrowings as close to the original as in Martin's case. But he himself testifies that he did not fully engage in the mental visualization exercise of make believe. In this respect, the problem could have been a methodical one and we failed to give Martin the space he would have needed for his make-believe world. On the other hand, it can also be an indication that make-believe worlds sometimes remain close to their origins and that children imagine being the character itself and relive the adventures this character was involved in.

Identification is also closely related to the notion of *idolization*, which can be understood to have two components, as well: *worship*, perceived as the admiration and reverence of the idol, and; *modeling*, defined as the desire to be and act like an idol (A. Raviv, Bar-Tal, A. Raviv, & Ben-Horin, 1996). These behaviors are promoted, supported, and rewarded by both peer groups and the media industry. However, only rarely did children in our study demonstrate such idolization. Dor (B, IS-13) worships a famous soccer player of the Maccabi Haifa team by the name of Yossi Benayun. He draws himself in this player's uniform receiving a trophy on an elevated podium, and even names himself after this player. He describes the scene as follows:

> I saw the stadium and in the middle a pyramid. You can see the palace of Maccabi Haifa where you can see Benayun who is the king of the team. He is the most important player so he is at the top. The weaker players are at the bottom. The airplane is carrying a Maccabi Haifa sign. I wrote my name—Dor, and added in parentheses, Benayun, because I am the best in my soccer team.

At the time this study was conducted, Yossi Benayun was a much admired front midfielder for the acclaimed Maccabi Haifa soccer club, known also as the Greens. The club is a seven-time winner of the Israeli Premier League championship and has also appeared 12 times throughout the years in the state cup finals, wining it five times. It is also known as the best opportunity-making club in Israel for players to join the top leagues in Europe. Benayun himself represented a success story of a young ambitious player from a peripheral small town who made it to the prestigious team in the big city, thus becoming a hero role model for many young boys of similar as well as other backgrounds.

As noted, idolization of real celebrities (e.g., athletes, pop singers), such as in Dor's case, was exceptional. In our study, almost all of the media-related characters appearing in children's stories were fictional. This might be explained by the potential openness for interpretation and manipulation that imaginary figures offer in comparison to real-live characters who are constrained by their obvious physical attributes such as gender, age, race, and appearance, as well as their personality characteristics. An additional explanation may have to do with the age of the children, who are barely preadolescent. One interesting twist to this interpretation is the finding that most of the characters chosen were either male or genderless. As previous research has documented (see, e.g., Hoffner, 1996; Reeves, 1979), physical power and activities (such as required in action–adventure types of texts) are predictors of the degree to which boys of different ages wished to be like or to do things like the various characters presented to them. We return to this point in the discussion of gender-related issues.

Parasocial Interaction

A second way that children employ media characters is not through the desire to be the characters themselves but to share a close friendship with them as does Robby (B, GR-43). He draws himself and his friend, a dragon, in red and brown, based on the media character "Draco" in the movie, *Dragon Heart*, which Robby saw a few months prior to the interview. During the interview, Robby reveals that he often daydreams about this fantasy and that he always talks to this kind of imaginary friend (see Taylor, 1999) in the evenings before going to sleep.

The film tells the story of an exemplary friendship between a successful dragon hunter and Draco, the last dragon. He tells us the following story (see Drawing 5.3):

> It's called "Me and My Dragon." The dragon and I are the world's best friends. I met him in a cave. He does what I want him to do. It's an ordinary cave, but there are more bats in it than usual. The dragon can spit fire. I'm going to see him quite often. Then we are just playing or we take a flying trip around the city to the sweets shop and to the school. We pass by the school and look through the windows during class. That's cool. He lives in the cave and is waiting for me. In the evenings, I always tell him who picked

Drawing 5.3. Robby (B, GR-43) "Me and My Dragon."

on me during the day. And, if someone did bother me, he can shock and terrify him or her. Or, if there are murderers around on our streets who want to kill somebody or so, the dragon would shock them. He could burn them all through a fire blow—but I tell him not do it. He *cannot* die, but he will die if he is killed. Well, a dragon will die if he's hit by an arrow or a knife or maybe something very sharp. If his heart is hit by it, he's almost dead. Then he's alive only a little. Otherwise this animal will not die. I can save him by telling the others that he [the evil king] shall let him go. But most of the times he saves me and not the other way round.

Robby employs the character of Draco in his big daydream, but he blurs the setting of the movie, a medieval world. He takes the dragon with him into his own world of a German suburb. Otherwise, as in the original story, the dragon lives in a cave and has compassionate traits. They have lots of fun together and have many adventures. The dragon with his huge size defends Robby if someone dares to pick on him, but Robby tells the dragon not to spit fire. The media character's abilities and features turn him into an ideal friend for Robby. They share some awesome moments and Robby is assured that he will not be troubled by criminals or schoolmates. The friendship itself is also secure and will last for a very long time because, according to Robby, such an animal cannot die unless it is killed by something sharp. This special feature as well as the whole plot are borrowed from the movie. When he is telling his story, Robby even quotes a specific scene when the hunter finds the dying dragon. However, in his fantasy story, Robby can save the dragon: *"I can save him by telling the others that he shall let him go"* (the "he" probably referring to the evil king in the original movie's plot line) and thus he is able to contribute equally to the friendship.

Tali (G, IS-6), for example, invents a complex story including being on stage with a famous singer as well as going on a journey with the cast of a popular children's telenovela. The whole fantasy develops within the routine of one day:

> I dream that my entire daily schedule is like this: In the morning I go to an animal clinic, because I love animals very much and I have animals at home … At noontime, I am at the Corner of Light [name of a boarding-school in a favorite Argentinean children's telenovela entitled Chiquititas]; here I wrote down all the children's names. I am one of the girls in the series, not really the main actress, but just one of them. They are shooting the episode I really liked; when they flew to Euro-Disney … in the evening—you can see the stage and spotlight and people say: "Applaud Tali!" I am on stage with Natalia Oreiro and we sing all of her songs that I like …, the next day it repeats itself … and the truth of the matter is that this way it integrates everything that I like, so I feel great. I have satisfaction and pleasure in helping out animals, in addition to all the fun of being on stage …

Tali stands on stage right next to her favorite real-life female singer and actress, Natalia Oreiro, from Uruguay, who was very popular at the time in Israel among preadolescents and teens. She imagines the spotlights and the applause of the audience yelling, *"Applaud Tali!"* The songs they sing are Natalia's songs.

Being with the character of Natalia boosts Tali's self-esteem and turns the fantasy dream into a potential reality. But the pop singer is not the only famous person Tali meets in her dreamworld. During the day, she takes part in a soap opera. Here she does not want to play the main character either; she simply wants to be one of the girls. She has little faith in her drawing abilities, so she writes the names of the characters in her drawing rather than paint the actual figures. Imagining being part of the famous soap's cast gives way to the idea of a community that shares a very special experience; they are all visiting Euro-Disney together. The imagined day has everything Tali loves. The media characters provide the setting and enable Tali to expand her abilities. Tali imagines herself to be part of a world of stars.

These relationships with media characters illustrate a phenomenon that is related to the concept of *parasocial interaction* (offered originally by Horton & Wohl, 1956). Parasocial interaction involves the process by which viewers feel that they have a personal acquaintance with the mediated characters and undertake imagined interactions with them. This form of quasifriendship allows children to process emotions and experiences and to experiment with various types of relationships with others of all shapes and sizes, all ages, genders, and species. Through these imagined relationships, they are able to practice social and communication skills under safe and self-controlled circumstances.

As with the category of *setting*, characters were adopted from a variety of media sources. The drawing styles of the characters, however, appeared to be restricted by their media appearance—most children took great pains to reproduce the characters in order to imitate the mediated original as closely as possible. Oftentimes, they were so successful that the researchers were able to make the connection virtually at first glance. This effort to replicate the original characters visually did not correspond, however, to any kind of limitation on the myriad roles the characters played in the children's stories. In other words, borrowing media characters did not seem to limit the wide-open range of narratives possible in the children's fantasies.

Clothing and Costume

Another way children borrowed from characters was to appropriate a character's clothing or costume. To do so opened up a symbolic world of possibilities for the child's narrative. Such was the case of Omer (B, IS-2), who combines the costumes of all his favorite superpowers to create a powerful self-character: Batman's mask, Spiderman's outfit and gloves, Superman's cape, a Star Wars' laser, and Pokémon belt (see Drawing 5.4):

> This world is only mine ... here I am the ruler. I can do whatever I want. Everything is allowed. I am wearing a suit. The red-cloak is like Superman's. The green are my hands so that I can climb on everything like Spiderman, those blue things in my hands are my

Drawing 5.4. Omer (B, IS-2) "Superpowers."

fire laser-ray weapons. The red is a belt like Pokémon's. The purple are my flying boots, and the horns I took from Batman's mask. I am the master and I also have a sword, like in Star Wars.

As he continues to describe his outfit in detail, we learn that the dark background of his drawing is his bedroom. It is colored black because he wants to draw attention to himself and his clothes, which are so central to his make-believe world. He continues with his story, combining a host of media sources, unrelated to the original superpowers, including books—new and old classics:

> There is a carpet and a bed and lots of things for training ... like in the Olympics. Also Pokémon figures, a huge Pikachu ... In this world there are good people and bad people, and also a school in a castle, like Hogwart's school in Harry Potter, that I have already graduated from ... In the middle of my world, there is a mystery island like Jules Verne's, with lots of whales, like Moby Dick. When I am asleep, I dream about the powers of television heroes, and I added a bit from my own imagination ...

Omer "slips" on the various superpowers as one slips on a dress, including the special skills he possesses as the master (*Star Wars*) and those he has learned at the school of magic (*Harry Potter*). He goes out armed for adventures in a world where the good and the bad co-exist, as on the famous *Treasure Island*, or in the fight with *Moby Dick*. Omer adopts the status of the media character (i.e., being a graduate of the school of magic and being the master), as well as the special skills and weapons of superheroes.

Omer's story is about the laser sword from *Star Wars*, but it does not include Anakin Skywalker and his changing allegiance with the evil. It employs Batman's mask but does not contain any traces of Batman's troubles in his identification process. Omer separates the media characters' accessories from the original stories and employs them as symbols of power. In fact, there is nothing extraordinary and powerful in Batman's mask itself or Superman's cape or Spiderman's gloves. For example, in the original story, Batman appears in disguise only to ensure his anonymity. Superman is born on another planet and therefore possesses some superpowers. His cape is of no significance in this respect. Spiderman can climb up the walls because he has been bitten by a genetically treated spider. His gloves do not bestow any powers on him. However, this does not matter to Omer, because for him, these items symbolize the skills he is able to use in his fantasy world. What is important to him is that he is armed against anything that might come his way.

Summary

In summarizing the category of characters, it is important to note that although the various settings opened up possibilities for the child, the characters themselves, their appearances, traits, and typical plotlines, resemble the media sources closely. The varied possibilities for the child seem therefore to not come necessarily from the character himself/herself, but rather from the type of the relationship with the character. The child may wish for a friendship with the character, to identify with him or her, and may even wish to be that character. Adopting a character's costume presents a subcategory of the desire to become like the character in some way. Through complementing themselves with qualities of their favorite characters (be it a personality trait, a custom, an accessory, and the like), children are able to experience their wishes for adventures, for being special or for having unusual power.

NARRATIVES

Through the discussion of both settings and characters, we have already touched on narratives as well, as these are all intertwined. In addition, children sometimes adopt a particular storyline from a media text and use it in their make-believe world as the backbone from which their own story develops. Sometime they stay close to the original narrative, on other occasions parts of the narrative are lifted and incorporated by children in their own stories. Interestingly, in our study, this phenomenon was strongly related to gender and genre.

Ruben (B, GR-44), for example, relives a trip in a spaceship to outer space following the narrative of the movie, *Armageddon*:

> I am an astronaut and fly in a rocket into space, together with my three friends. I'm in charge of the steering wheel ... We have just been to the moon. It looks as though a mouse has eaten parts of it, because meteorites have crushed into it and they have left behind holes ... On the moon there is a moon vehicle from the first man who was on the moon and the flag is still sticking there. We saw a meteorite there coming towards us. It was so fast that we flew away. Then we discovered a meteorite flying towards the earth. We destroyed it with our lasers and saved the earth ... now we keep on searching for meteorites in space and destroy them, because this is why we are in space.

Ruben imagines being on a journey into space. He and his three friends visited the moon. Ruben describes the flag and the vehicle of landing on the moon based on what his father told him. However, the main plot of his fantasy story deals with meteorites that threaten the earth. In his drawing, we can see that the moon has already been hit by many of them. In the interview, we learned that Ruben was allowed to watch *Armaggedon* at the young age of 7 although, according to him, it had been classified as appropriate only for 10 years and over. Even though he cannot remember the title of the movie, he recalls the particular scenes in full detail so they are easily traced back to the efforts in the film to save the Earth from an asteroid the size of Texas that is about to collide with it. Team members led by Harry (Bruce Willis) decide to ignite it manually by flying into the asteroid, sacrificing themselves for the sake of mankind.

Even though Ruben can recollect the entire story in detail, he only adopts particular parts of the original text; the team of equal friends, with himself as the captain, fly around continuously. During the interview, Ruben calls them "*meteorite chasers*," though the heroes of the original movie had not been specifically trained to cope with this task. Only by adding this kind of professionalism is Ruben able to overcome the existential threat and continue the chase after the meteorites. Ruben basically follows the inner structure of the film, but finds a rather simple way of expanding the original plot line by changing the unpleasant turn of events at the end.

The internal structure of computer games can also be followed by children. Jun'sik (B, SK-29), for example, explains his story about knights in a castle following the sequence of the narrative of the computer game, *Kingdom of the Wind*: "When they fight and a knight or a person dies, a leaf falls down from the tree—it is a tree of life."

In the original computer game, there is a tree that symbolizes the loss of life by shedding its leaves. Thus, in conclusion, children sometimes chose to include in their make-believe worlds only part of the narrative or a specifically personally appealing episode.

Formal Knowledge

In several cases, children abstracted one or more discrete bits of factual information from the mediated story and not necessarily a whole or partial plotline. Often, this "bit" serves as a springboard for an entire make-believe world. We accept as a given that any media trace is in itself evidence of the ability to retrieve information, interpret it, store it, and reuse it at will at a later point in time. Here, however, we refer specifically to formal knowledge of real-world events, places, people, and so forth, originating in nonfiction media texts; knowledge that is valued in our societies as part of formal education. Tessina (G, GR-3) develops her plotline around a piece of information on endangered animals that she picked up from a television documentary and she incorporates the knowledge of the importance of providing protected environments in her make-believe world. Similarly, Edith (G, GR-13) learned from a television program that spiders can be very useful, although they are often unnecessarily killed. She dreams about a garden where spiders can live in peace and do their useful work. In both of the cases, it is a documentary on television that presents these real-life facts about endangered aspects of nature to the children. In their imagination, the two girls solve these problems by offering the animals shelters.

However, it is not only information that involves them emotionally that inspires children's fantasies. Sometimes it is the knowledge of principles of natural science that triggers their imagination. Dam'dok (B, SK-40) uses his knowledge of the shape of the earth as seen from outer space to locate his own story. He describes this knowledge as follows (see Drawing 5.5):

> I travel to space with my family: my Dad, my big brother, and I. I watch the sun and the sky. Each one of us holds a balloon in his hand, so that we can't fall down. My father has a fish balloon; my brother a star balloon; and I have a butterfly balloon. I can see Korea, my land, the United States, and Africa. I also see the sun, the stars, and comets. Then I also see that there are many people on earth like insects. I can also see a zoo and watch animals. The sun is shining on all countries.

Dam'dok tries to figure out how it feels to be high up in the sky so that the people on earth would look like insects. He is able to recognize the United States and the continent of Africa that are far away from his own home. It does not matter to Dam'dok that his make-believe world is impossible in reality because various parts of it are factual; there are indeed different countries and continents on earth, the higher you fly, the smaller people down on earth will look, and a hot-air balloon rises in the air. Some of his knowledge has been nurtured by real experience; other facts he has learned from books, television, and from visiting the Museum of Natural History. Apparently, Dam'dok's fascination with various aspects of the world is so deep as to be included in his make-believe world.

Drawing 5.5. Dam'dok (B, SK-40) "The Exciting Spaceship Journey."

Clearly, children smoothly interweave formal knowledge picked up via media with wild imagination to create the narratives in their make-believe worlds.

Summary

In their imagination children adopt media narratives. However, it is not always the basic main plot they adopt, but mostly, the minor ones which specifically attract them. Stories that become part of the children's fantasy worlds are not merely limited to fictitious stories. Even realistic or technical information is integrated but leaves enough space to create new imaginary worlds. In addition, by using their imagination, sometimes children try to find solutions to real-life grievances and problems or to relive and even change real historical events for the better.

AESTHETICS

Apart from textual elements such as in the categories of *settings*, *characters*, and *narratives*, children acquire various presentational techniques through their experiences with media. We included these traces under the category of *aesthetics*. In line with the myriad ways in which children employ other media elements in their fantasies, media aesthetics are also used to varying extents. We found that some children copy specific aesthetic features from their favorite media texts (e.g., the dominance of the color purple used in the *Harry Potter* books; Pokémon figures; Minnie Mouse; or dinosaurs).

Children also used aesthetic conventions to represent various sensual experiences, such as the drawing of movement (flying, ball rolling); light (stage and studio spotlights, sun rays); sound (music notes, noisy explosions); action (collisions, fighting); and abstractions such as thoughts, ideas, and dreams (with captions in "bubbles," as is done in cartoons).

A third form of using media aesthetics was the use of conventions to symbolize complicated concepts. For example, indicating the concept of *time* by means of dividing the page into parts—night and day, or morning, afternoon, and evening—a code used in cartoons. The concept of *death* was presented through the shedding of leaves from a tree, taken directly from a computer game. The concept of *world peace* was expressed by means of the UNICEF emblem. And there are other such examples.

Conclusion

Our examination of media traces in the children's dream worlds leads to the conclusion that children use a variety of media texts in diverse and often creative ways. Although several significant gender and cultural differences have emerged (and are discussed later), it is clear that the media can play a role that is far from suppressing the fantasy world of children. On the contrary, our analysis suggests that children are active meaning-makers who use the texts, formats, and aesthetics offered to them in the media in purposeful ways for meaning-making. Furthermore, children are not just reading and interpreting the texts in active ways, but also selectively abstracting from them various elements and features and integrating them together with ideas of their own to create new worlds of meaning.

PORTRAIT OF PATRICIA (G, GR-54)

In sharing their make-believe worlds and examining the place media have in them, children enable us to gain entry into their consciousness, needs, problems, wishes, and aspirations. We were able to analyze their drawings, writings, and stories and to detect media traces in them and to interpret how the stories have been changed from the original source. However, it is much more complicated to understand why the children have used these particular elements and what motivated them to make those changes. Attaining such an in-depth analysis requires close acquaintance with the child, as well as a profound psychological understanding of his or her personality, which is not within the scope of this cross-cultural study. However, we would like to present one such analysis as a prototypical illustration of the potential of such an inquiry for understanding the role media serve in children's inner worlds. In the following single case, we demonstrate in detail how one particular child actively uses media texts for her own purposes and in her own way.[1]

Patricia is 9 years old and attends fourth grade in an elementary school. Her mother is an academic and her father a professional military person. She has an 8-year-old brother. German is the parents' native language, but Patricia has been raised bilingual (English/German). Her early childhood was spent with her parents living in small townhouses in the German towns of Passau, Gütersloh, and Mönchengladbach, as well as in Pacific Grove, California, in the United States. Since April 1999, she has been living in an apartment in downtown Munich. Her parents characterize her as a lively, curious child, interested in a lot of things. She is usually happy, but is sometimes extremely shy. According to her parents, the frequent moves and consequent need to adapt to new environments have presented her with a particular challenge. In her short life, she attended five different preschools and kindergartens. She also attended three different elementary schools—two of them in California, where she was required to learn a foreign language. At the time of the study, she was suffering acutely in the wake of the move from California to Munich in April 1999. In addition to the need to readjust to the German society, language, and school system, she also faced a new family arrangement. Her father is now posted in the north of Germany and she sees him only on weekends.

Patricia loves drawing and seems to have artistic talent. Most of all, she likes to play with other children, and prefers to be the one in charge. During the period of investigation, she was mostly engaged in imaginative role-play with Barbie dolls. According to her mother, harmony is a central feature of her play. For example, all her dolls are good friends and go on holiday together in a mobile home.

Patricia's preferred media are computer and Gameboy games. Her favorite computer game is the Gold Edition of *Pokémon*. Her favorite book is *The 35th of May*, by Erich Kästner. In her mother's apartment, there is no TV, but she watches it in her father's house, where she stays most weekends from Friday to Monday.

Fantasies are part of Patricia's everyday life. She says that she dreams a lot, in particular when she is bored. This is often the case during the time she is working on her homework, during math lessons, as well as in general education lessons. To describe this state of mind, she uses words like "sleeping" or "dreaming"

---

[1]In addition to the sources of information available to us through this project, we were aided in the analysis of this case by the interpretation of Patricia's mother as well as in-depth consultation with Dr. Ruth Etienne-Klemm in Zurich, a child and youth psychologist, who specializes in children and young people's fantasies and their meaning (see Etienne-Klemm, 2003a, 2003b).

and she is aware of the fact that it is not an acceptable behavior in school, yet still likes to do it often. This is how Patricia talks about her dreamland in the interview (shortened, summarized version; see Drawing 5.6):

"In the Land of Milk and Honey"

> In the "land of milk and honey": A Butterfree, a Snorlax, Vileplume, and a Mew are sleeping. And this was my dream. I dream of a "land of milk and honey." This is great, because there are so many beds to sleep in and I really like sleeping. And besides this, there are many fruit-trees that are permanently loaded with fruit. And in this "land of milk and honey" there are all kind of *Pokémon* characters. And there are also humans, but only those who believe in and love *Pokémon*. Others are not admitted. Here there are my favorite *Pokémon* (at the moment): this is Snorlax; he loves to sleep as much as I do. I'd also love to be Butterfree, because he can fly so nicely. Vileplume, a flower, and I like flowers, and Mew, my favorite *Pokémon*, who looks sooo cute and could explode half the globe, when angry, but that didn't happen so far. Well, then there is the *Pokémon* Togepi, but I play it as a moon mannikin. Togepi is always flying back and forth between the moon and the "land of milk and honey" because his parents live on the moon. And he also goes to school on the moon. There is also moon-general knowledge as a subject. I'd love to have that so that I wouldn't have to dream of the "land of milk and honey" during boring school lessons.

Media Traces Symbolizing Experiences and Self-Image

Media Trace 1: "The 35th of May" (Erich Kästner, 1970).   Patricia is talking about a land called "the land of milk and honey." As a feature of this

Drawing 5.6. Patricia (G, GR-54) "In the Land of Milk and Honey."

world, she repeatedly mentions extremely comfortable beds, where she can sleep soundly. The presence of fruit trees is also emphasized. Although she does not specify the media connection explicitly, an obvious implicit media trace is her favorite book. In Erich Kästner's classic book, *The 35th of May*, both heroes—Konrad and his uncle Ringelhuth—pass by "the land of milk and honey" on their strange journey to the South Seas (chap. 2). Here there are lots of comfortable beds from which the inhabitants rarely rise. They live off the fruit trees by processing the fruit into delicious food by pushing a button.

Out of "the land of milk and honey," Patricia picks out the humorous, loving way it is being described and the comfortable lifestyle. However, she only singles out this one chapter in her make-believe world. Other chapters, like "the up-side–down world," where children have the power over their parents and teach-ers (chap. 4), or the fully technological world (chap. 5) are not incorporated into her make-believe world. She also refrains from mentioning the male pro-tagonists in the book. Patricia adopts the part of the book that is most fascinat-ing to her—the setting in one chapter.

When referring to the creation of her fantasy in her mind she says: *"'the land of milk and honey' just slipped into my mind and then I thought of Snorlax, and then I thought that it can't just be a single Pokémon, and then I added three more."* Following the suggestion made in explaining the mental visualization exercise—of going to a place where she always wanted to be and where she could be her whole self, Patricia recalled "the land of milk and honey" in her favorite book, perhaps be-cause of her positive associations with sleeping. She chose to omit the original inhabitants of Kästner's land and to replace them with one of her own choice—a certain *Pokémon*: Snorlax. Patricia describes him as one that always sleeps for half a year and eats during the other half.

Media trace 2: Pokémon. Patricia's fantasy shows obvious explicit media traces of *Pokémon*, Patricia's favorite television series. She became acquainted with it through purchasing and collecting Pokémon trading cards. Later a friend of hers and her brother told her about the television series. Because there is no TV set at her mother's apartment, she can only watch the series at her father's apartment during weekend visits and during school breaks. Patricia owns two related Gameboy editions, the "yellow" and the "golden," and her brother has the "red" and the "silver" editions. She had seen and was fascinated by the movie, *Pokémon 1*. In her room there is a *Pokémon* poster, several plastic *Pokémon* characters, books, magazines, trading cards and stickers of *Pokémon*. It is there-fore fair to call her a serious *Pokémon* fan.

Snorlax, according to the *Pokédex* (a special lexicon for *Pokémon*), is a 2.1m tall, 460 kgs teddy-bear-like being. In Patricia's picture, he's lying in a bed. To make sure he is not alone, Patricia draws three additional Pokémon characters to keep him company, and even talks about adding a fifth. Although not shown in the picture, Patricia insists that all 250 Pokémon types exist in the land of milk and honey and that there are *"lots and lots"* from each species, all of whom are her friends. There are also other people, but there are clear limitations on who may enter the country. Only those *"who dreamt about Pokémon and stuff"* are allowed in the land. *"Yes. Those who don't believe in Pokémon are not allowed there."* This limitation is not taken from the media world of Pokémon (while they do, however, exist Kästner's land of milk and honey). Therefore Patricia combines in her make-believe world a setting that is traced to the book, *The 35th of May,* and characters that are traced to the *Pokémon* texts.

According to Patricia, she often goes to this same make-believe world and the characters within it are *"always the same."* In her land of milk and honey, Patricia draws four Pokémon that are easy to identify.

Interviewer:	(…) *Is there a reason why you chose these four?*
Patricia:	*Yes.*
Interviewer:	*Is it because you like them in particular, or what?*
Patricia:	*[laughs] Well, Snorlax loves to sleep, just like me!*
Interviewer:	*You like to sleep as much as Snorlax?*
Patricia:	*Yes! [agreeing enthusiastically]*
Interviewer:	*Do you also like to eat as much as Snorlax?*
Patricia:	*Well, so so.*
Interviewer:	*So so?*
Patricia:	*Mew, is my favorite Pokémon.*
Interviewer:	*Aha!*
Patricia:	*I'd like to be Butterfree, because he can fly nicely.*
Interviewer:	*Aha!*
Patricia:	*And Vileplume … because he's a flower.*
Interviewer:	*Because he's a flower.*
Patricia:	*And because I like flowers.*
Interviewer:	*You like flowers. Man, so you would like to change roles with all of these four characters? Really?*
Patricia:	*Uh huh. [agreeing]*

Patricia forms a relationship between herself and the characters and agrees to the direct question of the interviewer about identification processes. Snorlax loves to do something she loves to do as well—that is, to sleep. In contrast, Snorlax's love of eating is not so relevant for Patricia. Patricia identifies herself with the *Pokémon,* Snorlax. She also loves to sleep and lie in bed for long stretches of time, which is often judged negatively in everyday life. However, aided by the symbolic material inherent in the character of Snorlax, Patricia can reinterpret this characteristic in herself in a positive light.

Patricia not only paints a picture and describes the characters in it, but also invents a narrative based on this material, some of which is close to the original media text. In the interview, she explains that Snorlax, pictured in the bed, will wake up in half an hour and will try to eat the others. The only trouble is, it won't work, because not only is he way too heavy and lazy, he is not a meat eater, according to Patricia. The others have to run for cover to make sure they don't get squished when he trips. With this little story, Patricia relates her fantasy which she connects to the *Pokémon* 1 movie, where Snorlax chases other Pokémon characters. Presumably she enjoyed the movie scene and could imagine an interesting and humorous development of it in her make-believe world. Here, Snorlax is bestowed with a lot of power, in contrast to the original inhabitants of "The Land of Milk and Honey" book chapter. In the various media, he is characterized as lazy and comfort-loving. By endowing him with power, she creates a character that lends itself to a positive comparison to herself. With the employment of this media-trace, she can symbolize a particular aspect of herself, evaluate it positively, and integrate it into her own self-image. With the help of media texts, she can interpret individual characteristics positively, recognize her own preferences (e.g., for flowers), and imagine wonderful experiences, like being able to fly.

Mew, Patricia's favorite *Pokémon,* is of particular significance for her:

Interviewer:	*And this (points at Mew) is? And why …*
Patricia:	*Hum. And Mew can make half the earth explode. And his big brother can* [starts laughing] *make the whole earth explode.*
(…)	
Interviewer:	*And Mew is your favorite Pokémon?*
Patricia:	*Yes!*
Interviewer:	*Because he can make half the earth explode?*
Patricia:	*Noooo!* [louder]
Interviewer:	*But, because?*
Patricia:	*Hum …. he looks so cute.*

Patricia knows of Mew the character, from *Pokémon* the Movie, in which Ash and his friends meet Mew, the 151ˢᵗ Pokémon. He is introduced as the "most powerful *Pokémon* on earth," worshiped by cultures of the past, but is considered to be extinct in the present. In the cartoon drawings, the *Pokémon* culture is embedded within empires such as the South-American Mayas. In these scenes, the pink Pokémon can be seen and heard very briefly. Since her visit to the cinema to see *Pokémon the Movie,* Mew is Patricia's favorite Pokémon. He is powerful, surrounded by mystery, but also sweet and lovable. Patricia talks also about Mewtwo: *"This one can let the whole world explode, when he is angry."* Mewtwo, who is a genetically improved clone of Mew, is taller and more aggressive-looking than Mew (i.e., he has triangular eyes, gray color, is oblong, and has a ratlike shape). However, Patricia prefers Mew, whose features are childlike and gentle, combining the characteristics of power with cuteness, a unique source of attraction common to several Pokémon characters (Lemish & Bloch, 2004).

In order to produce a deeper understanding of this fascination with Pokémon, some additional information regarding Patricia's everyday life is helpful. During the investigation period, Patricia was involved in conflicts with her classmates. In one incident, she was accused of having stolen a missing marker. One classmate even swore to have seen the stolen marker in Patricia's home. This and several other events provide evidence that the class had singled out Patricia for quite some time and had ganged up on her and ostracized her. Patricia reacts to this group dynamic with withdrawal into herself. According to the home teacher, her withdrawal is interpreted by the class as arrogance. Her mother believes that this is Patricia's way of avoiding her own aggressive reactions to social attacks and further conflicts. She chooses another path of resistance—pretending that this has nothing to do with her.

This understanding allows us to make better sense of Patricia's great attraction to Mew, who never acts aggressively in the movie despite all the provocations and the power he has. Mew remains under all circumstances always joyful and lovable. He develops an air bubble around himself, allows the attacks to bounce back, squeaks happily, and finally paralyzes the opponent with one single beam. Patricia also does not actively fight back and admires this strategy of conflict management by Mew. Just like Mew, although seemingly "cute" on the surface, Patricia feels she too encompasses something rather "powerful," even when it is not immediately evident on the surface.

Another theme incorporated in Patricia's narration relates to Pokémon Togepi's role in symbolizing her own attempt to provide a positive interpretation of her academic failure at school. Patricia tells a story about Togepi, who is at school even if this is not obvious in her picture:

Patricia: *In break time, I dream wonderfully.*
Interviewer: *You're dreaming? What are you dreaming of?*
Patricia: *Of Mew!*
Interviewer: *Of Mew, wow! He is always with you in your thoughts so to speak?*

Patricia:	*Yes. The same way as the other. It is called Togepi and I play that it is a moon manikin.*
(...)	
Interviewer:	*And what are they doing all the time? Different things or stuff, what happens there?*
Patricia:	*Yes, well, Togepi is flown to the moon. He's visiting with his parents. And in the evening he flies back again.*
Interviewer:	*Hum! His parents live on the moon?*
Patricia:	*Yes. And he was sent down!*
Interviewer:	*From his parents?*
Patricia:	*Yes.*
Interviewer:	*Yes? And why did they send him down?*
Patricia:	*Well, in my case, it was the fact that he fell down. From the moon.*
Interviewer:	*And then he arrived at "the land of milk and honey?"*
Patricia:	*Yes.*
Interviewer:	*And he likes it there?*
Patricia:	*He likes it very much!*

Patricia invents her own story around Pokémon Togepi, a creature still in the egg, being cared for by Misty, the central girl character in the TV series. Patricia knows that she is deviating from the original media plot: "*I play that it is a moon manikin.*" In the repetition of this statement using "*always,*" she emphasizes that this is a repeated fantasy. In Patricia's fantasy, Togepi lives in two different worlds: on the moon, and in the land of milk and honey. Togepi is commuting between these two worlds. One possible way of understanding this feature of her story is to relate it to her own biography of moving back and forth from Germany to California. Patricia lived in two different worlds. Like Togepi, she was always brought into different worlds by others. This is naturally a challenge for a child and the implications cannot be easily assessed. Patricia works through these experiences in her make-believe world. The fact that Patricia is using the passive voice to describe this situation is significant for interpretation: "*Togepi is flown to the moon,*" and "*He is sent down.*" The coming home, however, is described in an active voice: "*And in the evening he flies back.*" The character was thrown (passively) into a foreign world, but finds an active form of returning. Patricia says that Togepi does not have to come back at all, but still does. In this narration, Patricia symbolizes her biographical experiences, and a plan of action (even symbolic) is offered to actively deal with it. In this sense, the story of Togepi is a way to productively deal with the challenges the girl is facing.

This is even more evident when taking into consideration an additional aspect of Togepi in Patricia's fantasy story, that in which the moon manikin attends a special school. Here he doesn't have to do so much homework and when he does, the others help him: "*Yes! And he is little and gets little homework. And the others are always doing it for him [Laughs].*"

Presumably, this reflects one of Patricia's wishes: that there will be somebody helpful and considerate toward her—qualities missing in her everyday experiences in the new German language school. Togepi also has to go to school, but it is a special school, where he learns special things. In the context of moving from the United States to Munich, Patricia found the change of schools extremely difficult. In California, she was well integrated socially and academically successful in school. She was very actively involved in several academic projects such as whale watching and marine biology. The transition from her Californian school experience, with an emphasis on individual projects, to a rather traditional form of Bavarian schooling was causing her great difficulty. Shortly before the interview, she was informed that she had been assigned to a lower level school because of her low academic achievements. According to her mother, the teacher saw her as a daydreamer, not participating in class and consequently she assigned her the lowest grade in oral performance. In the fantasy, Patricia tells how she retreats into her dreamland of *Pokémon* dreams, instead of facing the boring school curriculum that she feels has nothing to do with her. In these dreams, she processes her situation through symbolic means: Togepi, coming from a different world attends a special school, where contents relevant to him are taught. This enables Patricia to keep her self-esteem. She is not stupid, but in the wrong school, learning the wrong things.

This media-related make-believe world not only compensates for her daily academic and social hardships, but even more significantly, it helps her to understand her own situation and to find a way to come to terms with it. The *Pokémon* characters she selects provide her with symbolization material for various needs and characteristics (strong, powerful, tender, sweet, funny, needing protection). Events like frequently moving "happen" to her, as they do to Togepi, and she needs to find a way to deal with them as he does. Patricia can even make her school failures understandable through *Pokémon*-related experiences.

In summary, the move back to Munich and the teacher's feedback seem to be a major threat to Patricia's state of mind. She retreats depressively into her fantasy world. She is often tired and spends a lot of time daydreaming in Germany. She simply accepts attacks from classmates passively, although it would probably be more healthy for her to become angry. Instead, Patricia dreams herself back into an early phase, being symbolized by the newly hatched Togepi, needing protection. A state of regression can be found in the land of milk and honey, in which no demands are put on the child and he or she is allowed not to do anything, similar to being in the mother's womb. Everything is available in abundance and without any effort. Snorlax, in particular, is the icon of such a state, because he only sleeps and eats. However, Snorlax, like the favorite Mew, also symbolizes powerful characteristics. Mew in particular is suitable for identification, because he is officially extinct, perhaps a parallel to the "former" Patricia in the United States. In the movie, it is quite obvious that Mew still exists. Patricia may be creating a way to express her belief that the powerful girl she acknowledges herself to have been still exists in Germany—even if presently hidden. These are inner images full of power, in which Patricia sticks to the conviction: I am more powerful than I seem! This conviction may be keeping her from becoming depressed.

Media as a Shared Resource

Media traces do not only serve as an "inner dialog." They can be linked to another source of meaning. Patricia chose symbolic material that is shared and liked by her peer group. Shortly before the formal research procedure took place, the children in the research group informally discussed the different *Pokémon*. While painting, she noticed that some of her peers included *Pokémon* characters in their drawings. Patricia chose to use material commonly known and relevant to her peer group. In the interview, Patricia talked about that which she knew very well and on which she can appear as an expert. The interviewer encouraged Patricia by expressing interest and was impressed by the girl's vivid narration, which further encouraged her to continue. With the help of this media material, Patricia presented herself as a competent and interesting personality to the adult researcher. The honest and consistent reassurance of the interviewer allowed Patricia to feel appreciated. Even problematic areas, like her low school achievements, were shown in a completely different light.

Patricia as Prototype

The case study of Patricia, although highly individualized and detailed, is clearly prototypical. She uses TV characters to symbolize a part of herself, to invent her own story in which she processes events in her own life experience, justifies them for herself, and articulates desires. She communicates with others with the help of media material and presents herself as an expert.

To summarize this discussion, we suggest three ways by which children make active use of media material in their make-believe worlds:

Making Sense of Experiences.   Children use media content in order to symbolize and make sense of their own experiences. Through their choices of content and via their individual interpretations, they express their own feelings and needs. The media material becomes integrated within their self-image through the processes of transfer and symbolization.

Departure Point.   Children use media stories as a springboard for their own themes and their individual narratives in which they process their experiences. In their make-believe stories with media material, they represent their perceptions of their worlds and reconstruct them in a subjectively meaningful way. They can choose to stick closely to the original media story or use only parts of it. But it is always their own story that they choose to tell with the aid of material from the mass media.

Interpersonal Interaction.   Children use the media world to foster communication with others—children and adults alike, including the researchers who interviewed them. The media content serves as a common ground, a shared environment, a taken-for-granted world. On mentioning a name of a character, a program, or a particular episode, they assume that this shared world forms a basis for effective communication. This process is clearly evident in the research context, a brief exchange of words, a visual code in the drawing, hand gestures—all convey information that is assumed to be shared and to make sense to other participants in the social situation.

These conclusions have far-reaching implications for producers in terms of their responsibilities for offering children satisfying and nourishing media content; as well as for parents and educators in thinking about how to work with the world of children's understanding, imagination, and fantasy capabilities.

III

Central Themes: Gender and Culture

6

The Gendered
Nature of Children's
Make-Believe Worlds

The centrality of gender in children's make-believe worlds became immediately evident upon examination of the pictures and stories. In all four countries, the girls' pictures lean toward an emphasis on harmony and have notably fewer media traces than boys' pictures. Boys' pictures, in contrast, are characterized by conflict and fighting, and are loaded with obvious links to relevant media texts. Our intuitive first impressions are validated in a quantitative mapping. However, a more sensitive and in-depth analysis of the less obvious differences hidden behind what is considered as "typically girls" and "typically boys" reveals a much more complex picture that cannot be that easily forced into a neat scheme. The discussion in this chapter offers interpretation and analysis of gender-specific motifs found in our study and grounds it in what we know from related research on gender, childhood, and media.

A QUANTITATIVE OVERVIEW

Because the study is based on qualitative methods of investigation and evaluation, quantitative mapping serves to illustrate some of the gender-specific findings. However, the numbers refer to a nonrepresentative qualitative sample and therefore, are not meant to suggest any valid generalizations.

Of the 193 children studied, there were 110 girls, which comprised 57% of the sample. It was more difficult to solicit boys in the three countries where participation was optional and required an active decision to join in (Germany, Israel, and the United States), making it necessary to deliberately pursue boys' groups with greater efforts. Apparently, the topic of the study itself as well as the methods employed—drawing, talking about inner worlds—was more attractive to girls than to boys.

The breakdown of the children's make-believe world stories and pictures is presented in Table 6.1. Clear gendered emphases emerge from these cases: 55% of the girls' cases imagine worlds of harmony with nature, animals, and people. Lagging far behind are the make-believe worlds of foreign lands (13%), followed by the world of supernatural power (8%) and that of royalty (7%). The category of technology was the one most rarely identified in the girls' cases.

In the 83 boys' drawings and narratives, the themes characterizing their worlds are less clearly dominated by one category. However, there are clearly identifiable leanings toward the areas of fighting and threat (31%), and of amusement (20%). The next most popular category (16%) for boys is the world of harmony with nature and animals.

Some decisive gender-related differences are evident in the wishes to act as well. When counting only the most obvious and explicit wish to act, we find that almost 39% of the girls wish to experience well-being in their make-believe worlds followed by the wish to be connected to others (24%) (see Table 6.2).

As for boys, 43% express the wish to experience thrill, similar in proportion to the girls' wish to live in harmony.

TABLE 6.1

Girls' and Boys' Make-Believe Worlds

Worlds	Girls N = 110	Boys N = 83
Harmony and peace	60 (55%)	13 (16%)
Foreign land	14 (13%)	5 (6%)
Supernatural	9 (8%)	5 (6%)
Royalty	8 (7%)	1 (1%)
Sensual pleasures	7 (6%)	3 (4%)
Amusement	6 (5%)	17 (20%)
Travel	3 (3%)	7 (8%)
Conflict and threat	2 (2%)	26 (31%)
Technology	1 (1%)	6 (7%)

TABLE 6.2

Girls' and Boys' Wishes to Act

Wish to act	Girls N = 110	Boys N = 83
Experience well-being	43 (39%)	12 (14%)
Bonding with others	26 (24%)	10 (12%)
Experience thrill	12 (11%)	36 (43%)
Displaying specialness	10 (9%)	12 (14%)
Acting independently	19 (9%)	4 (5%)
Protecting/being protected	9 (8%)	9 (11%)

Overall, we can state that the prevailing wish for girls is to project themselves into a world of harmony, where the primary wish is to experience well-being and bonding with others. As for boys, the dominant wish is to experience thrill in a world of conflict and threat or a world of amusement. However, as is clear in the tables, a variety of alternatives to these dominant themes came out of the children's stories.

Media Traces in Make-Believe Worlds

Children's make-believe worlds have media traces of different and overlapping origins, as discussed in previous chapters. Our analysis identified gender-specific trends in relationship to specific media influence (see Table 6.3).

As already mentioned, the pictures of the boys seemed to be more media-oriented at first sight. Many dinosaurs and Pokémon and Digimon rule the make-believe worlds. The pictures of girls seemed to be less imprinted by media references. However, when we listen closely to the girls' stories, they themselves

TABLE 6.3

Gendered Media Traces

Media Traces	Girls N = 110	Boys N = 83
Media traces total	61 (55.5%)	61 (73.5%)
Explicit media traces	49 (80%)	48 (79%)
Implicit media traces	12 (20%)	13 (21%)
No media traces	49 (44.5%)	22 (26.5%)

mention references to media that we may not have identified on the basis of the stories and pictures alone. Even when including these implicit traces, a closer look suggests that the presence of media traces in girls' make-believe worlds are quantitatively lower than those of boys. This holds true in all four countries. The first impression therefore does not deceive, however it is less powerful than it appears to be at first sight.

Boys' fantasies have more media traces in nearly all the subcategories included in the quantitative breakdown (see Table 6.4). The widest difference shows up in relation to the incorporation of media-related characters.

Boys' stories connect more closely with, and are more deeply saturated by, the original media content. It is not unusual for their stories to incorporate a combination of settings, characters, and stories. In contrast, girls' stories are more likely to abstract a single element from the original media—for example, a specific object, costume, or piece of information. Twenty-six percent of boys' stories incorporated all three categories (*settings, characters, stories*) in individual make-believe worlds. Only 2% of the girls' worlds included media traces from all three categories. Twenty-eight percent of the boys incorporated two out of the three categories, in comparison to 19% of the girls. Forty-eight percent of the boys' stories included media traces in just one category, compared to 79% of the girls' stories. This helps explain why our first impression of boys' make-believe worlds is so strikingly dominated by the media, much more than the gap really proves to be. These findings beg questions such as: Are visual images more salient for boys or easier for them to draw? Do visual images play a bigger role in their imaginations, in terms of visualizing their fantasies? And, as a result, does borrowing from the media serve as a visual task?

TABLE 6.4

Gendered Media Traces' Contents

Contents		Sub-categories	Total Stories with Traces = 122	Girls N=110 Media Traces = 61	Boys N = 83 Media Traces = 61
Setting	77 (40%)	Setting	66 (54%)	31 (51%)	35 (57%)
		Object	11 (9%)	7 (12%)	4 (7%)
Character	65 (34%)	Character	59 (48%)	22 (36%)	37 (61%)
		Costume	6 (5%)	2 (3%)	4 (7%)
Story	52 (27%)	Story	29 (24%)	6 (10%)	23 (38%)
		Information	23 (19%)	10 (16%)	13 (21%)

GIRLS' MAKE-BELIEVE WORLDS OF HARMONY

In more than half of the make-believe worlds (56 %) girls represented themselves in their own pictures. It is striking, however, that this percentage differs from country to country. In Korea, more than 70% of the girls painted themselves, whereas in Israel, only about 30% did so. Despite our efforts, we were not able to provide any possible explanation for this difference.

Girls draw themselves with an obvious hairstyle, preferably braids or ponytails, across all countries. This is most striking in South Korea, where only one girl, Hyon'ah (G, SK-5), refrained from doing so as she was about to meet Jesus in her make-believe world. Apparently, the hairstyle for girls is an iconic way to symbolize their femininity as a girl or a young woman. Because the secondary sexual characteristics are not yet formed in this age group, the signification of hair becomes a clear gender sign. Clothes figure in a similar manner. Somewhat fewer than half the girls who represent themselves in their drawings are pictured wearing a skirt or a dress in their make-believe world. In South Korea, this may be based on the everyday experience of the school uniform.

Beyond what is considered everyday female clothing, some chose to dress themselves in old-fashioned baroque dresses or gowns. Women's attire according to the girls in our study, is a form of gendered-self-representation, a way of marking themselves as feminine and expressing themselves as beautiful. Appearances, as we know, are closely related to presumptions about "essence." The cultural connection between the construct of being a girl and a representation of the girl through the appearance code is highlighted through these choices (Tseelon, 1995). The centrality of physical appearance and attractiveness in the definition of femininity and the value of individual girls and women is nothing new in human societies. Our cultures strongly encourage girls to equate their physical appearance with their personal identity through the indoctrination of both traditional and mediated socializing agents in an everlasting quest for beautification. Through this highly commodified and commercialized process, girls are led to believe that they can achieve power, control, and their "ultimate" goal of heterosexual romance (Mazzarella, 1999; McRobbie, 1993; Peirce, 1990).

The analysis of the pictures of the make-believe worlds suggest that 8- to 10-year-old girls indeed define themselves to a large extent through appearance. However, surprisingly enough, they hardly ever refer to appearance or talk about it in the interviews. Paying close attention to appearance and drawing themselves in detail seem to be done unconsciously, inattentive to the meaning involved. The need to do so seems to go unnoticed by the girls, as a taken-for-granted, "natural" way of things, typical of uncritical adherence to social norms.

In addition to expressing who they are through beauty, in several of the stories, the girls reveal that their perception of themselves takes into account others' perspectives on them. Saya's (G, GR-4) make-believe world, for example, is located in a "land of Indians" (Native Americans). According to the girl, the starting point for this is that in her own environment, she is often mistakenly perceived to be "Indian." Because she has black hair (her parents are Vietnamese by ethnicity), she integrates this as a positive perspective on her own physical appearance. Reactions from others are incorporated here into the self-image in her make-believe world. In a different case, it is a personality trait that a girl uses to set herself apart. Güler (G, GR-14), of Turkish descent, describes her make-believe world like this:

> I always wanted to see the very hot Africa. I'm interested in the animals there. I see a lion, a kangaroo, a bird and also a rabbit. And, of course, many plants and trees. The lion and the rabbit look at me and the bird and the kangaroo are talking about me. What sort of girl I am? It is very interesting for them to see nice people and not only those who want to hunt them …. I have nearly all the jungle stories at home on tape and this is why I'm so interested in Africa.

Güler imagines how others talk about her. She portrays a moment that is experienced as pleasant because she is something special through being recognized by others as nice and not wanting to do harm. Tali (G, IS-6), expresses her desire for positive attention from others when she imagines herself appearing on stage with her favorite singer. Many spotlights are directed to the center of the stage and when she appears, the audience applauds her: *"You can see the stage and the spotlight and people say: 'Applaud Tali H.!'"* Young'son (G, SK-12), talks about her thoughts:

> My thoughts tell me that I have to prepare everything thoroughly. But now I can hear what the clock tells me. It says: "You have done a lot last week. You practiced the piano, read books, and slept. But best of all is that you have been good and donated something at church. You have shared your pocket money." I reply to the clock "thank you very much." In the future I also want to be good.

A case can be made for saying that these girls are internalizing other people's ideas about what constitutes being a "good girl" and, for them, this is important enough to play a key role in imagining their ideal selves.

This desire for positive judgment and praise from the outside was also found in the research situation itself. Tanja (G, GR-53), for example, draws herself in a romantic setting in the dress of princess Sissi. During the process of drawing her picture, a dialogue between Tanja and her friends is overheard by the field researcher. She reported that Tanja explains that she has originally drawn a queen or princess, but now she doesn't know if she can mention that in the interview:

"They may think I'm arrogant." The friend responds: *"Then just say it is only a court lady."* In the interview, Tanja takes the middle way out and says she is *"a court lady or a princess or so."* Even during the painting process, Tanja anticipates the outside judgment of the interviewers themselves and includes it in her self-presentation. Although taking into account all the subtleties involved in such moments, it seems that for many of the girls in the study, presenting themselves and their body in their make-believe worlds is a satisfying experience. This study provides evidence that the young girls who participated in this research process have already integrated into their self-image an outside perspective on their appearance and personality. Through the imagined self, they seem to experience the power to act. However, as Christian-Smith (1990) reminded us, in this process the girl accepts "another's version of reality as her own: how she should behave, think, and look. The ability to define reality for another is certainly one of the more important forms of social power" (p. 54).

Worlds of Harmony, Care, and Relationships

In all four countries the greatest number of girls prefer to dream of harmonious scenarios of nature with animals and sometimes people as well. A central characteristic of these paradise-like fantasy worlds is that all creatures live in harmony with themselves and others. As portrayed by girls from all four countries, each creature has its place in these worlds. There is a strict order of things so everything is integrated and in relationship to each another. The girls themselves are in most cases an integral part of this world. Sometimes they are positioned positively as ruling, while at other times they passively enjoy the world around them. This tendency is exhibited also as a form of the "aesthetics of order." The visual elements are often placed symmetrically or are somewhat ornamental as in You'jin's (G, SK-11) drawing of *"the wonderful garden in my dreamland,"* where everything is lined up symmetrically.

Only very rarely is there a potential threat in these fantasy worlds. If it is included at all, it is minimized in the narrative, as in the case of Carrie's story (G, US-10):

> I went to a land that had all the animals and mammals and reptiles and stuff. And there were no humans, but there were some dolphins and unicorns and some things that you couldn't usually see in real life. I also saw a unicorn who was running and found a food bowl and started eating. There are also sea creatures, but no sharks, because sharks might kill one of the animals if it goes in the water. There are alligators, but they are friendly and they won't bite. If they need fish, they fish for them. They just don't bite. There are all kinds of sea creatures, even whales, and there are all different kinds of birds, pelicans, and others. We don't have many hawks, because hawks would take up the squirrels and all the other land creatures that live on this land. There are not many predators. I'm near the unicorn, but not close enough to scare it. I can see the dolphin jumping out of the water in the sunshine from far away.

Carrie talks about a dreamland in which there are all sorts of animals, but only a few eat other creatures. She keeps potentially dangerous disturbances and threats to a minimum. Another girl, Isabel (G, GR-52), sends spies to the border of her country to keep bad people away from her territory. Tessina (G, GR-3) introduces strict rules that are to be obeyed by everyone. On her island, people who might potentially threaten animals can only come during the day. In the night when the animals come out, she is the only one allowed to stay on the island because she lives in harmony with them. By these precautions, girls seek to ensure that their worlds will remain harmonious. Everything that might interfere is outlawed or minimized through strategies created by the girls.

A central activity found in girls' worlds of harmony is that of care. Rona (G, IS-11), whose world was already described, concludes the description of her drawing as follows: *"I walked to the trees to climb on them, and found animals to raise, and flowers to grow, so as to improve heaven a little bit."*

They care for animals, feed, and look after them, and help them when they are hurt. In doing so, they see themselves in a position of responsibility and strength. This caring activity is proactive and positive. By putting the needs of others first and caring for them, the girls seem to gain a sense of empowerment and enjoyment. We did not get the impression from the stories they told that the girls felt exploited in their role as caregivers in their fantasies, but rather that being usefully connected with others in their make-believe worlds was pleasurable. This theme also demonstrates the complexity of the socializing processes into womanhood. Conforming to the expected role of caring for others is so deeply ingrained and internalized that it is experienced as an essential personality trait and a source of personal power. A rival interpretation would suggest that girls are subversively turning social expectations into a source of strength, a process by which girls gain authority for the otherwise marginalized female experience and worldview. This dialectical argument echoes much of the existing debate in the feminist literature over the trap proposed by the essentialist approach to gender differences (Lemish & Barzel, 2000).

Another motif that characterized a number of the girls' make-believe worlds is a stable relationship and partnership with one or few very close friends. Sharing the power and excitement of the fantasy world equally with a friend is a key element in the make-believe world. Thus, for girls, being part of a group is rather exceptional. This preference has been demonstrated in the gendered styles of children's peer relationships in other research as well. For example, in a study of the communication environment of children and youth in 12 European countries, it was found that girls exhibit a preference for more intimate relationships with a best friend, whereas boys have a stronger preference for group bonding (Lemish et al., 2001). A clear example of such a friendship in the fantasy world is told by Isabell (G, GR-52); in the make-believe world in which Isabell and her friend, Theresa, shared *"for a year or so,"* they created a world full of harmony in which their friendship is a defining element. A sense of justice, precautions toward potential threats, and a successful performance in the evening provide common ground for them and a perfect world for all participants. Here, as in many of the other girls' fantasies, relationships are defined and enjoyed.

The centrality of relationships in the upbringing of girls is widely discussed in the psychological literature, particularly that which is rooted in feminist perspectives. According to Chodorow (1974, 1981), a leading theorist in this area, with the current gendered distribution of work in most societies, where women are the dominant caregivers of babies and children, girls experience a strong bonding with their mothers and are relieved of the need to separate emotionally. The father symbolizes the outside world and can, in predominantly heterosexually oriented societies, become the object of love for this age group without any complications (Benjamin, 1990). Boys' personalities, on the other hand, are characterized by a need to separate from their mothers and to constantly establish themselves as different than the feminine.

The result of these processes, according to Chodorow and others, is that whereas the masculine personality is characterized by individuality and a quest for assertiveness and personal expansion, the feminine character is strongly characterized by cooperation, relationships, and a desire for closeness and belonging. At the risk of oversimplification, this line of argument can be summed up based on Gilligan's (1982) seminal book with the observation that girls learn to define themselves through their relationships with others, whereas boys learn to define themselves through separation and boundaries. Girls are socialized into a social model of interpersonal relationships, mutuality, and personal involvement and care, whereas boys are socialized into a social model of hierarchies, driven by competition and personal achievements. Clearly, the debate over the contributions of both nature and nurture to these processes continues, as evidenced by the ongoing discussion in the feminist scholarly community.

According to our study, children's make-believe worlds appear to provide further support for this analysis. The data presented for both the girls and the boys fall into place accordingly. Girls' worlds are characterized by expressions of needs and desires to envision themselves as responsible through caring for something or someone. The interrelationship between the need to care and the striving for harmony has been pointed out by Gilligan and colleagues (at the Harvard Project on the Psychology of Women and Girls' Development, see Brown, 1998; Brown & Gilligan; 1992; Pipher, 1995). Girls who are taught self-effacement by the culture around them are found to be in constant search for alternative forms of empowerment. In their make-believe worlds, they place themselves in the center and shape their environment from a powerful position through actively doing something to care for other creatures and to maintain a harmonious world. By creating mechanisms to minimize or eliminate threats to these worlds, they avert conflict and argument and their position remains unchallenged. They manage all this through skillful manipulation of their considerable communicative capabilities, with the support of close friends, animals, or natural forces, without the aid of technology or machinery and without help or interference from males. Finding the way to lead without the help of males may be another important source of empowerment for girls.

Worlds of Excitement and Adventure

Although harmony figures most prominently in girls' make-believe worlds, some of them do wish for worlds of excitement and adventure. In some ways, these dreams differ vastly from those characterized by harmony; however, some of them embodied similar motifs. These worlds are also generally different from the boys' fantasies of them, as we discuss below, because fighting is rarely found, even in these make-believe worlds.

Boram (G, SK-13), for example, imagines that she owns a superman rocket that she invented and humanized, and is flying to the sky to explore the stars and see aliens. She describes her make-believe world:

> I'm in dreamland for the first time. There are no other creatures and no animals. But I have a space ship—this is a superman rocket. It looks like a human being. The three purple fireballs at the rocket show that it's operating. I want to fly to the sky with my friend and explore the stars, watch aliens, and see the world from above. In a house with light blue walls, there are my dad, my mom, my siblings, and a parrot. The house has a roof with a pink chimney and on top of it there is a bell, hanging on a black rope. The rope reaches high into the sky and the bell signals the rocket to take off. Next time I will take my parents and my family up into the sky. You see, in the sky it is quiet and dark.

Boram imagines a technology she can master and use for her benefit. She fantasizes an exciting opportunity even though she does not describe it in detail. She is not on her own in this adventure, but with a friend and next time she wants to take her parents along. Boram does not describe the adventure itself, but the constellation of relationships that provide her with security. Within this setup, she wants to experience the adventure of seeing aliens and seeing things from above.

Lara (G, IS-25) imagines the thrills of an amusement park:

> We are here in the land of dreams. When we saw the place we were scared because the playthings were scary and we weren't allowed to go on them because they are danger-

ous ... there is a big train, and a big boat, and a waterfall that sprays water on us. I am here with my friends ... we came through here and went down there holding a metal handle. It was dark and we went down ...

Lara, a Christian-Arab girl from a remote village, goes on to describe the fun and thrill involved in being scared, explaining that in her home village, there is nothing pretty and exciting: *"You sit alone and you are bored and wonder what to do,"* while in her dreamland, *"There are lots of pretty things, lots of playthings."*

Teri (G, US-6) too is seeking excitement: *"My name is Strike. I'm the best hunter and the fastest runner. In Lions' Lair there are adventures, threats, and dangerous people ..."*

Like Boram, Lara, and Teri, many other girls in our study want to experience excitement. However, a world marked only by conflict and threat, as in many of the boys' fantasies, is not their idea of excitement. Furthermore, fights are specifically avoided by most of them. Rarely do exceptions to this rule occur, as in the case of Jody's (G, US-15) story. She describes her big daydream (see Drawing 6.1):

Drawing 6.1. Jody (G, US-15) "Saber-Tooth Tiger."

In my fantasy I am sleeping in my bed. My dream and I start to lift over the world and I land in the Arctic. There are lots of big mountains that are whitish-blue, and there's like an ocean, and polar bears, and icebergs, little mini-sized trees and plants and fungi. Colors start to turn around me. I morph into a saber tooth tiger. It is peaceful out. I sense something mysterious in the air. I hear a boom shot from a gun and I start to run toward it. I don't want the hunter to hurt any other animals in the Arctic. There are many extinct animals in the world and some of those were in the Arctic. I'm ready to fight, with my claws out and my teeth ready.

I see a hunter and his dogs. I don't kill the hunter, but I make him scared and I might scratch him and bite a little bit so he leaves the Arctic. In the end, I win the fight and the hunter goes home. I guess I felt really angry and disturbed that the hunter was there. I don't mind if people are there and they have no guns or knives or anything with them, and they're just exploring and taking photographs and stuff, but when they have a gun and I hear it shoot something or I just hear a boom, I really get very angry and disturbed about it and I don't want to run away because I don't want this hunter to stay and kill my friends and my family. After the fight, I go to catch some food and go to sleep and the dream ends.

Jody draws a saber-tooth tiger poised to strike. It leaps out from the page. This make-believe world is permeated by threat, but also embraces a demonstration of power. Jody explicitly links her story to Disney's classic animation movie, *Bambi*. She projects harmonious feelings, but also anger and aggression. Although she is protective, she is also aware of her responsibility and commitment to nonviolent values, trying to defend the animals without seriously injuring the hunter. Jody fends off threat, not for the enjoyment of the fight itself, but to protect others. Her fantasy, therefore, remains within the realm of gender-appropriate behavior, even though specific emotions and actions fall outside the norm in our study. Jody's make-believe world serves to enlighten us on how girls may be trying to align their own commonly labeled masculine desires, with the expectations of gender-appropriate desires and behaviors they have adopted through processes of socialization.

GIRLS' MEDIA TRACES

Our analysis revealed fewer media traces in girls' make-believe worlds than in boys' and the ones we found were less apparent on the surface. Girls integrate fewer media characters in their make-believe worlds; they seldom use a setting taken from the media, and rarely apply a media story. However, when we listened carefully to the girls in the interviews, we discovered that they do make media references, albeit more subtly and implicitly.

Media Settings. In 38 of the girls' stories, we identified an explicit connection to a media setting or object. In these cases, girls take a setting that helps them construct a world of ongoing harmony. Fairytale-like settings that readily enable magical narratives seem to be particularly attractive to them. Da'eun (G, SK-35), locates her make-believe world in such a fairytale setting. She describes it as follows:

> I come to my fantasyland and the fairy says: "Welcome to fantasyland!" There are people, fairies, and many animals: a rabbit, a baby elephant, a lion, a tiger, and a cat. All are welcoming me friendly. There is a castle, too. In there lives a king and a princess and a prince. In the castle there are many rooms and a big throne for the king and the queen … When I want to come here I fly, and when I want to go home—I fly back home.

In this land everybody present accepts Da'eun just the way she is, in a friendly manner (see Drawing 6.2).

Sometimes girls construct their make-believe worlds around real characters in their lives (e.g., family members, friends) within a media setting. Milena (G, GR-39), for example, invents a world set in the movie, *Faeries*, that was broadcast on prime-time television 3 days before the interview took place. She describes her land in the following:

> I am a fairy. I can fly like a bird and float through the magic land. There are animals that can speak, and other fairies, the wife of the Easter bunny. Lollipops and sweets are hanging on the trees and there are mountains of pudding. Of course, I'm tiny as a fairy and this is why everything else is so much bigger. All fairies live in the fairy oak and

Drawing 6.2. Da'eun (G, SK-35) "Fantasyland."

from there you get to the fairyland. In this land there are only women and girls. And all children have so much fun, because you're allowed to do everything you want: for example, to play a lot. In school you only have two subjects: Math and German, because they are my favorite; and there is a paradise fair, where there are sweets, lemonade, and Coca-Cola—as much as you want. And if you treat flowers really good, then you can even eat them. I'm a fairy and can naturally do magic whenever I want.

In the movie, *Faeries*, a girl named Nellie and her little brother, George, who are playing hide and seek in the forest, unintentionally come through a magic oak into the mystical land of fairies. Since George has eaten the magic food of the fairies, he has to stay forever, unless his sister can successfully complete three tasks. The children get caught in a power struggle between good and evil in the fairyland. Nellie finally succeeds in helping good prevail over evil and rescues her brother from the curse. The setting of the movie serves as the starting point for Milena's world and she talks about it with enthusiasm and in detail. In her world she eliminates everything from the movie which could threaten harmony, including the struggle between good and evil, the question of who rules the land, and all male characters. She even redefines the traditionally male Easter bunny into an Easter bunny woman.

Adva (G, IS-44) also refers to the very same movie, *Faeries* (she has seen it on television although she can't name it), when she shares her world:

I was a girl who came to a strange land with candies and dwarfs who played together and ate candy. The trees were made of candy and candy was hovering in the sky. Toffee and chocolate and lollipops, and a floor of chocolate, and ice cream. This dwarf is flying with a hat, like from Snow White. We are playing and eating candy. I've seen something on television—a boy and a girl who have a magic tree, and they enter it and there are other worlds in it.

Although adopting the details of the setting from the movie, she omits the prohibition of eating the candy, as well as all the possible dangers involved (such as not being able to leave the place), and modifies the setting to meet her own preferences. Similarly, Dana (G, IS-42), adopts a specific element from the setting of the animated Disney movie, *The Little Mermaid,* for her sea-life make-believe world—the swirling water in one of the opening scenes of the movie. She borrows neither the characters nor the narrative from the original movie. Her world is all about fishing with her brother—the two of them on their own.

Such fairyland media settings selected by girls serve to enable a make-believe-world of harmony. Many of them are based on traditional European fairytales as well as the Disney movies based on them.

Media Characters. In our study, 24 girls integrate a media character or parts of one in their make-believe worlds. Girls often adopt characters whose gender is ambiguous and furthermore cannot be identified according to age.

An example of this is the incorporation of *Pokémon* characters. Audrey (G, US-28), for example, imagines herself as a Pokémon in a sort of "land of milk and honey." She says: *"I always like to imagine that I am a Pokémon."* Pokémon are nearly all gender-neutral and are referred to as "it" in the series rather than as "he" or "she." However, many of them are marked by signs of masculinity through behavior or accessories, and sometimes children—including the girls—refer to them as "he." However, there is some space for individual gender interpretation.

Occasionally, girls take on the role of a female heroine. One such character is Ariel, the little mermaid from the Disney movie and television series, who was selected in several cases. She seems to provide a compelling ideal self for girls to project. However, in most of the cases, the issue is much more complex and when comparing the children's fantasies to the medium source, similarities can, in fact, be observed, but the differences clearly prevail. Such is the case of Karen (G, US-26), who describes her make-believe world in which she becomes Ariel, *The Little Mermaid:*

> In my fantasy, I pictured I was a mermaid. I was at my grandma's and I jumped into the sea. Under a big rock, there was a starfish who told me about the magical box. I found a box that would change me into a person or a mermaid. The box could sense when you are out of the water and want to have legs or when you are in the water and want to have a tail. In my fantasy, I get stung and chased by a shark, but I go through an anchor and the shark gets stuck in it, so I am saved. I love water and being a mermaid makes me feel like I am a fish in the water.

Karen changed into a mermaid and names the Walt Disney movie as the media source. Her drawing shows herself as a mermaid having a big fish tail. Next to her there is the magic box. The whole scene is located on the coast. The mermaid drawn by Karen resembles Disney's portrayal of Ariel's—the mermaid tail, the color (orange/red), and the length of her hair. Further features of the depiction of the mermaid in the Disney movie are not employed by Karen, like the very tiny bikini made of shells or the skinny waist. Karen's mermaid looks like a huge fish tail with a head on the top of it.

Karen's story tells of an adventurous encounter with a shark, similar to the film scene. Ariel and her little friend, Flounder, are attacked by a shark and try to escape by outwitting it. Finally, they succeed and the shark is stuck in an anchor. This particular scene is placed at the very beginning of the movie when Ariel is introduced. Through her language, her gestures, and her facial expressions, Ariel is characterized as courageous, witty, enthusiastic, and physically skilled. She is also represented as a good friend who is willing to risk her life for her friends. As soon as she meets her prince, however, these characteristics fade away and an emphasis is put on her more traditional feminine traits, including the transformation in her appearance (e.g., her lips become deeply red; her eyelashes longer and more pronounced).

The character of Ariel in Disney's, *The Little Mermaid,* and Disney's adaptation of Andersen's original fairytale, has provided fertile ground for much feminist analysis (see, e.g., Wasko, 2001). Karen, however, adopts those moments in the movie that present Ariel as a strong and nonsexualized person. In addition, she not only adopts that particular aspect of the character of the little mermaid, she also extends the fantasy to include a special role for the magic box, which knows exactly *"if you are in the water and need a mermaid's tail, or if you are on land and need some human legs."* The tragic moment Ariel experiences in the film is removed in Karen's imagination. What remains is the extension of Karen's personal potential and the experience of small adventures turning out well.

In some cases, it became obvious that girls imagine themselves "into" the plot and take on a position similar to male heroes but in a female character. Amelia (G, US-36), for example, tells her interviewer that her fantasy is similar to a part of the movie, *Shrek,* where the princess was in danger of being captured:

> In my dream, I saw a unicorn and fairies, and my dream was beautiful. The fairy gave me wings and made it so I learned how to fly and the flowers could talk, so I talked to them. The unicorn's name was Alisa. And she could fly. Sometimes she let me ride on her back. And her horn was pretty. She is shiny and her horn has the power to defend her and others. I have thought about this before. There are other people in a castle. A dragon and some trolls are trying to get into the castle and knights are fighting them off so that the knights can save the princess who is inside the castle. I help the princess—I am kind of like her maid, but I got out before the dragon came because I went to get some flowers. The flowers told me about the dragon and the trolls at the castle and said: "Don't pick us." I was going to go to the castle, but I was afraid. So I planned to go to the castle, to the back door cause there was nobody at the back door, but a little troll. The fairy was going to go with me and the unicorn. So they could like fight off the troll. This is kind of like the movie Shrek.

Amelia imagines herself in a similar position to Shrek, or the knights, in that she is a protector. But she uses her own tactics. Where the men prove themselves in a direct clash with a dragon, she uses the backdoor to avoid the confrontation and can overcome the troll with the help of her magical creature—the unicorn. The story of Shrek is a point of reference for her story, but the strategies she uses to save the princess are her own. Girls, as Amelia's illustration suggests, invent their own heroines in their make-believe worlds. This may be related to the lack of attractive female heroines missing in the bulk of mainstream media texts.

Tanja (G, GR-53), imagines herself falling through a pipe into a place full of candles where she is *"a princess wearing a magnificent wide gown and with upswept hair"* (see Drawing 6.3):

Drawing 6.3. Tanja (G, GR-53) "Candle Light."

Somehow I just fell through a pipe and suddenly I've came to stop in a forest. The sun was going down and complete darkness surrounded me. Then I stood amazed when I saw the candles all over the place. And I looked like a princess or a lady of the court wearing a magnificent wide gown and with upswept hair. There were candlesticks all around and even on the trees there were loads of candles. There was also a small hut full of straw. I entered it and nestled into the straw. Even there everything was lit by candles. It felt so romantic and I spent the night in the hut. Maybe outside there are some animals living, but you are not able to see them now. However, humans do not exist. In fact, I'm all by myself there.

The princess' gown, so she relates later in the interview, is borrowed from her favorite movie, *Sissi*. It is a classic Austrian movie from 1955 featuring Romy Schneider. It tells the story of Elisabeth, the Austrian Empress, in a very "kitsch-like" romanticized manner. All three parts of the movie are aired on a regular basis on German television around Christmastime. The first part, in which Franz Joseph, the Austrian Emperor, chooses Sissi for his bride is particularly popular with the audience. The Emperor falls in love with the 16-year-old Bavarian princess who loves nature and lives a very ordinary life in Possenhofen, next to Starnberg Lake (near Munich). His mother, however, would have loved to see him with Helene, Sissi's more suitable older sister. But the young Emperor has set his mind on Sissi and so a fabulous wedding scene concludes the first part of the trilogy.

During the movie, Sissi wears a variety of gorgeous dresses that must have left a deep impression on Tanja. However, she chooses to draw neither the spectacular white wedding gown, nor the azure gown that Sissi wears at the ball when Franz Joseph selects her. Instead, Tanja's drawing shows a girl in a red dress and a white apron that is a trace of a scene in the movie in which Sissi has a meeting with Franz Joseph in the forest. In fact, the dress is rather simple, consisting of a red skirt and top, as well as a white apron and ascot; exactly as Tanja depicts it. She also puts an emphasis on the hairstyle, which she adopts from this special scene in which Sissi's hair is tied so as to form a crown around her head.

However, aside from the clothing item and hairstyle taken from this particular scene in the forest, Tanja does not take anything else (at least on the surface) from the movie, in general, or from the character of Sissi, in particular. In the original movie, as in most traditional love stories, Sissi is defined through her relationship with the Prince; notably, there is no prince in Tanja's story. Whereas in the movie, Sissi works with her appearance to please the monarch and to improve her relationship with the public, Tanja's wish to be beautiful is connected with the need to feel good about herself. She takes over a stereotypical female character who is at the center of attention, but not the central themes of female dependency on romantic love or the oppression from the overall social environment that dominates the movie. In doing so, she creates a positive self-image.

Girls' lack of identification with male characters and systematic avoidance of males in their make-believe worlds in all four countries deserves special attention. This is particularly the case because producers of children's television often stress that it is unproblematic for girls to imagine themselves in the position of the male hero. In making this assumption and publicly defending it, the producers relieve themselves of the responsibility to produce programs that meet girls' needs for gender-specific hero identification. In only one case in our study did we find a form of appropriation of a male media hero that can be thought of as identification. Teri (G, US-6) imagines herself as a secret successor to the great lion king (of the Disney movie, *The Lion King*). She is Strike, the chosen one, and has magical powers similar to those possessed by Harry Potter; that is, she can make herself invisible and fly. Her opponent is a lion called Powell, who also has magical powers and threatens the king and the "chosen one." In all other instances, girls who took the role of a male hero reinterpreted and extended it to feminize it or at least to neutralize it in terms of gender. Even in Teri's unique case, it is interesting to point out that the chosen male character is an animal and not a human being.

Media Stories.   Of the 110 make-believe stories by girls, only six integrated part of a media story into their worlds, and even in these cases, for the most part, they excerpted bits of specific scenes rather than the entire narrative. Karen (G,

US-26), whose story has been described, provides such an example. She fantasizes herself as the little mermaid, Ariel, in a particular setting taken from the
Disney movie. She describes a scene the mermaid experienced, following the
exact plot in the movie itself: *"In my fantasy I get stung and chased by a shark, but I
go through an anchor and the shark gets stuck in it, so I am saved ..."* However, Karen's story is an exception among the girls because most of the media stories used
by them do not seem to function as a starting point for the girls' daydreams.

Quite a different version is provided by Chloe (G, US-4), who plays off the
fairytale character, Rapunzel:

> I just appeared on a cloud and I was looking down and this is what I saw. I went over to
> see what Chicken Boy was doing. I call him Chicken Boy because he has kind of a long
> neck and he has like chicken feet and hands and I use him in some of my dreams. In the
> castle is the princess named Samantha.

Chloe seems to be self-confident as she playfully pokes fun at the male character, Chicken Boy:

> Chicken Boy is trying to save her. He went up the staircase and then he got the prin-
> cess and they came down the marble stairway. The princess is kind of like a tomboy so
> she slid down the banister. She has long hair like Rapunzel, but Chicken Boy didn't
> read that story so he didn't know to climb up her hair.

In reversing the traditional gender roles, the princess becomes a tomboy
while the boy is at loss because literally, he does not know what to do:

> I followed Chicken Boy into the castle and I was talking to Samantha and she said that
> she thought that somebody was going to free her by climbing up her hair, but she said,
> "I hope they don't do that because you know I'm hoping to get a haircut as soon as I get
> out of this tower." She told Chicken Boy that if he ever saw another princess in a tower
> that he was supposed to use the hair.

The self-confident princess knows the expected roles, but also knows exactly
what she wants to do and instructs others accordingly.

> She got stuck up there, but not for the same reason as Rapunzel. She was supposed to
> be doing the dishes, but instead she was reading her sports book. Her punishment was
> that she had to go in the castle. The person that put her up there had to go on a vaca-
> tion for a business trip, and so she got stuck up there because he was the only one that
> had the key. Chicken Boy, since he has those claws on the end of his hand, put his claw
> into the lock and jiggled the handle and it opened.

In her imagination, Chloe is walking the thin line between maintaining traditional roles and reversing them, using a-typical fairytale elements:

> When they came back down, they went to the Apple Building, which is where all the
> apples are, and that's also where Chicken Boy's office is. He buys Samantha some ap-

ples and they didn't get married, but when I left my dream they were planning to get married on the soccer field. In my dream everyone just called the princess "Princess," but when I woke up I saw Samantha sitting next to me, so I called her Samantha. I kind of got the princess from Rapunzel and from the movie, Shrek ...

Chloe refers to the movie, *Shrek*, and the elements of princess Fiona as the captivated beauty in a tower. Most of all, she uses the humor of the movie, subverts the traditional stereotypes, and inserts intertextual references. *Shrek* is a production that, to a certain degree, turns around traditional gender roles. The beginning of the movie starts with a basic fairytale: a hero frees a captive princess. But the more the viewer gets to know the female character, the more she breaks away from traditional gender roles. She is self-sufficient, can do Kung-fu (intertextual relationship between Tiger and Dragon), and is not frightened away by the deadly provocation of a singing bird. Moreover, she ends up happily with a trolllike appearance, rather then her original stereotypical princess beauty. Chloe takes up the gender role reversal, counters existing stereotypes, and develops and extends it through her own funny variations.

Girls are also more likely to use factual information taken from media narratives. This seems to be particularly true for the German girls, who in several cases, mention documentary programs as starting points for their make-believe worlds. For example, Tessina (G, GR-3), imagines a world in which endangered animals are protected and can feel safe. It is easy to see connections between her personal history (the family had to flee from Kazakhstan for political reasons), and her fantasy world in which she protects animals and is also protected herself. However, she does not resort to a common traditional fairytale in which a princess is being saved by a prince. For Tessina, a girl we came to know personally as well as through her parents' description, as self-confident and self-sufficient, it is not this sort of story that opens up the possibility for an exciting make-believe world. Rather, she wants to be the one active in creating a protected space for herself and for others. An animal documentary on television, with which she becomes emotionally involved, introduces her to the fate of endangered animals. This becomes the starting point for a daydream introducing the "real fate" of animals in which she imagines herself in control, making up the rules. To this empowering situation, she brings in some elements, such as the castle, from more traditional narratives.

Girls Dealing With Media Content

In summary then, our results suggest that girls do not make sweeping use of the symbolic material from media content for their make-believe worlds. They seem to extract small discrete elements, while inserting their own characters and constructing something almost entirely new. Of particular interest is the way they handle stereotypes. The fact that female characters in media texts are often marginalized and portrayed stereotypically has been well documented in the literature (see, e.g., Carter & Steiner, 2004; Meyers, 1999; Ross & Byerly, 2004), especially in texts consumed by children and youth (see, e.g., Mazzarella & Pecora, 1999). Girls appear to deal with this phenomenon by incorporating fewer media references, by ignoring the male heroes, and by inventing their own characters. They also respond by using the same few salient characters time and again, like the fairy (which seems to be the most popular character in our sample), Ariel, or another, less familiar princess. Girls use creative strategies to adapt and incorporate female heroines from the slim selection provided through media offerings. In this regard, our study also illustrates the important function of texts that do seek to portray alternative portrayals of women, like *Shrek*, for girls' development in that they go beyond the gender clichés and offer diverse female characters. Girls wish to put themselves in the center of their fantasies and to emancipate themselves from the traditional and limited female characters provided by most of the available media texts. Our findings support the claim that diversity of mediated female role models lags significantly behind the realities of opportunities for self-actualization available and actualized by girls and women in many contemporary societies.

BOYS' MAKE-BELIEVE WORLDS OF ACTION[1]

Approximately half of the 84 boys who participated in the study drew themselves in the illustrations of their make-believe worlds. Technically their drawings seem rather sloppy and lack detail. No attention is paid to the figure itself and no attempts at an idealization of their bodies can be found, aside from the minimal representation of hair and/or glasses. What is striking is that boys were much more likely than girls to equip themselves with objects that render them powerful—such as weapons, accessories, and vehicles. Jeremy (B, US-20), finds a sword with which to fight a dragon; Omer (B, IS-2), equips himself with all sorts of weapons and clothing from superheroes; Christian (B, GR-28), drives his pluto scooter at 210 km per hour; Gyu'sang (B, SK- 34), flies with the assistance of a kite.

This is much in line with the traditional framing of masculinity that involves the use of technology to achieve domination, subordination and/or protection of others humans and nature—alike, as well as technology's use in occupational achievements and in engaging in daring activities outside the domestic sphere

---

[1]The analysis was aided by consultation with Dr. Reinhard Winter, a leading Germany psychologist specializing in boys (see Winter & Neubauer, 1998, 2001).

(Cockburn, 1992; Hanke, 1998). Historically, from the spear to the computer, from the plough to the rocket, technology has become part of the social construction of manhood. Artistic and media representations of men have traditionally reinforced this conception by associating men with weapons, gadgets, vehicles, as well as communication and technological devices (Craig, 1992).

Groups of friends play an important role in many of the make-believe worlds, in contrast to an attachment to one individual close friend, typical for the girls. *"There were many players and fans in my dream ... "* relates Dor (B, IS-13), when he describes a soccer game. Similarly, Jong'yun (B, SK-31) describes *"A land for us only"*: *"In my dreamland I played with Zolaman and my six friends. It was very exciting."* Chad (B, US-32) describes a magic waterfall and dam and reveals: *"There is a secret elevator behind the waterfall for going up. Only my friends and I know about it."* This is in line with what we know about boys' peer relationships and social development. Boys have a stronger preference for group bonding—playing sports, exploring the streets and public places. According to historical perspectives in gender studies, this behavior is reminiscent of what would be done in hunting in ancient cultures. Even in indoor activities, such as playing the computer or watching television, boys prefer to engage in typical male bonding behaviors in a group—such as loud shouting, back-slapping, grabbing things, and so forth (Drotner, 1999; Lemish et al., 2001).

Worlds of Excitement and Conflict

Many of the boys' make-believe worlds are characterized by conflict, action, and adventure. Fighting scenes often figure prominently in the pictures and stories. Boys deal with a constant onslaught of threats in their fantasy worlds in which they often imagine themselves under attack. In some cases, they take on the identity of imaginary creatures who are threatened and attacked. Joe (B, US-13), for example, describes his make-believe world:

> I was a big red dragon. I flew out of a castle—it was back in time in the age of castles and dragons. I could see all the little people down there and the fields. People back then didn't like red dragons. They only liked grey dragons. A bunch of people were coming after me with spears and arrows shot out of guns and trying to murder me. I would shoot back fireballs out of my mouth at the arrows and keep trying to hit them. I went into a cave inside a volcano. It was hot and I was getting sweaty. I knew the angry mob would come through the door, so I wouldn't take the cave door. There was a tunnel up there and I flew up and flew in there, and I had to make a fire with leaves and stuff so I could see. When I lit it there were dead people in there, like dead skulls and everything. I really wanted to get out of there, so I started using my tail to whip the concrete walls, and I was breaking it each time I whipped it. Then I started digging through the dirt and I got out. Just then the mob got in there and everything started caving in by the door and they got stuck in there and they died. Then I flew

home. There were some people who made trouble for my dad and they are the ones I was thinking of. So, when the volcano caved in on them I felt sad and happy at the same time.

Joe is chased while other boys are "simply attacked."

In the make-believe world, the issue of taking sides is of great importance. The boys are always the ones being attacked for no reason and they find themselves forced to fight to protect themselves, as does Joe. Joe has to throw fireballs or whip his tail in order to defend himself. Boys' fear of being attacked by other boys and men is well known in current boys' research (Winter & Neubauer, 1998, 2001) and is grounded in the reality of contemporary societies in which most violence is perpetrated by young males against other young males (Pollack, 1998). Although feeling unsafe and vulnerable, the boys imagine themselves as being able to put up a good fight. In doing so, they assume roles and try to live up to expectations of traditional, stereotypical, masculine behavior as projected in the "boy code" of toughness, emotional disconnection, and aggression (Pollack, 1998).

In the make-believe world, boys can recruit outside powers to help them to face all types of threats and dangers. Omer's case (B, IS-2) is prototypical of this desire. In his make-believe world, he is able to defend himself against all possible attacks through the incorporation of the powers of all his favorite superpowers—Spiderman, Superman, Batman, Pokémon. Similarly, the desire to be ready to face a fight is strongly expressed in Sandro's (B, GR-11), make-believe world as well:

> I'm in Pokémon land. I have seen Muk, who wanted to attack me. Slimok is a Psy-Pokémon. This is why I was launching my Pokéball into the air, when Exeggutor came out of it. This is a half Psy- and half Plant-Pokémon. And he is fighting Slimok for me. Exeggutor threw two Psy-balls toward Slimok and this is why he's getting weak right now and looking dumb. Exeggutor could also do Psycho kinesis, Stakote, and hypnosis. I'd love to be a trainer for my favorite Pokémon Electrode. This one can do thunderstruck. Then I could only throw my Pokéball and shout: "Go for it Electrode, thunderstruck!" I'd really love to be a trainer in reality.

In his fantasy world, Sandro has the capabilities and readiness to fight back. We learned that in the past, he preferred playing the roles of a knight or Zorro, but at the time of the study, he strongly wishes to be a Pokémon master. In everyday real-life circumstances, Sandro seems to lack personal power. He stutters and has to compete with a nimble sister and a strong, single-parent mother. Through his fantasy, Sandro counters the reality of his everyday life in which he does not feel powerful.

Sandro's case highlights the motifs that are deeply intertwined with socialization processes leading into manhood. Here, vulnerability is perceived as a sign of weakness, and the only expression of emotion allowed and accepted as masculine is that of anger. Masculinity research suggests that boys are prematurely pushed into harsh separation from an intense relationship with their mothers into proving their manhood. Accordingly, in their struggle to become ideal boys, they have limited role models, as their relationships with their fathers are usually quite restricted due to latter's limited presence in the private sphere. Other male characters available for interaction are scarce and those with whom there is a relationship are encountered in brief episodes with certain roles (soccer trainer, guitar teacher, etc.). Traditional images of men and masculinity still dominate the media (Craig, 1992) and offer a very limited range of alternative options. Women hold powerful positions over boys' everyday lives as their mothers, caregivers, and teachers. The daily routines of the school system encourage gender separation (Thorne, 1993) and the disassociation of boys from girls.

Within this already complicated situation, boys often receive ambivalent feedback and conflicting messages from their social environment. Mothers and educators reinforce the active, loud, and physical expressions of boys, while at the same time implicitly communicating ideas about traditional masculinity as a result of their own education and social conditioning. Consequently, boys' physical activity and behavior often become too loud and too aggressive, according to teachers. Indeed, the dominant perspective of the female caregivers in educational settings focuses on the boys as aggressors and disturbers of the social order. In doing so, caregivers' focus turns boys into disciplinary problems in a social setting that seeks the order desired by the dominant female in control (Pollack, 1998; Winter & Neubauer, 1998). The result is that boys are torn between traditional and new images of manhood, conflicting messages and expectations, and they receive contradictory or ambivalent feedback. Boys find themselves growing up preoccupied by the constant fear of inadequacy, asking themselves, "Am I man enough?" (Seidler, 1997).

A closer look at the case of Sandro, previously discussed, as revealed in the interviews with both him and his mother, further illustrates these points. Sandro is of Peruvian descent. His father, a bank manager, with whom he has a rather problematic relationship, stands for a traditional image of manhood. He expects Sandro to be "a man"; to be strong, not to let himself be dominated by women, to stand up for himself, and the like. However, Sandro is being raised by his severely handicapped mother, who is a bank manager in a higher position than his father. She has also been very successful as an athlete and has participated in the para-Olympics several times. In everyday life, Sandro finds himself inferior to his older sister and can only barely hold his own next to her. After school, Sandro attends daycare and the female caregivers describe him as helpful, reliable, and very quiet. Sandro's everyday life is marked by powerful women and it appears that he has no room to practice the kind of manhood that his father is modeling for him. It seems that he thinks that his masculine identity is threatened all the time. In his fantasy, he finds a way to ward off this threat through identification with specific media characters. Having watched the black and white classic on television in the past, it was the powerful masculine hero of Zorro. In the present, it is Ash, a Pokémon trainer. This allows him to legitimately combine the desire to fight—he always has a Pokémon to defend him—with the desire to nurture, because he also has to train and tend to Pokémon's needs. By combining masculine and feminine narratives, he finds a positive path for himself on the ambivalent road of boyhood (Lemish & Bloch, 2004). For his educators to deny Sandro these imaginary Pokémon fights may serve to additionally intensify his feeling of having his identity threatened.

In some of the make-believe worlds in which fighting plays an important role, the boys themselves are not actually threatened. They are the powerful ones whose benevolence or loyalty is sought and fought for. This is the case with Yon'uh (B, SK-20), for example. He is courted by two parties at war with one another: Mashimaro and Zolaman. Both characters, who are taken from an Internet animation, pull his arms into opposite directions, but he can chose which of the two to support. Another example is provided by Christian (B, GR-28), who imagines being captured by gangsters who want to talk him into changing sides in a conflict situation:

> I flew to the planet of Pluto with my rocket. Then it crashed, but I could jump out .... Once I wanted to go to a museum with my friend, since there were great exhibitions about outer space. Then two guys showed up, gangsters or so, whose meteorites unfortunately I had passed too close to and so they got angry, chased me, and wanted to force me to become a member of their group. But my friends helped me and fired the "paralyzer" at the gangster's space ship. Then they took them along, questioned them and everything is ok ....

In a world of make-believe in which Christian is an accomplished researcher and inventor, he is attacked by a group of gangsters. With the help of good friends and his personal invention, the "paralyzer," which can paralyze the enemy, he can escape and make sure the bad guys get their fair punishment. Threat here is an adventure and a competition that Christian wins, due to his outstanding intellect and access to technology. This combination of challenge and adventure is a frequent motif in the boys' make-believe stories of conflict. A variation on them involves sporting events in which boys are either the "stars" themselves or the avid fans of the winning team. Here they do succeed in meeting the challenge and winning important competitions. In these cases, and even more clearly in some of the dinosaur-related fantasies, we find a certain fascination with comparing oneself with someone else.

We found a few exceptions to the rule in which boys imagined themselves as a source of threat to others, as in the case of David (B, US-31):

> I was a Raptor, a giant dinosaur. I was walking through the forest and suddenly I saw this little animal, this other dinosaur, and I felt hungry and decided I wanted to eat it. I started to chase it, but it was faster than me so I couldn't catch it. I felt stupid. I wasn't watching where I was going because I was thinking, so I accidentally ran into a tree that was there and then I backed away and that sort of hurt. It was really fun to be a dinosaur, because I was about 20 feet long and I had long legs and I could run really fast. But you have to be careful not to run into things. In the forest, there were different types of trees everywhere and small underbrush and grass and stuff. Also, a huge tree—maybe 5 feet thick. There was also a little sapling. A dragonfly was passing through.

In his make-believe world, David is a tall and dangerous creature, remarkable to others and potentially quite dangerous. In the end, he does not really hurt anybody, but he would, if he wanted to. In his story, he diminishes his own dangerous powers through humor. Yet, he remains an awesome creature who does not have to fear any enemies.

Although boys' fantasies of fighting and aggression may seem problematic and raise many concerns, they could also be viewed as an expression and projection of their own desire for physical strength. In many of their favorite texts, such as *Pokémon* and *Digimon*, the creatures indeed fight with each other, but the focus is not on inflicting pain and suffering, neither is it about empathy, but rather seems to be undertaken as plain fun in competing and measuring themselves against others. In addition, it provides them with opportunities to experience the excitement of being a male hero in a fight situation. This interpretation incorporates the "aesthetics of fight," in its original Greek meaning of perception and understanding, closely connected to individual feelings and emotions. The boys seem to enjoy imagining a fighting situation. They draw it and talk about it in detail, as they comprehend the thrill of competition and the excitement of winning.

This interpretation has been posed and documented in other studies as well (Buckingham, 1996; Tobin, 2000; van der Voort, 1986). Accordingly, although experiencing their own triumphant participation in a fight, they ignore the perspective of the suffering loser and focus only on their personal elation as winners. This interpretation is much in line with Gilligan's (1982) theory on the development of gendered psychology, already described. While it is an oversimplification, the male psychology as depicted here assumes construction of hierarchies based on competition. At its core is decision making about who should lead according to criteria such as individual skills, talents, and achievements.

The image of a "pyramid" (such as in Dor's example) represents a pattern of response guided by the desire to be alone at the top, and the related fear of others reaching out as well.

In summary, we suggest an interpretation that claims that in boys' make-believe worlds they project their feelings of being threatened—both physically by other boys, as well as emotionally—in regard to the ambiguous messages received regarding their masculine identity. In their imagined worlds, they are ready and able to confront such threats. In so doing, they respond to two culturally dominant markers of manhood: physical activity and prevailing over one's opponents. It seems as though, in their fantasies, the boys are involved in a cycle of being threatened by and threatening others.

Worlds of Amusement

In addition to fighting, as the central focus or activity in boys' make-believe worlds, we found several examples of worlds of amusement in which the boys experience excitement without the presence of direct danger or serious threat. Amusement parks, in addition to sports events, are typical activities in this category. Pierre (B, GR-41) describes his make-believe world as follows:

> I always wanted to go to Disneyland Paris. And now, finally I'm here. I feel great. Now I have just arrived with my parents and my sister at the ghost train. From the outside, it looks like a monster, and has big teeth like this, but it is a very nice monster. Inside the ghost train, there are curves and there are also robots, scaring the people. Then it shakes and I get scared and have fun. And then you come back out again of the ghost train. If I ever get back there, then I'd pay for two nights and do everything there, and even go to the park in the evenings. Disneyland Paris, is where I feel good. That's great.

In Pierre's make-believe world, he can have a variety of nonthreatening, exciting experiences—he can *"get scared and have fun"* without putting himself at risk. Pierre goes so far as to make sure that the monster he drew is not dangerous but, is really *"a very nice monster."*

Boys' worlds of amusement are also full of friends. Byong'je's (B, SK- 2) story provides an example: *"I am going to an amusement park together with my best friend Young'jun. I want to enjoy lots of exciting playthings there. Vikings or Amazon or Safari, etc."* (names of amusement facilities in Seoul's famous park, Everland). The fun for Byong'je is mixed with concern for his friend, Hyong'uk, who has been hurt *"and I want to help him, so that my friend can also come along to the amusement park."* Thus, worlds of amusement provide an opportunity to experience thrill and to bond with friends, but without the dangers and threats associated with the worlds of conflict.

Worlds of Harmony

As in the girls' cases, there are exceptions to the norms in boys' stories that blur traditional gender divisions. Some boys also wanted to experience connection with others in a world marked by harmony with nature, animals, and people. Angelo (B, GR-42), for example, wants to fly on Pegasus to a secret, private land, inhabited only by many animals. He gets along well with all of them and they are looking forward to his visits. There are no fights in this world. But he describes in a very lively fashion how he takes various animals with him on his flying horse (a mouse and a leopard). When he is tired, Angelo can put his head on the fur of the leopard. Angelo is active in his fantasy, but it is action without fighting and without threats.

In another example, Matthias (B, GR-1), describes a make-believe world marked by being connected to others:

> I am a captain. My wife and I have just been shopping downtown on our boat. Now I stand up on the pole. From there I can see when land is in sight and make sure we don't lose our way. We live on an island. It is very hot there. There is a forest of palm trees. We built a house out of palm trees with a straw roof. We painted the wood with oranges. On top of the roof there is a parrot talking constantly. He warns us of dangers and likes to play marbles with my daughter at the beach. Moreover there is a magic fire. It's always burning. If we need certain things, like water for example, we only wish for it, and it's there.

Matthias enjoys harmony and being embedded in his family. He takes on the role of a caring partner and goes shopping with his wife. His daughter is waiting for him on an island, similar to a kingdom of one's own, where there are no disturbances from others. Inside the family, however, there is a clear hierarchy, as Matthias stands on the boat's lookout undoubtedly serving in the role of "head of the household," where he has everything under control.

Yoni (B, IS-5), imagines himself as a member of the community of children in the boarding school of *Chiquititas*, an Argentinean telenovela. He talks about this somewhat unconventional make-believe world (see Drawing 6.4):

> I draw a residence, because sometimes parents fight and punish and it is better to be in this special place because there are nice children there, good deeds, and lots and lots of adventures. This is the "Corner of Light" residence because there are only good things there. The sun is smiling above it, the door is wide and always open so many people can come in. There are all kinds of children there that are friends and play and have fun. There are also children there whose parents get a divorce and the mother is going to get remarried and they don't like her new boyfriend. The headmistress, Blen, is here and the cook, Sabario, who prepares croissants and meat patties and mashed potatoes … My friends and parents are not here. It's in a television series called the Chiquititas in Buenos Aires … They have things that we don't have. For example, the headmaster has a dream window that you open and dream your own dream, like the dream mirror in Harry Potter, but it's better here, because the mirror attracts you and does all kinds of things and here it only shows you your own dream, and only good dreams.

Drawing 6.4. Yoni (B, IS-5) "Chiquititas."

As a member of this residence, Yoni feels cared for and free from arguments with parents and potential punishment. The headmistress, Blen, a central caregiver cast in a very positive role in the television series, provides him with a sense of security as a kind of substitute mother. Interestingly enough, he does not mention that the telenovela itself is a very feminine world centering stereotypically on girls and their issues. Although it is tempting to read into Yoni's description possible signs of distress at home, it is quite clear that it is different from most other boys' stories. He uses a traditionally female genre and constructs a world characterized by harmony and a sense of belonging. In the interview, he speaks with reverence about a female caregiver, rather than a powerful male hero. This story stands out as unusual among the boys' make believe-worlds.

The fantasies of Angelo, Matthias, and Yoni allow them to experiment with less-frequently expressed male desires, while placing themselves in unique positions through which they may be learning to accept these desires as part of their being in the make-believe world that offers less-threatening social circumstances.

BOYS' MEDIA TRACES

In nearly 75% of boys' make-believe worlds, explicit and implicit media traces can be found. The connection to media is often immediately obvious to an observer when the boys readily talk about these media connections. This is particularly evident in fantasies categorized as falling into the world of the supernatural and the world of conflict and fight. All of these examples are strongly related to media texts.

Media Settings. Almost half of the male cases in our study—35 boys—envisioned their make-believe worlds in settings adopted from media and an additional four boys incorporated an object from a setting. Nearly all the stories involving conflict and threat are contextualized in media settings. In the Korean cases, for example, three of the stories take place in a dinosaur world that the boys connect to the movie, *Jurassic Park.* They use this setting to help visualize fighting and threats and to create a frightening atmosphere. Young'ho (B, SK-21), for example, draws and describes his dinosaurland in a fashion very similar to a specific scene in *Jurasic Park 3* (see Drawing 6.5):

> Here the dinosaurs are fighting. Here is the age of dinosaur. On the bottom there is water. The sun and the moon are also there. There is Tyrannosaurus and the pig dinosaur. I'm not there. In this dinosaur world, there are two groups, the good ones and the bad ones. The winners of the battle finally eat the losers. Blood is oozing out of a wound while fighting. In the beginning, a dinosaur drank water. Then Tyrannosaurus was creeping up behind him and beats the dinosaurs and then kills the dinosaurs, because

Drawing 6.5. Young'ho (B, SK-21) "Kill the Dinosaur."

they have killed several other dinosaurs before. Another dinosaur, I just painted for the heck of it, has sided with the bad ones. I like Tyrannosaurus, for no reason. When the dinosaurs lose the fight there is no need to interfere. Their killing is so exciting. They just fight and then they die. I'm not afraid of watching this.

Young'ho's story may seem quite bloodthirsty to us, with its pleasure of provocation and enjoyment of the gory scenario. Certainly the memory of the movie, *Jurassic Park,* as well as the excitement of the action in it play a role in this, evoking the feelings again while retelling the story. The emotions and pain of the suffering animals do not elicit sympathy from Young'ho. What is of importance from his perspective is that a fair punishment is being meted out by a powerful individual on a guilty one.

As with dinosaur worlds, in all cases in which boys' worlds deal with aliens and supernatural powers, explicit media traces are found. For example, Ohad (B, IS-34) describes his world:

> I love aliens and imagine them a lot. So I imagined that I am in a world of aliens, with little trees … These aliens don't have feet, it's like jelly at the bottom … This one just stands and looks. I call this one Venus, because it is on planet Venus. I imagined myself as a microbe, because a microbe is a very fast creature, and it can multiply within a second … I am a glaring microbe that flies around, but I have to be careful because he eats insects … He has this suspicious look, like in *Mission Impossible 2*—he looks at his prey and is ready to get his tongue out and catch me. But I got away. There are all kinds of aliens … some are in cultured villages, like people, in a more advanced culture, with machinery and all. Other kinds are wilder … I saw it in the *Invasion from Mars.* I draw the aliens and their weapons … and in *Men in Black* … and all these movies, and also cartoons or movies in English without translation …

Ohad mixes many fictional films on outer space—*Mission Impossible 2, Invasion from Mars,* and *Men in Black,* among others, to create his imaginary alien land, full of danger and excitement.

As the results imply, media settings provide the boys with a great amount of raw material for their imaginations in the areas of fight, conflict, and the supernatural. Media settings do not appear to trigger boys' imaginations as much with respect to worlds of harmony or amusement.

Via media settings, boys experience excitement and can imagine themselves as valuable and herolike. Jed (B, US-35), for example, fights like characters in *Dragon Ball Z* against Cell, who wants to destroy the earth. Udi (B, IS-1) fights evil forces in his *Harry Potter* setting. Sandro (B, GR-11), is fighting the enemies in Pokémon land. Similarly, boys can imagine themselves as heroes in sport settings, where they play an important role in the competition. Oz (B, IS-45) describes a soccer match where he imagines himself as a player who stands in the center and others recognize him as being special. The entire setting is taken from the soccer matches that he watches on a regular basis on television that seem to supply him with a lot of background material. Settings of action, so it seems, provide the boys with the space to imagine themselves as special, powerful, and active.

Media Characters.   Forty-one of the boys in our study integrated media characters of their customs in their make-believe worlds. All of these were male and most were powerful protagonists. An examination of the variety of characters they chose to adopt reveals some patterns of preference. Many boys placed media characters in the role of a friend. Jon'ho (B, SK-38), and Jong'yun (B, SK-31), and their friends are playing with the Internet animated character, Zolaman, who makes them laugh. A parasocial relationship is suggested by descriptions such as that of Ju'in (B, SK-47): "*In my dreamland all my friends in the computer game [Starcraft] are with me and play wonderfully together.*"

Ohad (B, IS-34), whose outer-space story was already described, interweaves characters as well as narratives from *E.T.* in his interview:

> And if one time there will be a crash of a UFO and I will be the first to see it and to check it out, it will be very beautiful, and if he will be as friendly as E.T., I won't tell anybody, and I would teach him to speak and he will teach me, and then I will let my family know but not my friends because there will be too much commotion and I don't like it around me …

Similar to the movie, when the alien creature arrives on earth, Ohad relives a bonding scene of care in a family setting, one very different from the outer space scene described previously.

In some cases, boys imagine themselves as the male heroes. Martin (B, US-22) imagines himself as Peter Pan flying as in the movie, *Hook,* and reexperiencing certain scenes in the film. Like Martin, other boys also borrow material from media characters to imagine themselves as strong and able to win in fights. An example of this is given by Christof (B, GR-49), who describes the following:

> I have painted Flendramon. It's a Digimon. It has eight different shapes—a teeny-weeny one, a bigger one, even a bigger one than that, and in the end, this one. This is not the strongest, but I like it most, since he looks so cool. I like the shape and color, most of all his face and horn. Because, if he's attacking, he can strike with his megahorn. Invisible right now is a mean Digimon. It wants to attack him, since the mean Digimon want to conquer Digiworld. But the nice ones prevent them from doing it. Some other nice ones are there as well, but they are invisible, like Schnurimon, that's a bird, who has sort of a knife in front. I would love to be in *Digimon* World, to win over the mean ones and then I'd love to be Flendramon. His appearance is simply cool!

Christof wants to be in the position of fighting the mean Digimon, but at the same time he is also attracted not only to power but also to "cool" appearances and wishes for the ability to transform himself to his favorite kind of Digimon.

Omer's (B, IS-2) fantasy is prototypical of this tendency in boys in that he combines elements from various admired media characters (Spiderman, Batman, Superman, Pokémon) to turn himself into a very powerful superhero who can do whatever he wants and proclaims *"here I am the ruler."* It seems that boys who imagine themselves in relationships with characters or as the main characters themselves seem to stay close to role models provided them by the media.

Media Stories.   Thirty-six boys in the study provided examples of reliving a story taken from a media text or using factual information from media stories as a starting point for their make-believe worlds. Most of these involve taking the position of the male hero in the media story and reenacting the story in "his shoes." As a captain of a spaceship, Ruben (B, GR-44) saves the earth from an approaching meteorite, as in the movie *Armageddon*. This is also the story of television programs he views, where there is a crew of individual men who have equal abilities and rights. Ruben sides with the "good guys," who win in the end, as do all of the boys who become media characters.

Jeremy (B, US-20) imagines himself as a noble knight complete with the expected costume of armor and sword on his way to the castle. He says in the interview, *"In my dream I was a noble paladin finding a magical sword to free a princess for the king. I am wearing silver armor and I have a shield and a sword ... "* and he goes on to detail the adventures he goes through. He saves the princess by order of the king because the only way to defeat the dragon is by using his magic sword. The dragon flees at the sight of the sword, Jeremy brings the princess back to her father, and is consequently rewarded for his brave deed. The boy explicitly names as an inspiration for his story the Disney movie, *Cinderella* (because the princess looks like Cinderella); the movie, *Gladiator*, an additional fantasy movie (the name of which he had forgotten); as well as a computer game that embodies a similar narrative. Following the expected traditional role and plotline, Jeremy tells us that he has to do *"what a man has to do"* (see Drawing 6.6)

Through these stories, it is evident that boys are being socialized by, among other sources, traditional narratives, and learn to internalize the desire to become saviors, particularly of helpless females, while overcoming evil forces and hardships.

Boys Dealing with Media Content

Boys appear to borrow contents more heavily from media than girls. At the same time, they interpret and rework what they extract from media to a lesser degree than do the girls. Our first impression seems then to have been correct; boys remain closer to media content in creating their make-believe worlds. This conclusion, already stated tentatively previously in our report of the quantitative findings, is further supported by qualitative analysis. Boys imag-

Drawing 6.6. Jeremy (B, US-20) "Noble Paladine."

ine themselves in action-filled media settings. They take over the role of male heroes, make minor adjustments in the originals, and imagine themselves in their places. Even in cases where the boys are only bystanders and viewers (e.g., of a soccer game), they identify strongly with the winners and are excited for them because of such identification.

Boys project themselves into original media plots and develop those plots further in their make-believe worlds. In contrast to the girls, they seem to exhibit fewer mechanisms for distancing themselves from existing narrative structures or positions, or of offering alternative, even subversive, readings and interpretations. However, much like the girls, who dismiss male media characters, the boys ignore female ones, with the exception of those they set out to rescue and defend. We did not find in our study any hints of boys attempting to reverse existing stereotypes. The few make-believe worlds of boys that differ from the mainstream masculine world either exhibited no media traces at all or referred to a female genre, such as in the case of Yoni, already described. Still, much like the other boys (and different from many of the girls), Yoni's employment of media content is limited; he stays close to the given characters, does not take them out of the surrounding context, and does not invent new ones. Rather, Yoni imagines himself inside a particular media setting and follows closely the ways of understanding that it offers.

PERFORMING GENDER

The fantasy worlds of girls and boys in our study are separate and quite different from one another. Girls use scenarios that emphasize harmony in constructive relationships. They are able to develop ideal environments according to their own desires in which caring for others is of great importance. Media texts are used as settings or to provide information to imagine worlds that are clearly connected to key concepts found in female socialization. The girls extract discrete elements from media content and exclude what limits them in their desires to act within worlds of their own making. Moreover, they redefine or ignore that which threatens the harmony of these worlds. They invent their own characters or describe themselves at a certain distance from the original media character. They are familiar with the classical female characters and find them rather attractive, but for projection and identification processes, they prefer to create alternatives.

For boys, excitement, action, and amusement in the make-believe worlds are most apparent. A central motif is that of being threatened and placed in a situation that calls for self-defense against such threats. Boys exhibit a pleasure from engaging in and witnessing action and enjoyment of fighting in media texts that are saturated with conflict and fights that provide settings, characters, and plots for such fantasies. They seem to express a wish to take on the role of a hero and exhibit little critical distance or evidence that they are producing counterreadings.

In attempting to gain insight into why boys and girls construct themselves in such obviously different ways in their fantasies, it is helpful to understand that the make-believe worlds and their expressions are ways of performing gender. As a general rule, girls and boys exclude each other in their make-believe worlds, that is, girls do not include boys and boys do not include girls in their make-believe worlds. Rather, they contextualize themselves in single-gender peer groups. This tendency is typical of this age group (Thorne, 1993). Even in the research context itself, they behaved in such age-related, gender-appropriate ways.

Understanding the quantitative as well as the qualitative differences in the media traces girls and boys bring to their make-believe worlds can be assisted by the analysis of media offerings for children and the related processes of meaning-making. Most media characters available to children today are not attractive for girls as models for identification, parasocial interaction, or wishful thinking.

This can be readily connected to relevant studies about the male and female representations on television. The well-documented underrepresentation of women in media and the limited scope of gender portrayals teach girls' self-effacement and constrain their development of an independent voice (Brown & Gilligan, 1992; Pipher, 1995).

Prevailing media messages continue to promote restrictive ideologies of femininity, glorify heterosexual romance as a central goal for girls, encourage male domination in relationships, and stress the importance of beautification through consumption (Mazzarella, 1999; McRobbie, 1993; Peirce, 1990). These ever-present messages indoctrinate girls into accepting the "beauty myth" (Wolf, 1991, 1997) and to dismissing the validity of their own sexual feelings and desires apart from masculine desire (Durham, 1998).

Changes in these images and messages are trickling into the media, but such changes are evolving too slowly and are limited. Overall, females are continuing to be presented primarily as helpless, dependent, ineffectual, emotional, vulnerable, subordinate, childish, and sexy. At the same time, there is a strikingly larger range of depictions of male figures. They are mostly presented in active, outgoing, independent, rational, and aggressive roles and are placed in positions of high status (see, e.g., summaries in Signorielli, 2001; van Zoonen, 1994; Witt, 2000).

Even children's television, an area of particular importance from an educational perspective, presents a significant underrepresentation of female main characters. Males—both younger and older—are the main heroes of children's programs. They succeed in overcoming everyday problems, they successfully deal with all sorts of dangers, and they have lots of adventures. Even non-gendered imaginary characters—such as creatures and animals are considered "naturally" male, unless they are specifically marked as female through processes of sexualizing their appearance (e.g., hair ribbons, long eyelashes, colored lips, short skirts). In this way, female characters continue to symbolize a deviation from the dominant male norm and remain the "second sex" in the classical sense presented by Simone de Beauvoir (1952). Female characters in most media texts for children are there to be saved and protected by the males and provide the background on which the adventure is set. Most of all, their position is defined by their meaning to the male heroes (Götz, 1999). Certain symbols, like a horse being drawn in soft colors, the dolphins jumping in front of a sunset, and bunnies and flowers, are gendered in our societies and reinforced by the market forces as "girlish". Other areas, such as technology, action, or fight, are always connected with boyhood themes and preinterpreted as masculine. Television advertising uses gender clichés excessively in presenting goods either as pastel glittery color for girls or action-packed blue for boys.

Given such circumstances, it is not surprising that girls tend to adopt fewer media characters and to engage in reinterpreting their positions in their make-believe worlds, whereas boys feel a lot more comfortable attached to the original characters and storylines. At the same time, boys are restricted in the social expectations for dominance and aggression, often situating themselves in the context of conflict and threats, and thus limiting their ability to experience desires for harmony and connections with nature and humans. So it seems that the mostly stereotypical popular media fare constrain the inner worlds of both girls and boys, and thus reproduce a limited range of cultural expectations.

7

Cultural Traces in Children's Make-Believe Worlds

Previous chapters presented unifying themes based on a collective analysis of all cases in the study: the types of make-believe worlds; the roles children occupied in these worlds and the wishes they had for themselves; the traces that the media used by children have left on their make-believe worlds; and finally, the overall gender differences that we detected in all four participating countries. In this final discussion of the empirical data, we concentrate not only on overall similarities, but also focus on themes of cultural differences that were identified.

The chapter is entitled "Cultural Traces" rather than "Cultural Differences," as we are cautious in suggesting that the study has a sufficiently solid base methodologically to develop such a comparison. Although in all four countries the same methodology was used, the sampling procedures differed greatly, as did the contexts in which the research encounters with the children took place. Further, it is not possible to claim that themes that emerged in the empirical data are "typical" of the particular cultures studied nor are they "generalizable," due to the small nature of the sample. Rather, our purpose was to identify those different cultural traces that emerged in the four countries and to describe, analyze, and understand them. Thus, there is no intention to compare the same themes across the four countries. This is in line with the arguments put forth in Livingstone's (2003) discussion of the challenges of cross-national comparisons and particularly Chislom's (1995) argument that "societies and cultures are fundamentally non-comparable and certainly cannot be evaluated against each other" (p. 22).

150

Thus, at the foundation of this analysis is the assumption that make-believe worlds are contextualized. Everyday experiences—such as living conditions, family composition, demographics, media, and other factors—clearly impact children's make-believe worlds, as demonstrated in the previous chapters. Now the question remains as to whether, and if so, the more mid-macrolevel of contextualization—the cultural level—plays a role in children's expressions of their inner world. The approach adopted to confront this question is based on the cultural studies tradition of examining audiences, not as a conglomerate of individuals, but rather as "interpretive communities" (e.g., Fish, 1980; Liebes & Katz, 1990; Radway, 1984; Schroder, 1994). Media meanings attained by children are understood to result, not only from individual cognitive processes, but also from their learning orientations and expectations about texts that are shared socially (Buckingham, 1993a). This suggests that social class, race, and gender play significant roles in the process of meaning production. As we have argued in the methodology chapter, studies on children and media that considered macrosystem variables and involved relations at the level of subculture or culture, referred mainly to occupation, income, education, and ethnicity, but overlooked the more general concerns that differ across cultures—national identity, deep social or political conflicts, national goals, and the like.

As we specified in the methodological chapter, the four countries differ greatly from one another on many dimensions including history, ethnic and religious roots, geographical location, language and heritage, current economic and political situations, and media environment, to name but a few. How are the cultural traces expressed in children's make-believe worlds? Do their fantasies reflect a cultural lens through which their fantasy worlds are filtered? Is there evidence of a meeting with global cultural forces, creation of a glocalized children's culture, or new forms of hybridity? These are the main issues at the heart of this chapter. To begin with, signs of the globalized culture evident in children's make-believe worlds are traced, then specific attention is devoted to each of the four cultures and the unique themes that emerged in their children's make-believe worlds.

TRACES OF THE GLOBAL-LOCAL AXIS

Studies of the role of media in the lives of children and young people in the world throughout the last decade have highlighted the operations of two seemingly conflicting forces—globalization and localization. Previous studies (see, e.g., Livingstone & Bovill, 2001) found that children born into a world that is global and local at the same time accept this situation as the normal state of affairs; they engage in similar activities as well as sharing media preferences and interests with children from very diverse backgrounds from all over the world. The children in the four countries of our study were watching the Japanese series, *Pokémon*, reading the English book series, *Harry Potter*, watching the Disney videotapes, visiting movie theaters to see *Jurassic Park* or *Spiderman*, and playing action-adventure computer games. Similar consumption habits were found in other cross-cultural studies as well (see, e.g., the discussion of *Pokémon* in Tobin, 2004; and the discussion of Disney in Wasko, Phillips, & Meehan, 2001).

Previous studies have found that mediated globalization is closely linked to age and class; the older the child from the middle and upper class, the more he and she relate to the wider world and position themselves within it. "Taste markers" such as media products (mainly American in origin, or marketed through the United States) and media language (mainly English) play an important role in this positioning process. Mastering the English language, playing computer games, surfing the Internet, preferring American movies and television series—are all associated worldwide with children's exercising of a sense of social belonging and personal distinction (Lemish, Drotner, Liebes, Maigret, & Stald, 1998).

The four countries studied here differ greatly in regard to their position toward the globalization of children's culture. For the children residing in the United States, globalization equals localization, as they are both part of their same culture. Even the popularity of texts originating in other parts of the world can be explained through what Bloch and Lemish (2003) coined *The Megaphone Effect*, according to which "many cultural texts are widely adopted internationally only after having been successfully integrated into the culture of the United States" (p. 159). Children's culture, in particular, demonstrates the workings of the megaphone effect whether it is through books (e.g., *Harry Potter*) or a convergence of various media (e.g., *Pokémon*).

Indeed, *Pokémon* has been the recent and most extreme mania in children's culture (Tobin, 2004). It began as a game for *Gameboy* by Nintendo, turned into a popular TV series, a card game, movies, and a massive market of merchandising. From Japan it traveled to the United States and from there to the rest of the world to become an unprecedented success. Effective localizing of the television series has been credited as being responsible for this phenomenon. For example, the original Japanese product was geared to a wider audience, including adults, whereas the American product was directed at young children and thus required significant adaptation. The American version thus became more dynamic, with brighter colors, faster pace, and sharper and more clear-cut editing. Five of the original episodes ("The Lost Episodes") were understood to be unacceptable by American audiences (for being too suggestive and violent and not "politically correct") and as a result were omitted. Names of characters were changed in order to be pleasing to the English-speaking audience and overt Japanese elements were eliminated so as not to interfere with fantasy for American audiences (Allison, 2004; Bloch & Lemish, 2003; Katsumo & Maret, 2004).

The *Pokémon* phenomenon thus illustrates the complexity of the globalization discourse. It is not an issue of children around the world merely being exposed to a homogenized American culture. Rather the situation is one in which children are part of a global audience that transcends physical and cultural boundaries in their consumption of multicultural texts (Drotner, 2001; Lemish et al., 1998). These texts are packaged as "American" for the local audience, and in turn are masqueraded as "global" for children worldwide.

For the three countries other than the United States, the situation is much more complex. Following Lemish et al.'s (1998) analysis of children's leisure in Denmark, France, and Israel, we argue that for children in our study the issue of globalization and localization, too,

> is not a matter of oppositions. That is, we should not view this phenomenon via dichotomies such as globalization versus localization, international versus national, or universal versus particular. Rather, globalization involves the linking by children of their own locales to the wider world. At the same time, localization already incorporates trends of globalization. (pp. 552–553)

We contend that our children's media worlds provide evidence for at least three forms of mediation between the two polarities of the global and the local (Lemish, 2002). First is the consumption of original local texts saturated with local values and worldviews alongside transnational, sometimes ideologically clashing, texts. For example, we found in Tanja's (G, GR-53) make-believe world reference to the movie, *Sissy*, describing a biography grounded in Bavarian history, famous all over the world. For Tanja, however, this story has a particular meaning because she lives in Bavaria near the location of some of the events accounted for in *Sissy*.

The second form of mediation is through the consumption of local media texts that exemplify the local domesticated version of another culture's product. For example, references are made by several Korean boys to unique local computerized animations. These are a source of much pride—*Mashimaro* ("naughty" Rabbit) and *Zolaman*, but are formulated according to and adopt typical action-adventure narrative known worldwide.

Finally, there is process of glocalization (Robertson, 1994); that is, consumption of global texts within a local context and the process of endowing them with meanings made relevant to one's own situation. Such for example is Udi's (B, IS-1) interpretation of *Harry Potter* that is adapted to an Israeli frame of military conflict, as discussed later.

The simultaneous working of all these mediation processes supports Robertson's (1994) argument regarding the increasing interconnectedness of global culture as it involves and includes many seemingly clashing local cultures. The present study suggests that, indeed, children do not share a perspective that assumes a tension, or even a contradiction, between traditional local values and global (i.e., American or late modernity) values, as typified primarily by commercialism, globalization, privatization, and individualization (Fornäs & Bolin, 1995; Livingstone, 2002). In fact, as we have demonstrated, the children in our study perceive universal values—such as friendship, love, and cooperation—as global.

As noted previously in detail, our study found that young audiences seek symbolic spaces where they can feel harmony, experience thrill, bond with others, display their specialness, protect and be protected, and act independently in a variety of make-believe worlds. It seems that when these children were following their imagination into their make-believe worlds, they were not thinking about their local identities, but rather seeking relief from them, perhaps suggesting that their cultural identities are expressed less overtly than one would have expected.

However, on closer examination, these worlds had many traces of locality, but less formal signs of such than adults might expect. There are few references to specific familiar places (e.g., famous locations, capitols, tourist attractions); to famous people (e.g., local celebrities, politicians, historical or cultural heroes); to symbols and icons (e.g., national flags, religious symbols, local signs); to local events (e.g., conflicts, rituals, celebrations, tragedies) and the like. There is also very little mention of a deity or religion in any of the four countries. Indeed, these children's make-believe worlds are almost completely secular in nature, with very few exceptions mainly of Korean children (including two immigrants who were included in the U.S. sample).

However, there were many local traces of special meaning for the children themselves. In Germany, for example, Dominique (G, GR-40) makes a reference to her family's tending of their garden plot—a typical East German weekend activity of families living in big apartment houses. Arab–Israeli Yasmeen (G, IS-26) draws a *shababa*—an Arab musical instrument. In South Korea, Hyon'ah (G, SK-37) presents a girl coming out of a snowball bush, the Korean national flower. In the United States, Jorge (B, US-30) sets his fantasy in his Midwestern hometown surrounded by cornfields, yet with tall buildings and busy traffic akin to New York or Chicago.

The Meaning of "Country" and Perceptions of "Self" and "Other"

One obvious expression of cultural awareness that is possibly a side-effect of the process of globalization is the knowledge of the existence and the naming of foreign countries. We found several cases of such a phenomenon. German children located their make-believe worlds in continents and countries such as Africa, Australia, "Indian Land," Mexico, New York, North Sea, Paris, planet Pluto, Spain (included in the same story were also "Arabia," Russia, and England), and resort areas such as Disneyland Paris, the Grand Canary islands, Lanzarote, and Seychelles. Israelis mentioned America, Brazil, Buenos Aires, Cyprus, England, Euro-Disney, Switzerland, and the United States. South Korean children mentioned the United States, Japan, and Africa as countries on the globe, and another talked about the land of Mongol, following a television program. Finally, American children mentioned Africa-Asia-Australia in one story, Arctic, and Japan, but also California three times and Florida once (which for midwestern children is perhaps a reference to an exotic land). Interestingly enough, then, the concept of a *country* is most commonly used in reference to a place somewhere else—a fantasyland, a vacation land—whether it is a real or an invented place.

Occasionally, another country is clearly referenced, but not central to the make-believe world, as is the case with the presentation of windmills from the Netherlands seen on television in South Korean drawings, as well as medieval European castles borrowed from fairytale books. Similarly, Peter (B, US-33), uses a stained-glass warrior who, according to Peter, is from ancient Japan to design a radar detector. It is a creative adaptation of an artifact from another culture that Peter develops in his fantasy. Rather than being about Japan, however, as a country, it is Peter's artistic and creative talents that figure prominently in the expression of his fantasy.

The concept of country is hardly ever used in reference to one's own country by name. For the most part, the children do not seem to be consciously occupied with the notion of national belonging. It is simply assumed and rather subconscious in its expression. Therefore, when they do refer to their country, it is particularly meaningful for them. In the entire study, we had three mentions of Germany by German children, five mentions of Korea by Korean children, and two mentions of the United States by American children.

Kevin's (B, US-27) patriotic make-believe world is quite an exception to this comprehensive general finding. He talks about being in a rocket with the US astronaut Neil Armstrong: *"I am in the rocket with Neil Armstrong and his crew. I am getting all the switches ready. I am in charge. In my fantasy I travel on a rocket to a planet that the US and only the US knows about. The space shuttle launches from Florida."*

The description of the launch clearly reflects Cape Canaveral in Florida. Interestingly, Kevin's picture is largely done in red, white, and blue—the colors of the U.S. flag, emphasizing his perception of the United States as conqueror of outer space, too. None of the Israeli children named their country as a whole, but made several references to particular cities—Tel Aviv and Haifa, in their discussion of sports teams; the Sea of Galilee also was mentioned in reference to a resort area in the north. It seems that the abstract concept of a country is not a frame used by most of our children to perceive of their own reality, but rather as reference to a reality somewhere else, a reality that opens up possibilities for the imagination. Similarly, typical fairytale exposition of "once upon a time" sets the stage for perceiving foreign lands as the arena for fantasy. However, when the children do use the concept of their own country, it is always in juxtaposition to another country, in a form of hierarchy with their own country being "better"—either in winning a sports competition (as in Raviv's [B, IS-18] and Dong'sung's [B, SK-15] soccer matches), or when offering "others" something "better" as is the case of Katharina (G, GR-16), who wants to bring sausages, cheese, and apples from Germany to her dreamland so that the people there would not eat meat:

> They are hunters, their food is animal meat … they eat animal meat and drink water. But I am with my friends and my family don't want this and therefore we want to try to bring new things to the dreamland, from Germany, such as sausages and other things. So they do not eat the animals anymore. Because they do not have anything to eat.

Germany, in Katharina's fantasy, becomes the country from which she brings good things with her in order to help the other country and its animals. Responding to the question about how large the country is, she answers: *"It's about as large as Germany."* For Katharina, Germany is a reference dimension and a country from which others can benefit. Katharina repeatedly begins speaking about how she tried to teach the inhabitants: *"But they do not understand! … [first signs of laughter] Yes, we tell them but it's so, they are silly!"*

Katharina's intention to protect the animals and keep the inhabitants from eating meat suggests a form of hierarchy as Germany is the country where people know a lot and behave in the right way whereas the other foreign country does not know anything and people there are "silly." This self-elevation can be understood from a subjective perspective, yet it is nevertheless problematic as it connotes negative stereotypes toward other people (particularly because Katharina herself does not seem to understand what the ingredients of sausages are).

An exception to the preference to one's own country is Claudia's story (G, GR-50), who mentions Germany in the interview in contrast to her dream country, Mexico. *"Well, there won't be as much dirt there maybe as here in Germany and maybe more expressed commitment for the, um, dolphins. Because some dolphins are simply caught during some fishing. [In a low voice] I simply think it's sad."*

In her dreamland, Mexico, there is less dirt lying on the streets and people are more committed to saving dolphins. For Claudia, Germany is a country that does not care enough about waste and its disposal and about animal protection. Kathy (G, US-17) also expresses fascination with another country, India, which she has knowledge of from a visit, and incorporates in her picture long and floating interwoven lines on the houses ending in spirals and squiggles, characteristic symbols representing parts of popular Indian art. She also provides a portrayal of the sharp mountains and unique colorful sunsets that are typical of the particular area she visited (see Drawing 7.1).

An interesting make-believe world about the process of developing new relationships and winning the trust and acceptance of someone a child might consider as "other" comes from South Korea. Hyon'ah (G, SK-5) is concerned with friendship and overcoming borders. In her fantasy, she flies by Korean Airlines to a country called *Mongol* (i.e., a name of a television series). There she overcomes her initial distrust and makes friends with two boys.

> Today I was in my make-believe world for the first time. It's called Mongol. I got there in a hot-air balloon. Every now and then I go to Mongol and live there, but then I go back again to Korea. When it is morning in Korea, it is evening in Mongol and vice versa. In Mongol there are mainly lions and horses. This is why Mongol people are experts in riding and also they shoot arrows at animals and then eat them. Mongol boys are riding, too, and they are painting the whole day. In the beginning the boys thought that I am an enemy, but then I told them that I want to be their friend and then they

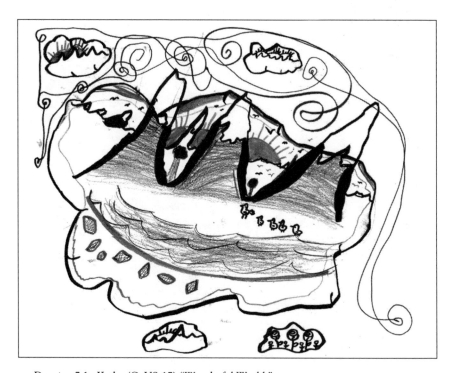

Drawing 7.1. Kathy (G, US-17) "Wonderful World."

became more friendly. Now many adults and children come here to play. The Mongol friends are stronger than me, but they are my friends nevertheless. A boy is handing me a coconut. The other boy is his younger brother. But he is shy. I brought him 12 new crayons, because my Mongol friend has broken mine.

Hyon'ah's story is all about a cultural encounter and creating a bridge to the "other." She finds a way to form a friendship with the two Mongols whom she describes as a mixture of Native Americans and Asian Mongols, but who are depicted in the drawing as African; they have dark skin, black curly hair, and they wear colorful garments covering only parts of their bodies (an image that has probably been constructed from various sources). They exchange presents as a sign of connectedness, which conforms to a typical Asian ritual. Hyon'ah also demonstrates a benevolent behavior for, as she relates, she is not angry because her new friends have broken her crayons, but even gives them new ones (see Drawing 7.2).

The concept of *other* that surfaces in these children's make-believe worlds seems to focus on their curiosity about differences: What does the other look like? What does the other know or have that we do not and vice versa? What do we know or have that the other does not?

Drawing 7.2. Hyon'ah (G, SK-5) "Mongol."

The Missing Traces of Globalization

A theme that would have been expected, based on the globalization discourse, but was surprisingly missing in our findings, is the domination of the English language. Yet, English was hardly present in the non-American children's make-believe worlds, neither in the drawings themselves, nor in the verbal discussions. In each country, several children added written explanations or signs to their drawings in their native languages: German in Germany, Hebrew and Arabic in Israel, Korean in South Korea, and obviously, English in the United States. Although clearly our age group may be too young to show the effect of the internalization of the English language, it would have been at least expected to creep into the Israeli and South Korean make-believe worlds because English is a mandatory second language from early school age in these countries, and is very highly regarded as a central skill for higher education and social mobility. An interesting exception to this was offered by two drawings of Israeli boys from the same research session, who specified names of their favorite Israeli basketball teams in English to resemble a scoreboard on a televised game.

In addition, a surprising finding was the absence of overt signs of the culture of consumerism. In contrast to our expectations, the children were not preoccupied with materialistic desires, pursuit of objects, money, or economic status. There were just a handful of references to ownership of brand name products. The one obvious exception is the case of Jack (B, US-25), who wants to be the *"best millionaire in my dreamland,"* and draws himself on stage under a rain of green dollars. However, his desire may also be interpreted as a wish to stand out on center stage, rather than for having the money as purchasing power.

Similarly, there was very little evidence of desire to join the glimmering world of celebrities. None of our children expressed deep desires to become fashion models or beauty queens. Only Tali (G, IS-6) expressed a wish to become a television actress like a famous singer whom she identified by name, and Dor (B, IS-13) identified himself by name with a famous soccer player.

Obviously, these findings do not dismiss the workings of consumer culture in much more subtle and subliminal ways, such as wishes concerning vacations and trips, ownership of horses, or leisure activities. Yet the absence of direct reference to shopping for goods (with one American exception) is in itself a marker of the complexity of these issues at this developmental stage.

LOCAL CULTURAL TRACES

So far we have argued that we did not find persuasive evidence for either one of Barber's (1995) two dynamic processes: on one hand, of McWorld, the moving force of a borderless market toward global homogeneity; and on the other, Jihad, the rival process of localization that originates in cultural, religious, ethnic, and linguistic boundaries. The children's make-believe worlds seem to offer, for the most part, mostly references to shared human values and ideals. Therefore, when we do find expressions of cultural contextualization, we need to ask ourselves why is this an exception and what does it mean? We turn now to highlighting two cultural themes that seem more prominent in each of the four countries, using some excerpts of children's own voices as were expressed in the interviews themselves . Although, as we have argued, they are not comparable, these themes do nevertheless reveal quite a bit about the interplay of local cultures and lifestyles and children's inner worlds.

CULTURAL TRACES
IN GERMAN MAKE-BELIEVE WORLDS

Two main themes stand out in the German sample in comparison to the other three cultural groups: interest in and concern for animals and ecological awareness.

Interest in and Concern for Animals

Children in all four countries were found to have a special affinity for animals. However, this theme had a particular prominence in the German group. Animals can be seen in 73% of all fantasy drawings in the German sample, in comparison to 61% in the Korean sample, 45% in the Israeli sample, and 40% in the U.S. sample. Nearly all girls who drew animals chose real animals, while boys also drew animal-like fantasy figures such as *Pokémon* and dragons.

The German children's favorite animal is the horse, followed by rabbits and hares, birds, butterflies, dolphins, and snakes, respectively. Boys draw different *Pokémon, Digimon,* and dinosaurs, putting them at the center of attention. A smaller group of children use animals, especially butterflies and schematically depicted birds, mainly as decorative elements. But for a majority of the children, the animals have a specific meaning. This is reflected in the efforts made, for example, and in the investment put into drawing colored feathers or fur. The importance of the animals also becomes apparent in the stories and in the roles that the animals are assigned.

What roles do these animals have in children's drawings? Animals facilitate aspects of the plots such as extending children's abilities. Thus, as she explains in the interview, Charlotte (G, GR-12) needs a horse to make the long way from Arabia to Spain in order to help people there (see Drawing 7.3):

> Well, this is Spain here and this is my horse. And I sit on it and I want to ride through the whole of Spain. And the, and the poor people, help, that, and go to their dwellings and some money and things like that …. I have been riding for many hours and many days and weeks.

Drawing 7.3. Charlotte (G, GR-12) "Trip to Spain."

In this case, the horse is more of a companion, supporting and assisting her. Thus, because Charlotte has to hold the reins, her horse picks up a flower with its mouth that has been offered to Princess Charlotte by "the crowd." The horse not only becomes part of a scenario in which the girl experiences her uniqueness, but the horse also facilitates her fantasy and supports her. Such a role can also be found in the make-believe worlds of boys, who often fantasize about animallike creatures. In Robbie's case (B, GR- 43), this is a dragon that can avenge everyday teasing, thereby extending Robbie's possibilities for taking action against the teasing. In other cases, *Pokémon* characters defend children against powerful attackers or participate in contests on behalf of the boys, who are their trainers.

Fantasy creatures or animals that are endowed with extended abilities enable children to share another very common fantasy—being able to fly. In three stories, children begin by describing the movements of a horse jumping over an obstacle, but then they continue and make their horses take off. In only one case does the flying horse refer explicitly to the myth of Pegasus. Having once been told about the story by his mother, Angelo (B, GR-42) describes how he draws a jumping horse that is supposed to be Pegasus. In contrast, the remaining fantasies refer to girls' real-life experiences with horses or riding them. Indeed, riding horses is a very popular activity in Germany, particularly for girls. Professional horseback riding as a sport has a strong tradition, including consistent winning of riding competitions, including the Olympic games. For children in southern and eastern Germany, this is rather wishful thinking due to limited experiences for beginning riders of this age group, whereas in northern Germany, there are specific references to real experiences riding high-quality horses and children enjoying longer visits to riding schools. Accordingly, the sample from northern Germany contains about twice as many make-believe worlds that focus on horses.

Riding horses can also be related to the desire for control that seems to have a special place in the German sample. More specifically, it is the control over the movement of the horse, rather than over the animal itself that is at the heart of the wish. Lena (G, GR-22) draws a dream in which she dashes through the desert with a cowboy. She says that she herself rides too. She has already galloped once, with the horse striding forward, and this appealed to her very much. She feels insecure while trotting and she tells of how she "nearly" fell off. In her fantasy, she gallops bareback without a saddle, which is especially difficult for beginning riders, but it also shows great attachment to and confidence in the horse. She extends her fantasy even more by imagining herself on wild horses. She explains to the interviewer that these horses are free and more difficult to ride. In her fantasy, she transcends her previous riding skills and gallops through the desert at a *"very fast gallop which is hardly a gallop anymore"* without any difficulty on the bare backs of wild horses. The cowboy, who knows a lot about horses is all the security and safety she needs because she is competent and controls the situation completely.

"Being concerned and caring for animals" is a very important aspect of several animal make-believe stories. In their fantasies, girls as well as boys describe how they take responsibility for animals, helping them if necessary. As has already been demonstrated in the discussion about the word "care," this caring for another being is not a self-sacrificing moment, but is of mutual benefit to both sides. The task of taking care of something or someone gives rise to its own significance and is connected with a good feeling. This is discernible when Sarah (G, GR-5) tells in her interview how she cares for the animals in her kingdom: *"Well, I never leave my horses and hares, well I don't neglect them. Instead I care for them every day, so that they have a beautiful life and I do as well!"*

In their imaginations, children do not only want to care for animals, but some of them clearly aim at actively protecting them. Such is the case of Tessina (G, GR-3) who wants to create a refuge for threatened animals, and Edith (G, GR-13) who dreams of a land in which animals, especially spiders, are not endangered. Both of the girls have decided to deny other humans access, because the humans are the ones to be blamed for threatening the animals. Although these two girls have learned from television that there are endangered species,

Saya (G, GR-4) has had a personal experience and therefore knows that animals might die. She had a jackrabbit living at her grandfather's home in Vietnam who died after being fed the wrong food. Saya takes care of her jackrabbit in her fantasy; there is always enough fresh water and pasture for him. Saya is standing on a rock above, calm and pleased, and is watching over him. *"I simply watched him eating,"* Saya says during the interview. These girls are designing a living space that, according to them, is the most adequate for the animals.

A related theme in the German sample deals with a concern for eating and being eaten. Güler (G, GR-14), for example, thinks that some animals are definitely *"dumb,"* because they eat other animals and therefore she prevents their entrance into her imagined African world. She draws a laughing mouth on the lion to symbolize him as *"sweet"* and *"nice."* The topic of eating animals pervades the interview and Güler, who is a Muslim, explains her own problem with eating meat:

Güler: *Yes! God has, well has given the animals to us because we really have to consume them. Otherwise we could not live! Therefore.*

Interviewer: *And therefore they exist as well.*

Güler: *Yes.*

Interviewer: *And the animals?*

Güler: *Hmm. But I think it's dumb with animals because they could also eat their grass. And we could also, hum, eat vegetables and the like, we do not always have to eat meat. Hmm, hmm, well when there is a good meal with meat, I like it. But when there is a bad one, then I cannot eat it somehow.*

Interviewer: *Aha! And what is good and bad?*

Güler: *Well, when I do not like meat in my mouth, then it is comfortable and it tastes good but when my mother says afterward this is meat and then I feel sick somehow. But otherwise I like meat .... And well, I don't want to consume the animals somehow! But you have to! Otherwise, hmm, you don't have vitamins. And you don't grow. And get older and so, therefore!*

Güler says that she likes the taste of meat but if she is told afterward that she has eaten meat, she feels "sick." Basically, she does not want to consume animals but she feels she has to. Her frame of reference: God gave it to us and without meat people do not have enough vitamins, they do not grow up and get older. The topic of liking animals but still eating meat concerns Güler at the moment. For her and for three other German children, their make-believe worlds mirror this special moral conflict, which is not even mentioned in any of the other countries. They find themselves in a dilemma between their love for animals and eating meat. In their fantasy world, they find ways to deal with this situation. Güler finds a justification for why she eats meat, but still loves animals and wants to protect them.

Locating this focus on animals in a national culture is extremely difficult. A Europewide comparison found that Germany is among those countries where people love pets the most (Central Committee of Zoological Companies, 2002). Therefore, one possible reason for the high number of animals in German children's fantasies is the concrete experience with a pet at home. In addition, although the centrality of television programs in children's lives was common to all children in our study, the German children made references to nonfictional formats, such as documentary and information programs, that mostly having to do with animals much more often than others (in 23 of the cases). Twelve of the children inserted information directly derived from such documentaries into their fantasy worlds. In comparison with other countries, this specific feature was quite striking.

Ecological Awareness

The concern for animals is interwoven with a strong ecological awareness. The vital characteristic of these make-believe worlds is always a safe, natural environment. Peter (B, GR-10), for example, wants to buy a piece of land: *"If I had more than a million, I would buy a huge sanctuary for animals."* He wants to build a sanctuary in which nature can recover and afterward he merely wants to watch it grow. During the interview, he provides us with some reasons (see Drawing 7.4):

Peter:	*Because, hmm, because first came the animals, not the humans. And, we the humans remove everything, we remove everything from nature.*
Interviewer:	*We remove everything? What are we removing?*
Peter:	*Well, the whole scenery, hmm, the beautiful flowers which once existed, and the birds.*
Interviewer:	*What will happen to the animals if we remove them?*
Peter:	*They will become ill from exhaust gases if the cars are driving for too long, and, hmm and they do not have enough space, I mean, not as many forests as there used to be and so they cannot exist any more.*

Peter has recognized some "big truths" that are moving him. Humans are robbing nature although they have no right to. In his make-believe sanctuary, he tries to solve these problems aided by ideas he has gained from his favorite television program, *Dandelion*. He has already been practicing additional ideas

Drawing 7.4. Peter (B, GR-10) "The Great Paradise of Animals."

in the ponds of the family garden and in his own little fish tanks. What is important for him is to create a living space where animals are safe and not threatened by intrusive humans.

The wish for active environmental protection is not only common in children's fantasies from Germany; it plays a role all over the world. In South Korea, for example, You'jin (G, SK-11) tells about the environmental pollution endangering animals and nature that she prevents in her make-believe world. In the United States Jody (G, US-15) imagines herself turning into a ferocious saber-tooth tiger who protects threatened animals in the Arctic. However, in Germany this theme is much more prominent, as more children include some traces of environmental awareness. Christian (B, GR-28) wants to drive nonpolluting cars, such as his "Pluto" scooter, which runs without fuel. Yamir (B, GR-55) tells about his fantasy world, Hongcity, where he and his friend always set their imaginary play. Hongcity is an ecofriendly fantasy city where cars go without any fuel and a factory recycles the waste. Even the buildings in Yamir's imagination are glad of the situation as once a house bent over to him and said: *"I'm glad you came here. The other cities are not as ecofriendly as we are. I'm happy that we have such nice friends as you."* In this case, animal and environmental protection is tied up with images of appreciation, power, and expertise.

Conclusion

Animals, in particular, horses, are often integrated into the fantasies of German children, and serve a variety of functions for them. In their imaginations, German children want to play an active role in nature conservation, they want to reduce waste and act in an ecofriendly way. Apart from the prevalence of television programs about nature and the environment, this emphasis can probably be accounted for due to several sources: (a) The curriculum in elementary schools that has had an impact on the children in Germany, (b) the public discourse and regulations regarding recycling behaviors, and (c) the centrality of the Green Party. All of these are promoting children's ecological awareness in Germany.

CULTURAL TRACES IN ISRAELI MAKE-BELIEVE WORLDS

The absence of explicit traces to living within a deeply conflicted society as well as cultural differences between the Jewish and Arab Israeli children compose the two unique themes of discussion for the Israeli sample.

Traces of Living Within a Conflicted Society

The study took place in the winter and spring of 2002, only a few months after the emergence of the second uprising in the occupied Palestinian territories, with its terrorist attacks on the civilian Israeli population on one hand, and the tightening of the Israeli occupation and military actions against the Palestinian population on the other hand. It was a period of growing violence, anxiety, and despair within Israel, and a time of growing polarization between the Jewish and Arab populations, as well as within those populations themselves. Accordingly, in the children's make-believe worlds we expected references to their attitudes toward this situation as well as to their own concerns, anxieties, and wishes.

However, contrary to our expectations, the conflict did not surface in children's make-believe worlds. Neither Jewish nor Arab children explicitly wished for worlds where there were no terrorist attacks, no suicide bombers, no military occupation, and no racism. All in all, we found only a few references to the political situation, and even those were mostly in passing. Only one Jewish girl, Amanda (G, IS-48), seemed preoccupied with terrorist attacks and made an explicit wish for a world without them. In her utopian world, she drew a bomb and crossed it out with a thick X explaining: "*I draw an X on it, so there are no wars and no terrorist attacks.*" Later in the interview she described her make believe world in detail (see Drawing 7.5):

> There is no school and there are no studies, and there is no need to work there because they have everything, and there is no need for money ... this is why I draw it in a cloud, so it means it is imaginary, where I really want to live, a place without terrorist attacks.

Drawing 7.5. Amanda (G, IS-48) "Utopia."

Similarly, there were no stories in which children imagined themselves as military heroes fighting against the enemy or defending their own people. We found neither Jewish nor Arabic nationalistic symbols in the fantasies. There were no national flags or slogans, no religious symbols or cultural icons, and virtually no mention of the collective—either in a religious or in a nationalist context (the one exception being three Jewish boys' wishes for a victory by an Israeli soccer team). The sole indication that children are aware of the situation and are concerned came indirectly. Several Jewish and Arab children said that they tried to avoid reading newspapers or watching television news because they were troubled by the contents. Omer (B, IS-02), a Jewish boy, doesn't like to read the papers *"because the headline always has bad things."* Ravit (G, IS-36), a Jewish girl, declares that she does not like to watch the news on television *"because it causes me nightmares."* Similarly, Sahar (G, IS-23), a Christian-Arab girl, says: *"I don't like to watch the news because there are pictures and terrifying scenes that bother me."*

If anything, the striking difference in these children's drawings was the absence of any explicit form of fighting—no gory bloody scenes of brutality such as were found in some drawings from the other countries. Presumably the children partly suppress the political situation, are inclined to create in their fantasies a kind of counterworld where the conflict and the threats it poses to their well-being, identity, and morality are nonexistent. However, two of the boys—Udi (B, IS-1), and Omer (B, IS-2)—positioned themselves in a state of "being prepared" to defend oneself with appropriate arms and gear against an unknown threat. In none of the other stories did we find such a form of defense without attack that could be hypothetically related to the country's general narrative of living a life of defense against possible future attacks. It should be noted, however, that in the period that has passed since that time, the situation in the region has escalated even further, and it is possible that the cumulative effect would have prevented children from avoiding the issue if the study had been conducted at the time of this writing.

It is possible that the dominant role of travel to foreign lands as a form of relief is related to suppression of the local conflict. Although this theme was evident in all four countries, and traces of holidays and vacations could be found in many children's make-believe worlds, their emotional centrality in some of the Israeli children's interviews seemed to stand out. Children's reminiscing over trips to the United States, England, Australia, the Netherlands, and Cyprus, seemed to color their wishes and dreams. Aviv (G, IS-47), for example, was strongly affected by her past trip to the United States:

> I picked purple because it is a bit dark and a bit happy ... and I also wrote USA, because I was there and I remember it all the time ... it was an amazing experience and I draw it orange, because it is really shining and happy color ... and it is in the center, because it is all the time in my mind ... and I draw fruits that I saw in the USA .... and my brain is telling me that my thoughts flew and they are all now in my dreamland which is the USA .... and the boy just returned from an exam at school, and he told his mother and remembered the USA and Disney ... and although his mother is calling him and the cat is wailing and the dog barking, he is really deep into Disney, and he looks at the Disney pencil and starts smiling ....

The dominant role of trips abroad be could perhaps explained by the high priority that Israeli society puts on traveling within and outside the country. This is commonly understood as a symptom of the need to break away from a sense of closure within a very small geographical territory constrained by enemy borders or the sea on all fronts, as well as by a psychological sense of suffocation, anxiety, and intense pressure caused by the constant state of war. Israeli children, so it seems, have internalized this passion for travel and search for a sense of freedom and escape.

Ethnic/Religious Differences

Differences between the Jewish and Arab children in our sample became obvious from the start. The Arab children were interviewed by an Arab female student in their own language—Arabic. Their reverence toward her was in sharp contrast to the way the Jewish children treated their Jewish female field researchers. The Arab research assistant was treated as a respected authority figure. Personal distance was strictly maintained, both physically and verbally, and the children were obedient and tried to perform as "good students." The Jewish research assistants, on the other hand, were treated much less formally. They were called by first names, were physically touched, and children occasionally even roughhoused with them or provoked them verbally. In addition, the Arab research assistant felt on occasion that she was treated by the children's families with suspicion—perhaps as a collaborator with the dominant Jewish society, and that the study attempted to be a cover-up for lack of sincere interest in Arab children. One mother went as far as openly resisting cooperation for political reasons. Jewish mothers, on the other hand, seemed very interested and supportive of the study and cooperated willingly.

The Jewish and Arab children in our sample also seemed to be living in very different media cultures. The Jewish children were consumers of both Hebrew and imported popular programs (mainly in English) on commercial and cable television and read Hebrew as well as translated books—from classic children books (e.g., Jules Verne's) to the most current ones (e.g., the *Harry Potter* series). Arab children, on the other hand, were primarily consumers of programs in Arabic produced by Arab TV stations (e.g., Syria, Lebanon, Saudi Arabia) or dubbed and received through satellite broadcasts. They read Arabic books and listened to Arabic music. In this regard, the Jewish children can be said to be more culturally globalized, whereas the Arab children were more culturally localized. Moreover, the Jewish children's make-believe worlds had significantly more media traces than did the Arab children ones.

As anticipated, in the study we found several differences between Arab and Jewish children's make-believe worlds. Due to the limited number of cases, however, they are presented as ideas for consideration and tendencies for discussion, rather than firm results. The make-believe worlds of the Jewish children revealed more traces of an individual orientation: *"for myself," "to be all by myself," "to be independent," "to do only things I want," "to have no parents telling me what to do," "nobody is there to discipline me."*

The Arab children, on the other hand, seemed to be more oriented toward the collective; in their make-believe worlds, they tended to be with other people, mainly with their relatives or friends. Rima (G, IS-9), for example, fantasizes riding horses (see Drawing 7.6):

> I arrived at the city of dreams and found a beautiful nature scenery. I am in the middle and people greet me nicely, and I found a stable with two horses: one white and one

Drawing 7.6. Rima (G, IS-9) "Riding."

black. Later I went to a different place and found children riding horses. I rode a horse. I walked and found a pretty villa. There are people who live there.

In her interview, Rima emphasizes that she feels happy there. She also pointed out that the light in the house is turned on—symbolizing to her the hospitality of the people greeting her at the villa.

One possible interpretation of this difference can be associated with their collective cultural-social orientations. On the whole, Jewish children currently raised in Israel are oriented toward a Western, modernized society, highly Americanized and characterized by the typical processes of individualization, commercialization, and privatization. Arab-Israeli children, on the other hand, although raised in the same country, usually grow up amid traditional social institutions much more resistant to change. The traditional society focuses heavily on the extended family as well as responsibility for the Arab minority collective, which has been systematically discriminated against due to the complexity of the political situation in the region.

One possible indication of the sense of alienation in which these Arab-Israeli children are raised, is their lack of acknowledgment and identification with the state of Israel as an entity. In their stories, these children referred to their village or town, but never to the country or state, directly or indirectly. Although Jewish boys, for example, identified with Israeli soccer teams and proudly wished for their victories, the Arab boys chose to skip their country of citizenship and to identify with a faraway team from Brazil, or drew a flag of Switzerland.

An additional difference that we detected in the make-believe worlds is the central role that pets played for many of the Jewish children and their absence in the Arab children's world. Many of the Jewish children included their pets (real ones or imaginary) in their drawings and related stories, or associated animals with peaceful and harmonious worlds. None of the Arab children had pets in their make-believe worlds, except for horses in two of the drawings. Here too, we are cautious of overgeneralizing, based on the limited number of cases, yet it is interesting to note that raising pets is not a common custom in most traditional societies. In the Islamic tradition, for example, animals are perceived as impure and as a cause for health problems. Raising pets is also a matter of resources—traditional and poorer societies with large families do not have the resources and conditions to invest in pets. In secular modern societies, however, pets are looked on positively as an educational resource, fostering qualities of responsibility, caring, sharing, expressing emotions, and developing friendship skills. Horses, on the other hand, as an exception, have a very prestigious role in Arab culture, and riding a horse may well be associated with positive experiences of status and joy.

Conclusion

Within very unique social circumstances, Israeli children seem to have more in common with children in Germany, South Korea, and the United States than one might have expected. In their make-believe worlds, they seem to push aside concerns for the harsh sociopolitical context in which they are raised and the real daily threats to their existence. They accept global culture as their own, seasoning it with signs of local roots. The most interesting differences, however, come from the analysis of Arab-Israeli children, which can be interpreted as signs of being raised in a traditional minority culture. We point out these differences as directions for further exploration rather than as firm conclusions.

CULTURAL TRACES IN SOUTH KOREAN MAKE-BELIEVE WORLDS

The analysis of the make-believe worlds from South Korea suggests an interesting co-existence of tradition and the latest multimedia technology. These two aspects in particular stand out in this group's make-believe worlds.

Confucian Influence on Children's Fantasies

Confucian doctrine and principles are deeply ingrained in South Korean society to this very day, affecting family structures and daily habits, education at home, and at school. Some of these Confucian principles could be found in the South Korean children's make-believe worlds. The high esteem placed on education puts a lot of pressure on Korean children to excel in their studies, to compete for admission to elite universities, and in general to work hard and to succeed academically. Attending private schools after public-school hours, as early as preschool age, which is a widespread phenomenon in South Korea, is an illustration of these rigorous educational expectations. It is the most common activity Korean children do after school and much more prevalent than any leisure activity. In our sample of elementary-school children in Seoul, over 85% participated in private lessons in such formal institutions (mostly in mathematics and English, but also in Korean, natural and social sciences; Korea Education Development Institute, 2002).

In all four countries, there were children who wished to live carefree lives relieved of pressure and responsibilities. However, the wish to be free of the tremendous pressure to perform and excel in school and to have more free time was particularly noticeable in the South Korean sample. Some children strongly stated the desire to be set free from pressure placed on them by adults. For example, Hyon'ah (G, SK-5) talks in the interview about her desire to fly to the United States by a hot-air balloon or an airplane belonging to Korean Airlines because she thinks that children in the United States do not have to study so much.

Children and young people in South Korea have the impression that pupils in the United States and Europe are not exposed to as much pressure to perform by adults and have more free time than do pupils in South Korea. They base this idealized image on many television series about everyday school life in the United States and Europe. The United States and Europe become the land of make-believe, in which pupils have to learn less and in different ways. Another example of looking for a place to escape to is Seyong's (B, SK-18) story where he flies to his land of make-believe that is symbolized by concentric circles in the sky. This land is something special for him, a place that he goes to in order to relax.

> …Here I run a lot, play with my friends and have fun …. I just want to play there …. except for me there are only my friends and a dog but not adults, because I like my friends most and do not want to have any pressure …. It is great to be on my own. It is fun to run ….

It is important to note in Seyong's fantasy that there are no adults, and children do not exert any pressure on him. In his everyday life, he is a model student, but he wishes to enjoy his freedom with his friends without adult pressure.

Children try to escape high adult expectations by building up make-believe counterworlds. In his picture, Jong'yun (B, SK-31) draws a special land "just for us"; it is a lazy, exciting life where he does not need to behave, just like in the book he loves to read, *The Adventures of Tom Sawyer*. His fantasyland is completely different from his everyday life, where he is controlled by a strict father, a mother who pays attention to orderliness and cleanliness, and a younger brother whom he has to look after. In his fantasyland, he wants to live by himself with his friends, without parents and adults. All those things denied him in the real world are allowed in this land:

> … Here I play with six of my friends. We can do as we please and what I want. I can always play without asking Mom and Dad. The animals, the birds, and the sun with the sunglasses are also playing. The eye, the nose, and the mouth are all tanned by the sun … We play on the mountain, in the water, and also in the rain … we play until one o'clock in the morning, we play computer games, get tired, then we sleep …. we get dirty because we didn't wash for two days. Ticks are bothering us because we played too close to the tree … the birds finally tell us "This can't go on!." Then the birds wash our clothes for us in the evening …. There is a car for taking a ride with my friends. I'm driving the car and my dad is sitting in the back seat … my parents did not allow me to come here, because they think it is too dangerous. I don't want to take my little brother there, because he would give away my secret to the parents. Moreover, I'll have to play the water game with him. This is why I go to the land with my friends …. the cloud comes along and tells us, "Please wash often!" "Please clean your teeth," "Please wash your clothes." This is what my mom says, too ….

Jong'yong develops a counterworld to his real life. This is a world where anything goes, a world where he can play as long as he wants, where even clear power positions are reversed, for example, while he is driving the car, the father sits in the backseat. However, the child can not escape a sort of a "alterego," as a cloud and birds continue to discipline him, because the sense of duty is so deeply rooted in him.

Young'son (G, SK-12) inserts a clock into her make-believe world that provides her with feedback about her behavior and reassures her that she has been "good." She draws herself in the middle of her picture with the clock right above her head. Three thoughts expressed in Korean scripts fly around her: *"me," "thought,"* and *"work." "My thoughts tell me that I have to prepare everything thoroughly."* She also hears the clock complimenting her on her behavior of the previous week, for which she politely thanks him. In her fantasy world, Young'son accepts the things she is expected to do (e.g., practice the piano, read books, sleep, donate money to church), takes pleasure in the fact that she is appreciated for such actions and adds: *"In the future I also want to be good"* (see Drawing 7.7).

Another expression of Confucian influence in the pictures was evident in the strong awareness of being a member of a group and a desire not to stand out as an individual. This is particularly true for children who are excluded from their circle

Drawing 7.7. Young'son (G, SK-12) "The Clock Tower."

of friends; when they try to be special, they are treated negatively. Indeed, in the South Korean sample, there are hardly any drawings where the desire of "being special" is the center of attention. Only Ji'yun (G, SK-25), mentions the desire to sing like a diva. She tells us in the interview that she wants to be a famous singer and perform onstage for many people. She thinks she can make people happy by telling them beautiful stories and singing. However, in her drawing she assigned this role to a bird.

> … Here a bird is flying and looking for a village where everyone likes music. The people there enjoy the bird's singing … this bird knows that I like music very much. You can make the bird sing, when you wish for it deep in your heart …. It is my desire to become a singer. When the bird is too tired to sing, deep in my heart I think "Please stop now!" But the bird likes the people very much, who love its songs. This is why it continues singing although it is really tired.

The bird thus becomes a projection of Jiyun's desires. But when asked directly, she denies being the bird herself (see Drawing 7.8).

Centrality of Computers in the Children's Lives

Although media figured heavily in children's make-believe worlds, computers were particularly prominent in those of South Korean children, in comparison to the other countries. In about half of the South Korean boys' drawings in our

Drawing 7.8. Ji'yun (G, SK-25) "A Singing Bird."

study, we found media traces of computers serving various functions, in comparison with none in Germany, one boy in Israel, and one third of the boys in the United States.

As mentioned, the domestic market of computerized flash animation is very notable in children's leisure in South Korea. *Mashimaro* and *Zolaman* top the list of the most popular characters that are downloaded for a small fee from the Internet. The content of the computer world was central for some of the children in the study. Yon'uh (B, SK-20) draws "Zolaman and the Mashimaro" characters from the Internet flash animation. He depicts two divided kingdoms, a land where *"Zolaman is the king"* and a land where *"the Mashimaro is king."* In his story, the two kingdoms are fighting in a manner similar to the situation in the computer game (see Drawing 7.9):

In my fantasyland, I stand in the middle of a border between two separate countries. One country is owned by Mashimaro and the other belongs to Zolaman. Mashimaro has a silver fur and a red cap. Normally he is white, but because he is the king in this country—he has a silver fur. In both countries there are numerous tanks and they fight each other, because Mashimaro and Zolaman wage war against each other. The tanks are called "Potank," "Multank," "Bang-gutank," and "Missile-tank" and they are produced in the castles of both countries waging war. King Mashimaro and King Zolaman both want me to help them to defeat the other country; this is why they are both pulling my arms. But when the war ends a 100 million years from now, the Zolaman will win, because its 1,500 inhabitants are technicians.

Drawing 7.9. Yon'uh (B, SK-20) "Zolaman and Mashimaro."

The two characters in his very accurate picture are drawn on either side of him. He stands in the center of the picture, each hand held by one of the characters. In the foreground of the picture are fleets of opposing tanks. The two media characters who have command of Asian martial arts, are the leaders of their countries who are at war with each other. Yon'uh combines the two characters in his daydream by making them fight against each other and depicts himself as a popular ally. In the original medium, the two characters do not appear in the same cartoons, nor is one of them involved in warlike activities. Nevertheless, Yon'uh imagines such a conflict and bases an entire story on them.

Jun'sik (B, SK-29), too, imitated in his "fantasy castle" story the plot of a computer game:

> ... All people in this land are in the castle now. I watch them from behind the mountain .... The knights are just revolting against the king. They want to kill him .... In front of the castle there is a tree. If one of the people dies in the fight, one leaf falls from the tree. The leaf on the ground is later reborn as a human .... I saw that from a computer game, which is called "the Kingdom of the Wind." I extend my level up to 99 [this is how he generates soldiers] and send them to the army, then I generate more soldiers ....

Fascination with violence and brutality emphasized in computer content seems to be another source of pleasure for these children. Although some characters in the drawings, dinosaurs, for instance, were influenced by picture books, animated films, or in movies like *Jurassic Park*, the way the story unfolded in the interviews revealed that violent elements unique to computer games were integrated into their fantasy world. Young'ho (B, SK-21), for example, drew an interesting world with dinosaurs, but titled it, "Kill the Dinosaur!" He told a very brutal story about his drawing, containing lots of killing, revenge and plenty of blood: "*... Here two dinosaurs are fighting, just for fun. I don't know why they bite each other ... they kill each other in an interesting way. They fight and die. Some dinosaurs drink water, and suddenly a Tyrannosaurus appears from the sea and they fight.*"

Hyon'gu (B, SK-3) drew in his "The Land of Dinosaurs" picture many small, funny, and strange creatures, characters or actors directly drawn from computer games (e.g., the fairy of electricity, the star fairy, the thinking balloon, etc.) The two dinosaurs were already bitten by someone and show bones and blood, but they eat peacefully. The display of this scene is copied from the computer game as well. This boy is not in the fantasy world himself, but depicts the scene from a distance, as if viewing it on a computer monitor.

Another piece of evidence that children adapt motifs from computer games into their make-believe worlds is the display of settings of the action that is taken directly from computer games. A good example of this is the use of castles. Various computer games, popular with children and young people, are based on Medieval European history and thus castles are an important setting for action. A few of the Korean children drew castles that are closely similar to those of the games. Some even directly mention computer games as their source of information regarding the castle.

For some children, it is more about skills and competence in using the computer, rather than the content per se. Seyong (B, SK-18) admits that he borrowed the idea for his make-believe world from a feature on the computer. As the entrance to his fantasyland, he drew a tornado, an image he found while surfing the Internet. Gyu'sang (B, SK-34) loves cars and knows nearly all the names of car brands, even the difficult ones, by heart. He uses the computer frequently, mostly for educational reasons and homework. In his picture he drew a car with eyes, the same way cars are displayed in computer games for children.:

> ... When I type into the computer, "let's go," then the car is driving automatically ... I can drive the car very well ... yes really. When I play [computer] car games, I never bump anywhere. And, I know everything about cars. When I play computer games, I only play car games ....

Jae'jun (B, SK-22) "transferred" his computer to his favorite garden. Based on his everyday experience, he believes the computer can be used in many ways. In his make-believe "Garden of Cartoons," he can use it when he wants to know something new or to find out something. In his favorite garden, all animals and plants can play peacefully with people and, in particular, with him and his friends. Even the animals he likes—the cat, the turtle, and the fish—can use the computer, just like he does.

The central role of computers in South Korean boys' make-believe worlds seems to reflect the multimedia developments in this country and the prevalence of computers in children's schooling as well as leisure lives. In 2000, 66% of the population owned a computer (Information Culture Center of Korea, 2000) and the numbers have been on the increase since then. The proportion of people subscribing to the Internet in South Korea was 51.5% in 2002, the highest in Asia (compared, for example to Hong Kong, 39.3%; Japan, 37.8%; Taiwan, 35.1%; Singapore, 29.9%). Close to 90% of all elementary-school students use the Internet at school and home (Korea Network Information Center, 2002). Since the 1990s, the high-tech area in economy and education has been strongly supported by the government, including provision to each classroom of various media and linkage of the entire school system to the Internet. Each school has a special computer lab for computer literacy that pupils attend beginning in the second year of elementary school. Many children start using personal computers (PCs) in early childhood and close to 60% of 6-year-olds have experience with the Internet (Korea Network Information Center, 2002).

The Art Work

Finally, what is most striking at first glance about the Korean sample is the children's unique drawing style. Their drawings are vivid and colorful, often very ordered, and almost always use the entire space provided by the page, covering it completely from corner to corner. Although we refrain here from analyzing these differences based on the rich artistic traditions of the East, we would like to point out two complementary explanations: first, the special writing skills of the complicated configuration of the Korean script mastered at a young age may develop pupils' proclivity for drawing. Second, the school context in which the Korean study was performed could also have affected children's desire to "complete" the drawing assignment to the best of their abilities.

More specifically, overt visual signs of Korean society can be found in the pictures: The children often draw "Asian eyes," in particular, the Korean variety of the half moon with its downward crescent. The girls often wear a hairdo with typical ponytails and bows, as well as traditional dresses. In addition, the contexts of the make-believe worlds are linked to Korean culture. This is demonstrated by the shape of the houses, the combination of skyscrapers with gardens and small Korean garden chalets, and the mention of real amusement parks, familiar to the children.

Conclusion

In South Korea, Confucian mentality meets with multimedia in children's make-believe worlds to demonstrate how both the cultural context as well as the popular mass media within it are expressed in children's fantasy worlds. Participating in this project was a wonderfully unique experience with adults for these children. Feedback following the study highlighted the joy brought about by the possibility of freely sharing their inner worlds with caring adults and being acknowledged by them. While this was clearly the case in all four countries, it seemed significantly more so for South Korean children, perhaps due to the fact that common patterns of parenthood and education are much more hierarchical and based on Confucian principles of loyalty, reverence, and respect for authority, parents, and adults in general.

CULTURAL TRACES IN U.S. MAKE-BELIEVE WORLDS

The analysis of the U.S. study, conducted in a midsized university town in the midwest, highlights, not surprisingly, two central themes embedded in their culture—consumerism and individualism.

The All-Consuming American Dream

One striking characteristic of the American cases is the predominance of media traces in their make-believe worlds. Overall, the U.S. children referred directly and indirectly to a wide range of media. Box office movies such as *Shrek, Tomb Rider, Spiderman, Roger Rabbit,* and *Jurassic Park,* as well as popular Disney movies such as *Aladdin, Bambi, Cinderella, Lion King, Peter Pan,* and *The Little Mermaid;* a list of television channels including the Discovery Channel, Disney Channel, and Nickelodeon; many cartoons and animated series such as *Pokémon, Dragon Ball Z, The Simpsons;* as well as a long list of video games and book titles—were integrated in American children's drawings and stories. On the other hand, although we often think of U.S. children as leading a highly wired childhood, the media texts most frequently (10 times) referred to were the *Harry Potter* book series. This would lead us to think that even with all the new media available, certain books still have a prominent place in the fantasy lives of U.S. children, lending credence to the idea (pointed out also by Roberts & Foehr, 2004) that new media do not replace older media, but are better viewed as augmenting the older media.

Close to half of the boys' fantasies were almost entirely derived from media: Martin (B, US-22) imagines himself as Peter Pan in the adventures of the video, *Hook;* Jeremy (B, US-20) is a Noble Paladin on a mission to free a princess; Jack

(B, US-25) is the Best Millionaire in the television quiz show, *Who Wants to Be a Millionaire?*; Jorge (B, US-30) plans the future *Jurassic Park*; David (B, US-31) is a Raptor, a giant dinosaur; Ricky (B, US-34) becomes the greatest *Pokémon* master in the gold version of the Gameboy; and Jed (B, US-35), imagines himself in a fight in the *Manga* world of Japanese cartoons, where he combines the characters of Tecnchi Muyo and Dragon Ball Z (see Drawing 7.10).

One could argue that especially with regard to boys—the media scripts that are integrated into their fantasies provide evidence for the role of the market in their imaginary worlds—although in a more subtle way. It can be argued that these programs are in themselves marketing tools and by internalizing them, the children's fantasy lives have, in a sense, become commercialized. This of course, raises questions regarding creativity and originality in their imaginative thinking and fantasy lives.

These findings need to be understood in light of commercial culture in the United States, which has expanded its reach in recent decades along several dimensions with respect to children. There is both a wider range of products and services available and they are targeted to younger and younger audi-

Drawing 7.10. Jed (B, US-35) "Dragon Ball Z."

ences. Along with the proliferation of products and services for children, advertising and marketing have become ubiquitous—even in schools to a certain degree—although this is controversial (Aidman, 1995; United States General Accounting Office, 2000). The drive to create synergy between programs and products that appeal to children, with product tie-ins through movies, fast-food chains, toys, and a wide range of children's products, is self-evident today. New, interactive media have also come into play as vehicles for advertisers to deliver their messages to children, as well as for marketers to collect personal information from and sell products to children. U.S. children grow up in a media-saturated environment that has at its heart the creation of desires in children for a wide range of products (Kline, 1993; McNeal, 1999). While this trend is common to all four countries, it is particularly so in the U.S. case.

Through cable television, children have entire channels that are devoted to entertaining them and selling products to them. Movies in the United States serve as a focal point of attention for children's media properties. Characters from television shows often spin-off into movies that are then promoted on television, and through other foci in children's culture. Marketing campaigns aim to build excitement around the release of a movie with product tie-ins and promotions that often include fast-food restaurants and other child-friendly retail outlets. The fast-food chains are involved in movie promotions by including free toys, such as plastic figures of movie characters, in special children's meals. Children are urged through television advertising to collect these toys. The goal is for the characters' images to become a ubiquitous presence in children's popular culture even before the release of a movie.

Following the theater run, it is routine practice for a movie to go directly into video release within several months. There is then commercial hype around the video release. For example, even before the video release of the movie, *Harry Potter and the Sorcerer's Stone*, children were made aware of the upcoming release via television. Furthermore, video rental chains promote the video, even before its release in order to create a buzz among young fans. Once the children acquire the video of the movie, they are likely to watch it repeatedly. This promotion; involving movies and then the acquisition and repeated home viewing, may help explain the prominent role movies play in the fantasy world of the U.S. children. Interestingly, four children mentioned the movie *Shrek*, which had been in the theaters at the time of the study.

It is interesting to note, however, that desires for products did not dominate the children's fantasies. We had expected to see more direct influence of consumer culture on the children's desires to come through in the fantasies. It was thought that wishes for particular products would be evident. This was not the case. There was one child whose fantasy was a kind of shopping mall, but this was the exception rather than the rule, as the make-believe worlds were not directly about consuming behavior or wishes for products.

The American Dream—A Celebration of Personal Power

In the United States, an ideal projected culturally encourages Americans to succeed through their own personal power. This ideal is reflected in some of the children's stories. American children have agency in their make-believe worlds. They put themselves in a position to act upon the world, rather than to have the world act upon them. They are powerful. They are in control and make decisions. In many cases, they portray themselves to be, in some way, the underdog, yet they prevail.

For instance, in the "Lion's Lair," Teri (G, US-6) is the smallest lion, yet the most powerful one, who outsmarts the evil lion and protects the good ones. In "I am a Dragon," Joe (B, US-13), as a dragon, is the protector and the underdog. This is also a part of the American dream—children are often told that the poorest, most underprivileged person can grow up to be President. The idea that "You can do or be anything" is central in the philosophy of parenting and education. This myth is also a dominant theme in U.S. media, certainly in children's media, and is employed in stories across all media platforms. It is the classic "rags to riches" myth—just work hard and you can overcome all obstacles and succeed. Of course, a little magic, such as that which Hollywood brings to a story, never hurts.

In a cross-cultural analysis of cultural norms in childcare, some specific differences in societal values are spelled out:

> Most Western, industrialized societies tend to emphasize individualistic over collectivist goals for a variety of historical and cultural reasons. Accordingly, traits of independence and assertiveness are generally valued in individuals and directly encouraged by parents in these societies. (De Loache & Gottlieb, 2000, p.13)

Independence and self-confidence are encouraged in contrast to interdependence and self-effacement. It is okay to be different and it is good to stand out in a crowd, quite in opposition to the values that South Korean children are being brought up to adopt! These values come through in the U.S. children's fantasies, in which the child's individuality and competence are highlighted and celebrated.

In the "Land of Witches and Wizards," Marsha (G, US-16) points out that she has always thought of herself as different, as a kind of a witch. In her fantasy she develops that aspect of herself that she believes makes her special (see Drawing 7.11).

In "Best Millionaire," Jack (B, US-25) takes pleasure in being in the spotlight and having the audience applaud for him. Rather than feeling embar-

Drawing 7.11. Marsha (G, US-16) "Land of Witches and Wizards."

rassed, as such attention might do to children with a more collectivist upbringing, he rejoices in the attention. It makes him feel as though he is a part of a "good family." These children, who would like to feel positive self-value draw themselves in the center of their pictures. Jeremy (B, US-20) is a very special noble paladin out to free a princess. Sometimes, however, being the center of attention also puts them in a dangerous position, as in the case for Joe (B, US-13). He imagines himself as a big red dragon, but also states that *"People do not like red dragons—they only like gray dragons,"* and therefore they chase after him.

It is interesting to note that the prominence of individuality comes across in the U.S. sample even from glancing through the drawings , many of which present the child on his or her own, detached from a family, peer group, or community, often at the center of the world, with little concern for others.

The Artwork

Overall the U.S. children's drawings appear more abstract or even symbolic than those in other countries. An initial appraisal and comparison to the drawings of the children in other countries might leave one with the idea that those of the U.S. children are somewhat impressionistic and, in some cases haphazard, or sloppy. However, having watched the children draw, it is difficult to support that opinion. In fact, our point of view is that the pictures were done with care, but that the overarching goal was to convey something conceptual; therefore, the attention to order and aesthetics was secondary. It may also be the case that the camp setting (even the context of the arts camp) is a relaxed atmosphere in which the process of what the child is doing is more important than the product. In a more formal setting, such as in school (like in the South Korean study), the U.S. children might have been more product-oriented.

One other possible explanation for the less-formal approach to the drawing part of the exercise is that, in general, the arts are not highly valued in the education of U.S. children. Considering the ever-waning support for the arts in society and in education, it might be said that the arts are not as valued in U.S. society as they are in some other countries.

Conclusion

It is clear that U.S. children are growing up in a world that is highly attuned to media (Roberts & Foehr, 2004), and their make-believe worlds give testimony to that. However, there are other influences in U.S. culture that also come through in the children's fantasies. Beyond the market, there is also evidence of the individuality and independence that are inherent in U.S. child-rearing that make their way into children's dreams. It is interesting to note that many of the other prevalent themes in these cases—such as gender differences, concern with resolving violence, fantasies of coasts, water, and the like, were much in line with those of their counterparts in the other three countries. One may speculate that it is the American culture as the "mobilizing force of globalization" that leaves little space for a unique local voice.

CONCLUDING NOTE

As stated, we are not arguing that the themes highlighted in each country are unique solely to that particular context. The contrary is probably just as true. We have found Israeli children dreaming about horses; German children traveling to other countries; American children setting their fantasies in local contexts; and South Korean children concerned about the environment.

What we are emphasizing, however, is that the prevalence of the aforementioned themes in the different countries cast them in a particular cultural light. Thus, we come full circle from our opening discussion of globalization and culture in concluding that, for our children, the local and the global meet in their everyday lives as well as in their make-believe worlds symbiotically, to create a desired world of fantasy and wishes. In the following portrait of Udi, we demonstrate this process in detail.

PORTRAIT OF UDI[1] (B, IS-1)

Udi (see Drawing 7.12) is an extraordinarily intelligent and sensitive 10-years-old boy with a rich and diverse inner world who is in fourth grade. His outstanding ability to create his own fantasyworld is reflected by his detailed drawings and descriptions. His mother is a special-education teacher and his father, a director of special education projects. He lives with his family, which includes four children (three boys and a girl) in a small peripheral town. His parents define themselves as Jewish nationalistic and lead an active religious life.

Drawing 7.12. Udi (B, IS-1) "Harry Potter."

[1]The interpretation of Udi's drawing and interview was assisted by Dr. Ruth Etienne Klemm.

The father describes Udi as very sensitive, shy, and introverted. During the research meeting, he was extremely quiet and reserved, perhaps even stressed and uncomfortable. During the guided imagination journey, he hid his head between his hands on his knees, and had a very hard time letting go of the make-believe world and returning to reality. During the drawing session, he hardly made contact with the other children and was deeply involved in his own picture. Upon completing his fully detailed drawing, he had a need to continue the process and asked for a second piece of paper, which he filled with more animals in the same spirit. Apparently, it was difficult for him to restrict himself and to control his many thoughts, ideas, and feelings. During the interview, he spoke very softly, to the point that it was very difficult to hear him. However, after a short warm-up exchange, he became very engaged in talking about his imaginary world and provided short, concise replies.

The father also described Udi as a very intelligent and knowledgeable child, very creative and imaginative, who demonstrates talents in both verbal (e.g., foreign-language learning, word games, expressive abilities, creative writing) and artistic forms (drawing and playing musical instruments). His favorite leisure activities, according to the father, include watching television programs (such as *Pokémon,* and videos such as *Mary Poppins* and Walt Disney animated movies); reading books (particularly the *Harry Potter* series); and playing computer soccer games. Mostly, according to Udi's father, he seems to be attracted to the world of fantasy and imagination—including magic, dreams, and the humanization of animals. Udi's make-believe world and interview, as we will shortly see, demonstrate these observations very clearly.

Udi's story takes place in *Harry Potter's* land as depicted in the book series. Udi calls his big daydream "Harry Potter," which guarantees that the source will not go unnoticed. At that time, the Harry Potter stories were only available in printed form and Udi admits to being an avid reader of the books. It is a type of springboard for his own imaginative mind, following his own needs, desires, talents, and interests.

> My land is called "Magicia." It is a country in the shape of a star that has magic in it. I drew a map of it on a separate page. In the picture there is a palace. The eagles, lion and tiger guard it. There are four princes in the palace, including my brothers and myself. I control the water, the ice, and the sky, the animals in the water like fish, the animals in the ice like penguins, and the animals in the sky like birds. The princess in the second tower from the left is the sister, she controls the sun, the fires, and the lava. She has her own volcano and she lives in it sometimes. The third brother controls the land, the sand, and the plants. He is holding the crown and the sword with the magic wand. The fourth brother in the fourth tower controls the air. All of us control the magicians, because all of us are princes, and our father and mother are the King and the Queen. There is another planet called "Evilina," where the dragons and witches who want to conquer the world live. They started by trying to conquer

Magicia, so they can control all of the magic … The prince is going to tell us what to do, using his special computer and the animals outside … there is also another planet, a television planet that has many countries, such as Pokémon country. We've got friends there who will help us during wartime.

At first glance, it is obvious from his drawing that Udi has borrowed many things from the setting of Hogwarts in the *Harry Potter* stories. For example, he draws some of the icons involved in the original adventures, such as an eagle and a sword. The purple is dominant, a color of central meaning to the magic world. Additionally, the drawing includes a detailed picture of a castle that resembles the Hogwarts School of Witchcraft as it appears on the back cover of the Hebrew edition of the first book in the series. It presents four towers representing the four Houses. In Udi's story, he and his three siblings work together to defend themselves, resembling the structure of the stories in J. K. Rowling's books. In Udi's fantasy-world, each child has unique powers and only working together guarantees defeat of the dark forces. Similar to the original, in Udi's story there is evidence of the threat to the world of magicians and witches (and ferocious dragons dissimilar to the original ones in the book) by those who want to control all the magic forces and to rule the world through use of the dark forces.

However, Udi's verbal story, as revealed in the interview, is an imaginative plot that embarks on its own path, one far removed from its original *Harry Potter* setting. The division of the houses follows a structure that is the same as the original storyline. In Rowling's story, the houses are occupied by many students. A single emblem symbolizes the house residents' characteristics. Slytherin students are cunning, ambitious, and so use any means to be successful. Their emblem shows a snake. The ones from Gryffindor, symbolized by a lion, are characterized by bravery and chivalry. Students living in Hufflepuff are loyal and true, their emblem showing a badger. In Ravenclaw, the house symbolized by the raven, the students have wit and a thirst for knowledge (for an analysis of the books, see Gupta, 2003).

In Udi's story, the houses are inhabited by him and his siblings. They are each characterized by different abilities. However, these are not personal characteristics, but rather unique magic powers that enable them to control nature. They rule the water, the ice, the skies, the animals, the sun, the fire, the earth, the sands, the plants, and so on. The siblings control everything and each one has his or her own specific sphere of control. They already have powers and do not have to learn them, as do the heroes and the heroine in the world of Harry Potter. Because they have such powers, Udi and his siblings are protected against attacks by the evil ones. They cannot be threatened seriously as it is the case in the original story.

The menace the three protagonists in the Rowling books have to deal with is Lord Voldemort. Further minor attacks are committed by their classmates,

Draco Malfoy and his two friends, Goyle and Crabbe, and by Draco's father, Lucius Malfoy. In addition to obvious provocation and discrimination, we can find some allusions referring to racism. After all, we can say that, to date, any trouble Harry encounters that threatens the magic world has been overcome and he is always able to save his siblings in the end (at least up to the fourth book that Udi was reading at the time). Every person involved in the action reported has been or is a student in Hogwarts. Thus, evil is embedded in the building, like the basilisk, hides within a magic diary that appears in the school toilet or slumbers in harmless-looking pets or in weird teachers.

However, in Udi's story, the basic setting is different because the siblings keep together to defeat attacks from another planet. In contrast, in Rowling's books, support is provided by adults like Dumbledore or Sirius Black as well as by magic creatures like dragons or a phoenix, as well as by magic objects, such as time clocks. In comparison, Udi employs support from outside, from an alien TV planet consisting of many countries, like, for example, the land of the *Pokémon*.

It becomes clear that although on the surface the borrowed setting may be equal to the original medium and the boy calls it by the same name, a closer look reveals significant differences. This illustrates that children may adopt, but also omit, many elements. They employ some basic structures, but others they picture differently from the original text.

Udi's interview includes many additional media references. Surprisingly, when asked about the origin of his story idea, he did not quote a *Harry Potter* narrative, but a computer game. Computer games have apparently had a very central role in his world of imagination:

Interviewer: *Tell, me, where did you get this idea, of this entire story?*
Udi: *When I was in 2ⁿᵈ grade, me and my friend played some computer game. It was about magic. So we decided then that we also want to be magicians and then, every time we had a break at school, we planned more and more things and then we developed this game and we played as if … we are magicians.*
Interviewer: *So you programmed a computer game?*
Udi: *No, we did it as an imagination game.*
Interviewer: *What do you mean you did it as an imagination game?*
Udi: *We imagined it out loud.*

As the interview unfolds, it becomes clear that Udi is referring to a role-playing game inspired by a computer game that he and his friend played during school breaks. Later in the summer, *"he left my school and then I made up other things alone and played them with my sister."* Following a long and detailed exchange regarding magical animals, the field researcher continued to ask:

Interviewer: *Tell me, all of this is from the computer game? Is it possible that you have seen this kind of story somewhere else? Or something similar to it?*

Udi: *It's not similar to the computer anymore, because we invented other things. But sometimes we are missing some ideas, so we make up new things from what we have.*

Interviewer: *For example?*

Udi: *For example, we turn our computer into a magic computer so it can help us solve all kinds of problems.*

Udi continues to explain that the computer can photograph their ideas and give instructions to the various animals on how to handle the evil forces. The computer is thus interwoven into Udi's make-believe world both as a specific game that inspired his interest in magic and as a communication device, as a "being," perhaps a kind of "robot" that completes action and participates in the adventures.

Later in the interview, when asked about his favorite books, Udi returns to *Harry Potter* and enriches our understanding of its role in his make-believe world:

Interviewer: *… and tell me, what kind of books do you like to read?*

Udi: *Harry Potter.*

Interviewer: *Harry Potter? Do you like Harry Potter?*

Udi: *Yes. Harry Potter helps us complete our game.*

Interviewer: *Harry Potter helps you complete the game?*

Udi: *Yes.*

Interviewer: *What in Harry Potter helps you complete the game?*

Udi: *The magic words.*

Interviewer: *The magic words?*

Udi: *Yes.*

Interviewer: *What kind of magic words, for example?*

Udi: *Lumes.*

Interviewer: *What does this word do?*

Udi: *It lights up the wand.*

Interviewer: *And then what?*

Udi: *It's like a flashlight that you can turn on and off as you wish, and it can be a strong or a weak light.*

Interviewer: *And what else did you take from Harry Potter? How else does it help you?*

Udi: *With their animals, the dragons.*

Interviewer: *Oh, they have dragons there?*

Udi: *They have all kinds of animals that they made up.*

Interviewer: *They made up?*

Udi:	*J. K. Rowling made it up.*
Interviewer:	*So … did you also get some of the ideas for the adventures from Harry Potter?*
Udi:	*Yes.*
Interviewer:	*For example?*
Udi:	*The battle against the dragon.*

Following this long exchange, Udi continues to tell about another favorite book of his, an original Hebrew book that describes a grandfather who is able to "fix" bad dreams and turn them into the positive. Knowing that "*J. K. Rowling made it up*" is a form of confirmation for him that other people too, have the ability to create fantasy-worlds and to cope with them, and they even become famous and recognized for these abilities.

Television, too, can be heavily traced in Udi's interview. As he explains, "*I take from it those [creatures] from the programs that I like.*" In his list of favorites are the *Pokémon* "*because they are cute,*" *Nils* (from the animated story of *Nils Holgerson*—the boy who flew around Sweden with a flock of geese) "*because it is also about magic, because he became tiny and was able to talk to animals,*" and *Digimon* "*because it is like Pokémon.*" Udi relates his great interest in fantasy and in particular, flying, and his collection of favorite videotapes of English-speaking fantasy movies (with Hebrew subtitles). These include *Mary Poppins, Chitty-Chitty Bang-Bang, My Dragon Friend Elliott,* and *Song of the South.*

Although heavily dominated by foreign popular texts, well known in many places, closer reading suggests that Udi's make-believe world provides us with a fascinating illustration of the smooth workings and reconciliation of the tension between global and local forces. As an Israeli child raised in a nationalistic, religious environment, Udi constructs an imaginary world within the general framework of a very marketable cultural phenomenon, set in the world of magic. The *Harry Potter* book series, although a global success, is clearly grounded in a specific British environment (including typical cultural icons such as the Underground, boarding schools, English names and manners, and the like). On the face of it, this cultural world might be very foreign to the typical Israeli child growing up in a small remote town who attends a Jewish religious school.

Within this *Harry Potter* framework, Udi's strong family attachments, too, come to life. He divides the major roles between himself and his three siblings: "*We are all princes. And our father and mother are the King and Queen,*" he explains in the interview. Both parents are at the top of the hierarchy, unchallenged. The only human drawn in the picture is one of Udi's brothers, who has a crown on his head and a sword in his hand. Udi himself is not drawn in the picture. When asked about it, he answers:

Interviewer: *And why are you not in the picture?*
Udi: *Because I haven't decided yet what I look like.*

Udi, so it seems, is still observing everything from the outside and is not able—or willing—to take a stand just yet. Perhaps at this point in time he wants to avoid the corresponding confrontation of opinions and values involved in such a move.

The centrality of the family, the loyalty of the family members to each other and to their joint "cause" of ruling the world and protecting their universe, conforming to family expectations, and the united front they present to all of the outside threats constitute a central underlying theme in the interview, as well as in Israeli society involved in a fight for its existence. Udi traverses from occasional mentions of the family in the make-believe world to the real world. For example, he makes an incidental comment about watching television together as a family on Saturday evening (a special evening for religious Jewish families, as they are not allowed to watch television during the Sabbath):

Udi: *It's a program that shows how they were able to use a computer to create things that look like dinosaurs ... it looks real.*
Interviewer: *And any other programs that you watch with your parents on Saturday evening?*
Udi: *Who Wants to be a Millionaire.*

In addition, Udi echoes parental discourse when he talks, for example, about the unsuitable nature of certain books for him. Following a long conversation about various books that Udi likes to read:

Interviewer: *And are there any books that you don't like?*
Udi: *... it's like programs. When I am told that the book is really not nice then I [don't read it].*
Interviewer: *When is a book not a nice book? Can you tell me what kind of books you are told are not nice books?*
Udi: *Yes.*
Interviewer: *For example?*
Udi: *For example, books that are inappropriate.*
Interviewer: *What kind of books are inappropriate for you?*
Udi: *With scary things. They are appropriate for children, but mostly for children that are 14 or 15 years old.*

The drawing and story of Udi can thus be best captured by the expression, "my home is my castle," with a special emphasis on finding a safe place for the family. Family values and rules are shared without challenging or scrutinizing them. The immediate family bond that is so evident in Udi's story has been well established as central to Jewish tradition in general and the Jewish–Israeli ethos in particular (see, e.g., Fogiel-Bijaoui, 2003). This strong solidarity within the family is probably also reinforced by the domestic conditions he lives in, because during times of crisis and life-threatening hardship, the mental need for a strong closeness within the family is much more urgent.

However, Udi's story also resonates a strong commitment to the wider "imagined community," to apply Anderson's (1987) term regarding the nation. Magicia, in Udi's story, is quite a mythological country, where control of all of nature's forces is divided among the four siblings. In his story, Udi then establishes an order by creating different spheres of competence that he allocates to himself and to his siblings. Interestingly, he gives his sister the power over the sun, the fire, and the lava—an intuitive attribution of female elements. This division of "labor" is reminiscent of the biblical story of Genesis, as well as stories that form Greek mythology, and is endowed with additional meaning in Udi's reference to his country as being "the capital" of all other countries. This clearly resonates the nationalistic "collective memory" of Jewish traditions that perceives Jerusalem to be the center of the world, the holiest of all cities.

One central theme that binds Israeli society in its self-perception and self-definition of identity boundaries is that of the "siege mentality." Israel's enduring conflict with Arab countries since its establishment, the hovering fear of another Holocaust, and the mental state of constant anxiety and suspicion, as well as the geographic isolation from the rest of the world due to the fact that it is surrounded by practically closed borders, all contribute to a national state of mind labeled as *siege mentality* (Bar-Tal, 1986; Bar-Tal & Antebi, 1992). This mentality is very deeply engraved in the consciousness of Israeli society and is characterized, first and foremost, by the conviction that most of the world has malicious intentions toward the country and thus cannot be trusted. This sociopsychological state of being (independent of a discussion of the real objective geopolitical situation, which is not the focus of concern here) reinforces a strong belief of distrust toward others, a need for self-reliance, and motivates a drive for internal integration against the rest of the world.

Udi demonstrates this siege mentality in narrating his make-believe story. He and his family live in Magicia, but the rest of the world is evil. There is much concern with "borders": setting the boundaries, drawing of borders, defending the borders, and protecting them, whether they are external earthy borders or the internal psychological ones. Udi needs to establish an order and define clear borders because, on one hand, his own inner images, fantasies, and fears may be threatening to overwhelm him and need to be controlled. On the other hand, the real circumstances of everyday life in Israel also pose a constant external threat. Therefore he creates a fantasy-world clearly defined by borders, with a special order and a clear-cut allocation of rights and duties, including support by the family and mutual assistance. His interview is loaded with the motif of "conquest," alerts for war, and the need to control the environment. There is the country of Evilina, where the witches and sorcerers reside, and there are other threats, such as dragons and robots. The forces of Evilina were able to conquer some of the family's territory, but not all of it, as Magicia remains intact. (While it might be farfetched to suggest the possible similarity to the history of Israel's geopolitical situation, this comes immediately to mind). Udi does not trust anyone except family members in the struggle against the evil forces. However, there is one exception as Udi puts it: *"There is also another planet, a television planet that has many countries, such as Pokémon country. We've got friends there that will help us in wartime."* Could that other country that has many states and whose residents are "our friends" be the United States of America? Possibly, since growing up in Israel entails a very strong awareness of the role and influence of the United States in Israeli politics and culture. Further, Israeli society is undergoing intense processes of Americanization, as well as a development of strong emotional ties to the United States as the "only friend we can trust" (see, e.g., Avraham & First, 2003).

Finally, there is an interesting local-linguistic angle to Udi's story. Following the linguistic rules of some word games in the original English story (which he read in its accurate translation into Hebrew), Udi creates his own word games in Hebrew. He invents the name of Kosmia (created from the Hebrew word *Kosem*, that is, magician, translated into English as Magicia, from the word "magician"), and Ra'utshka (created from the Hebrew word, *Ra*, that is, bad, translated into English as Evilina). Both words in Hebrew have a female suffix, as the words "country," "land," and "State" in Hebrew are all female (and thus we translated them into English using what sound like female names). Udi, we conclude, internalized Harry Potter's author, J. K. Rowling's word-games and adapted them to his native Hebrew language by making up his own word games.

Udi's make-believe world, so it seems, is representative of the hybrid nature of children's culture these days, as he interweaves his own local roots and collective beliefs with those coming from the outside world to create a world that is meaningful to him and that allows him to find his place and to express his needs, desires, and dreams in the most appealing way for him. Above all, Udi seems to be concerned with the issue of "power"—the power of magic, the power to control the world around him, the power to defend against outside aggressors, the division of power between friends and siblings. Within this context, he seems to be in search of his inner balance through his attempts to cope with both internal and external threats. His intelligence and his capabilities allow him to use his fantasy-world and particularly the power of magic. Being raised in Israeli society today, it is no surprise that he focuses on the issue of a "power-struggle" and a need to control the world, which in reality is quite chaotic and unpredictable.

IV

Conclusion

❧ 8 ❧

Conclusion:
Media and Children's
Make-Believe Worlds

Our journey through the make-believe worlds of 193 children in Germany, Israel, South Korea, and the United States is coming to an end. Through grounded analyses of their drawings, writings, and interviews, as well as adults' questionnaires, we have learned an enormous amount about the worlds they dream about and the places they envision for themselves in these worlds. The study revealed that regardless of children's country of origin, overall, worlds of either *harmony and peace* for girls, *worlds of conflict and threat* as well as *amusement* for boys, are the major contexts for their fantasies. In addition to these, a number of other world types, including *worlds of foreign lands, supernatural, travel, sensual pleasure, royalty* and *technology* were identified as typical locations for some children's make-believe worlds.

It became evident, via the analysis, that children build upon a wealth of information gathered from a wide range of sources, including their own personal experience and mediated sources, and freely interweave them to create rich fantasy backdrops for playing out their wishes to act. They wish for acts that are self-empowering: to experience feelings of well-being and thrill; to bond with others; to protect and be protected; to demonstrate their own specialness and independence. The opportunity to fantasize is used also to connect to their everyday lives: to play out their special interests; to elaborate on stories related to

197

them by significant others; to expand on their own positive real-life experiences, and to correct negative ones.

The roles the media have in these make-believe worlds have been the main focus of this study, and the results present compelling evidence of the centrality of diverse media in children's fantasies, particularly the audiovisual ones (television, videos, films, computer), especially for boys. The type of media traces found, their degree of integration into the make-believe worlds, and their centrality, range from very "thick" ones, which would include adoption of media settings, characters, and plotlines, to "thin" traces, in which a media reference was found, but was of peripheral importance to the overall nature of the story.

A few cases—in particular those created by boys, and more so in the U.S. sample—stay closer to the original text in their make-believe worlds. These fantasies seem to be a reenactment of the kind of action-hero media script that is designed to engage boys at the deep level of their wishes to have power, be strong, and overcome adversity. Through a market that saturates their media and play environments, these scripts are repeatedly reenacted. This raises the question of whether such media texts inhibit children's imagination, so that there is less originality and more imitation in the fantasy. According to our study, this is the exception rather than the rule, but one that deserves further consideration.

Our data suggest that, perhaps, the more time children have to dwell upon their own interpretation, the more they move away from the original media content. For example, those children whose make-believe worlds were developed over an extended period of time, and were returned to repeatedly, showed great diversity from the original media story that inspired them. Make-believe worlds that were "thick" with media traces belonged mainly to boys, who seemed to be inventing them through the course of the interview and had neither the time nor the opportunity beforehand to develop them in their more unique and original ways. However, in a few cases mostly involving *Pokémon*-related fantasies, we found "thick" media traces and make-believe worlds that have been evolving over time. This is much in line with the analysis of a cultural phenomenon such as *Pokémon* as a complete multimedia environment.

Contrary to popular belief, children make sophisticated use of these mediated worlds. They mix and match settings and specific objects within them in ways that facilitate their own fantasy-worlds and allow them to best experience their wishes to act in these worlds. They highlight and expand on those aspects of the original media worlds that are particularly attractive to them and adapt or erase those that hinder or are not relevant to the wished for experience. One might say they play the role of editor, as they formulate their own stories, using original elements of their own creation and dipping into the files of mediated materials as needed for the finished product. In some instances, a media setting serves as a springboard for a child's fantasy-world, providing space for his or her own drama to evolve.

Children used media characters in their fantasies, but rarely adopted them completely. They felt free to make changes in the characters to suit their own needs. They imagined themselves in these characters' shoes and/or used the most attractive traits and behaviors of the original media characters, ignoring or simply omitting nonrelevant or contradictory parts of the characters' personalities. More often, however, they conducted imaginary relationships with characters in which case the original media depiction is retained. This kind of integration of a media character leaves more space for emergence of their own wishes to act. Interestingly, even when the media characters' personalities are changed, they are still easily identified in the drawing as they look very much like the original, providing children's fantasies with a concrete structure, shape, and form. As a result, the range of "ideal" appearances of friends and self are limited.

In adopting the media plotlines to fit their make-believe worlds, children seem to break down the original narrative sequences into fragments that are central to their wishes to act. Often they choose those scenes that occupy a central role in the original story such as the exposition sequence at the beginning of the story or a dramatic peak of the plot. They also make use of various kinds of information acquired from different sources. For example, from documentaries, they might incorporate exciting locations and reuse them in their fantasies to try to resolve real-life problems of the human and natural world. This finding suggests that even children as young as age 8 to age 10 may want to be engaged in real-world issues and have a need for diverse media offerings in a variety of genres that go beyond the common fiction narratives of "perfect worlds and happy endings."

Thus, overall, according to our study, the media do play a central role in children's make-believe worlds. The in-depth analysis suggests that media elements come into play in ways that are used mainly to help children symbolize their own experiences and self-image and as a springboard for their own narration of a world that allows them a personal space for developing who they wish to be. Media reception processes of appropriation of the content are integrated within inner pictures that are interpreted, reflected upon, molded, saved in individualized ways, and used to form connections between the original content and the child's own imaginary world. Thus, the child negotiates the meaning between the external media content and his or her own inner world. Visual media, so it seems, participate in this process in a more powerful manner, thus leaving stronger imprints on children's fantasies.

We are clearly aware that there is a lot more to children's incorporations of media's symbolic material in their make-believe worlds than we were able to ascertain. We probably were not able to identify all media traces available let alone understand them. We realized, by returning to the empirical cases again and again, that we were able to attain new depths of understanding with each additional analysis. We have learned that even when children only adopt a tiny incidental detail from a television program, a book, or a computer game, this detail may be laden with symbolic meaning that is lasting and significant. We are also aware that our methodology has its own limitations. For one, the research situation, although less restrictive then experimental settings, was still a rather structured one, more akin to an informal classroom situation than to children's private leisure environments. We hope that further investigations will be helpful in overcoming some of these issues.

Central to our study were issues of diversity, in particular with respect to gender construction and cultural forces. In regard to gender, our study supports the accumulating body of knowledge that demonstrates that preadolescent boys and girls live in very different cultural worlds. Traditional gender roles are still very much ingrained in their perceptions of themselves. Boys, armed with a host of accessories, seem to be seeking the thrills involved in action and overcoming dangers and conflicts, whereas girls imagine worlds of harmony with people and nature that result in general feelings of positive well-being. As a rule, boys and girls also tend to exclude each other in their make-believe worlds, preferring a unisex world, free from countergender perspectives. The exception to this was the incorporation of immediate family members of the other gender, and a few boys who included girls in their make-believe story as the cause for the plot (e.g., a princess to be saved).

The genders differ in the ways they integrate the media in their stories. Boys are much more media-centered than girls and imagine themselves as media characters, often as heroes that advance the narrative. The media offer them plenty of symbolic material for this type of fantasy. Girls, on the other hand, have a limited range of favorable female role models, who are mainly traditional and sexualized. We found that, perhaps as a result, girls in our study seemed to invest much more energy than boys in altering the original media content to meet their needs and to reinterpret their positions in their make-believe worlds. Thus, they move away from the original plot and seem to take only fragments or moments out of the narratives and reinterpret them to express their diverse inner wishes. Perhaps girls' general position in society, as well as media offerings that restrict their worlds of possibilities, drive them to work harder at finding creative outlets for themselves. Boys' role models are restricted in a different way; their desire to be engaged in action is often unnecessarily conflated in the media images linked to aggression, therby limiting the scope of the roles they can take upon themselves.

Although these are the main findings, we had many exceptions and variations that break traditional gender roles and gendered expectations, helping to
highlight the complexity of the issues involved.

Finally, we also found that the children in our study integrate global cultural
forces with their unique local cultural world to create a meaningful and relevant
world for themselves. In these hybrid worlds, different emphases are placed on
local issues that are deeply embedded in the culture in which they are growing
up and are perceived as natural and taken for granted. Accordingly, it seems
that children appropriate and integrate media content and forms that are relevant to their special concerns. In Germany, for example, we found evidence of
input from television documentaries regarding environmental concerns.
Avoiding conflict on one hand, while developing strong emotional attachments
to fiction books and telenovelas, on the other hand, were more pronounced in
Israel. South Korean children, who are struggling with social pressures and high
expectations, seemed to find a greater interest in computers and use Internet
characters in their make-believe worlds. Perhaps the high value attached to
new technologies in their society encourages them to channel their interests
into this medium. In the United States, we found that blockbuster movies, both
in their theater runs and later when released in video, brought great affinity, and
became very important to children's culture, which seems to be typified by
strong individualization.

We also found common coping mechanisms that children adopted in their
make-believe worlds for handling these themes; they either confront the issue
by trying to repair or solve it (as in the case of German children and environmental concerns) or repress and avoid it (as in the case of South Korean children and academic pressure). They are aware of the world around them and
view other countries as an open space in which to enjoy unique experiences of
their imagination. Here, too, we see the influence of media on their conceptions
of "exotic" others—both people and places.

These findings attest to the complexity of the concept of *glocalization* being advocated currently in the discourse of globalization processes. The dynamics of this
process include the negotiation of the global with the local, either within the texts
themselves and/or within the meaning-making audience. However, many of the
parameters of this process are yet to be sorted out. What, if any, are the particular
aspects of the global on one hand, and the local on the other, that take over the
individual person's reception of a text? Can we formalize specific notions of how
this process is formulated, or does each case operate individually in
nonpredictable ways? In our study, for example, we found that the format or appearance of many of the make-believe worlds could be traced to global popular
media texts (like the appearance of the characters and settings), whereas the indi-

vidual contents that fill these worlds were often local and personal in nature. Children, so it seems, integrate global media texts to represent experiences, self-image, and personal narrations that are central to their lives. Children's habitualized consumption of global media texts is a form of institutionalization in Berger and Luckmann's (1966) sense of the way things "look": What are normal, appropriate physical appearances?; what should friends look like?; how do "others" look?; how do the wishful worlds look?; what is an exciting story?; what is a "good" thing to do?; and so forth. Institutionalization can thus be examined on the personal level, as we find that the global media are highly influential even when they are individually appropriated.

However, our study suggests that perhaps not all local issues can get a global look, as media texts do not provide outlets for the variety of issues facing children around the world. For example, we could not find media traces in several of the Korean cases for those children dealing with the heavy social pressure of their culture. It is possible that the media do not supply enough relevant symbolic material for this kind of issue in their make-believe worlds. Accordingly, this can also help to explain the relatively flat discussion of the local in the U.S. sample, as the gap between what is perceived as global and local is the narrowest of the four nations. Perhaps this is also why we found more media traces in the U.S. sample—because the global is much more readily available for children to represent their world. Interestingly enough, however, more than anything else, what dominated the content of the make-believe worlds of the children who participated in this study were universal human themes of harmony, relationships, wish to overcome conflict, and search for excitement and fun.

Our encounters with the children included many moments of empowerment: Children placed themselves in their make-believe worlds and in their research situation in positions of strength, expressing their wishes and unique identities. The sincere adult interest and positive reinforcement that was built into the research procedure seemed particularly valuable for them and attests to the need children may have for opportunities to share their inner worlds with compassionate and positive adults.

So does "television kill the imagination"? Our study would certainly not support such a populist argument. Our findings suggest that the media are another resource in children's environments that they use in creating worlds of fantasy. The diversity we found is related, among other things, to gender, to the media offerings and roles in their particular cultures, but also to the opportunities children have to develop their make-believe worlds outside the research situation.

What does all this mean for academics, parents, educators, and producers of media material for children and other caring adults? More than anything else, it probably means that the role media have for children should be taken very seriously and responsibly. In particular, parents and educators should make efforts to give children the space needed to develop and expand their own fantasy-worlds, in accordance with their individual needs, and to provide opportunities to express these mental and emotional processes in verbal and artistic forms. This may be of particular importance to boys who, overall, encounter more difficulties in our societies in expressing their inner worlds and who are often negatively sanctioned for imitating aggressive behavior stimulated by media. Producers have a responsibility to offer children texts and characters that open up possibilities for experimenting with a wide range of roles and plots that are not constrained by gender, race, and other common stereotypes, and that are characterized by diverse interests and issues of concern for children. As we have seen, there is a lot more to children's inner worlds than a superficial attraction to action based on aggressive conflict. And academics, such as ourselves, have the exciting task of continuing to study the multifaceted relationships of children and their favorite media worlds as they come together in the world of children's imaginations.

References

Aidman, A. (1995, December). Advertising in the schools. *Eric Digest* (EDO-PS-95-12).

Aidman, A. (1999). Disney's Pocahontas: Conversations with Native American and Euro-American Girls. In S. Mazzarella & N. Pecora (Eds.), *Growing up girls: Popular culture and the construction of identity* (pp. 133–158). New York: Peter Lang Publishing.

Allison, A. (2004). Cuteness as Japan's millennial product. In J. Tobin (Ed.), *Pikachu's global adventure: The rise and fall of Pokémon* (pp. 34–49). Durham, NC: Duke University.

Anderson, B. (1987). *Imagined communities.* London: Verso.

Anderson, C., & Collins, P. (1988). *The impact on children's education: Television's influence on cognitive development* (Office of Research Working Paper No. 2). Washington, DC: U.S. Office of Education, Office of Educational Research and Improvement.

Aries, P. (1962). *Centuries of childhood: A social history of family life.* New York: A. A. Knopf.

Atkin, D. J., Greenberg, B. S., & Baldwin, T. F. (1991). The home ecology of children's television viewing: Parental mediation and the new video environment. *Journal of Communication, 41*(3), 40–52.

Avraham, E., & First, A. (2003). "I buy American": The American image as reflected in Israeli advertising. *Journal of Communication 53*(2), 282–299.

Bachmair, B. (1984). *Symbolischer verarbeitung von fernseherlebnissen in assoziativen freiräumen: Fernsehspurn im handeln von kindern* [Symbolic meaning making of television experiences in associative spaces: Television traces in the acting of children.] Kassel: Gesamthochschule. Opladen: Westdeutscher Verlag.

Bachmair, B. (1993). Tiefenstrukturen entdecken—medienanalyse und Massenkommunikation [Deep structure—media analysis and mass communication]. In: W. Holly, & U. Püschel, (Eds.), *Medienrezeption als aneignung* [Media reception as appropriation] (pp. 43–57). Opladen: Westdeutscher Verlag.

Bachmair, B. (1996). *Fernsehkultur—subjektivität in einer welt bewegter bilder* [Television culture—subjectivity in a world of moving pictures]. Opladen: Westdeutscher Verlag.

Barber, B. R. (1995). *Jihad vs. McWorld: How globalism and tribalism are reshaping the world.* New York: Random House.

Barron, F. (1969). *Creative person and creative process.* New York: Holt, Rinehart & Winston.

Bar-Tal, D. (1986). The Massada Syndrome: A case of central belief. In N. A. Milgram (Ed.), *Stress and coping in time of war: Generalizations from the Israeli experience* (pp. 32–51). New York: Brunner/Mazel.

Bar-Tal, D., & Antebi, D. (1992). Siege mentality in Israel. *International Journal of Intercultural Relations, 16,* 251–275.

Baumgardt, U. (1985). *Kinderzeichnungen: Spiegel der Seele* [Children's drawings: Mirrors of the soul]. Zürich: Kreuz-Verl. (Original work published 1969).

Benjamin, J. (1990). *Die Fesseln der Liebe—Psychoanalyse, Feminismus und das Problem der Macht* [The bonds of love—Psychoanalysis, feminism and the problem of power] Basel: Stroemfeld/Roter Stern.

Berger, P. L., & Luckmann, T. (1966). *The social construction of reality.* New York: Anchor Books.

Bettelheim, B. (1976). *The uses of enchantment.* London: Thames & Hudson.

Bianculli, D. (1992). *Teleliteracy: Taking television seriously.* New York: Continuum.

Bloch, L.-R., & Lemish, D. (2003). The megaphone effect: The international diffusion of culture via the USA. In P. Kalbfleisch (Ed.), *Communication Yearbook 27* (pp. 159–190). Mahwah, NJ: Lawrence Erlbaum Associates.

Blumer, H. (1964). What is wrong with social theory. *American Sociological Review 19,* 3–10.

Brann, E. T. H. (1991). *The world of the imagination: Sum and substance.* Savage, MD: Rowman & Littlefield.

Brown, L. M. (1998). *Raising their voices.* Cambridge, MA: Harvard University Press.

Brown, L. M., & Gilligan, C. (1992). *Meeting at the crossroads.* Cambridge, MA: Harvard University Press.

Buckingham, D. (1993a). *Children talking television: The making of television literacy.* London: Falmer Press.

Buckingham, D. (Ed.).(1993b). *Reading audiences: Young people and the media.* Manchester, England: Manchester University Press.

Buckingham, D. (1996). *Moving images: Understanding children's emotional responses to television.* Manchester, England: Manchester University Press.

Buckingham, D. (2000). *After the death of childhood: Growing up in the media age.* London: Polity.

Buckingham, D., & Bragg, S. (2004). *Young people, sex and the media: The facts of life?* New York: Palgrave Macmillan.

Carter, C., & Steiner, L. (2004). *Critical readings: Media and gender.* Maidenhead, England: Open University Press.

Caspi, D., & Limor, Y. (1999). *The in/outsiders: Mass media in Israel.* Cresskill, NJ: Hampton Press.

Central Committee of Zoological Companies. (2002). Zahlen zur Heimtierhaltung in Deutschland und Europa [Figures on pets in Germany and Europe]. Available at www.zzf.de/presse/03htp04d.html

Chandler, D. (1997). Children's understanding of what is 'real' on television: A review of the literature. *Journal of Educational Media, 22*(1), 65–80.

Chislom, L. (1995). European youth research: Tour de Force or Turmbau zu Babel? In L. Chislom, P. Buchner, H. H. Kruger, & M. Bois-Reymond (Eds.), *Growing up in Europe: Contemporary horizons in childhood and youth studies* (pp. 21–32). Berlin: Walter de Gruyter.

Chodorow, N. (1974). Family structure and feminine personality. In M. Z. Rosaldo & S. Lamphere (Eds.), *Women, culture and society* (pp. 43–66). Stanford, CA: Stanford University Press.

Chodorow, N. (1981). Oedipal asymmetries and heterosexual knots. In S. Cox (Ed.), *Female psychology: The emerging self* (pp. 228–247). New York: St. Martin's Press.

Christian-Smith, L. K. (1990). *Becoming a woman through romance.* New York: Routledge.

Cockburn, C. (1992). The circuit of technology: Gender, identity and power. In R. Silverstone & H. Hirsch (Eds.), *Consuming technologies: Media and information in domestic spaces* (pp. 32–37). London: Routledge.

Cohen, D., & MacKeith, S. A. (1991). *The development of imagination: The private worlds of childhood*. London: Routledge.

Cox, M. V. (1993). *Children's drawings of the human figure*. Hillsdale, NJ: Lawrence Erlbaum Associates.

Craig, S. (Ed.). (1992). *Men, masculinity, and the media*. Newbury Park, CA: Sage.

De Beauvoir, S. (1952). *The second sex*. New York: Knopf.

De Loache, J., & Gottleib, A. (2000). If Dr. Spock were born in Bali. In J. DeLoache & A. Gottlieb, (Eds.), *A world of babies: Imagined childcare guides for seven societies*. Cambridge, England: Cambridge University Press.

Dorr, A. (1983). No shortcuts to judging reality. In J. Bryant and D. R. Anderson (Eds.), *Children's understanding of television: Research on attention and comprehension* (pp. 190–220). New York: Academic Press.

Drotner, K. (1992). Modernity and moral panics. In M. Skovmand & K. C. Schroeder (Eds.), *Media cultures: Reappraising transnational media*. London: Routledge.

Drotner, K. (1999). Netsurfers and game navigators: New media and youthful leisure cultures in Denmark. *Reseaux: French Sociology Review, 7*(1), 83–108.

Drotner, K. (2001). Global media through youthful eyes. In S. Livingstone & M. Bovill (Eds.), *Children and their changing media environment: A European comparative study* (pp. 283–305). Mahwah, NJ: Lawrence Erlbaum Associates.

Durham, M. G. (1998). Dilemmas of desire: Representations of adolescent sexuality in two teen magazines. *Youth and Society, 29*, 369–389.

Dyson, A. H. (1997). *Writing superheroes: Contemporary childhood, popular culture, and classroom literacy*. New York: Teachers College.

Etienne-Klemm, R. (2003a). *Die Kraft der inneren Bilder. Entstehung, Ausdruck und therapeutisches Potential* [The power of imagination: Development, expression and therapeutical potential]. Basel, Switzerland: Schwabe.

Etienne-Klemm, R. (2003b). The formation of inner pictures—an overview. *TelevIZIon, 16*, 6–10.

Fein, G. G. (1981). Pretend play in childhood: An integrative review. *Child Development 52*, 1095–1118.

Feshbach, S. (1955). The drive-reducing function of fantasy behavior. *Journal of Abnormal and Social Psychology, 50*, 3–11.

Fish, S. (1980). *Is there a text in this class?: The authority of interpretative communities*. Cambridge, MA: Harvard University Press.

Fisherkeller, J. (2002). *Growing up with television: Everyday learning among young adolescents*. Philadelphia: Temple University Press.

Fitch, M., Huston, A. C., & Wright, J. C. (1993). From television forms to genre schemata: Children's perceptions of television reality. In G. L. Berry & J. K. Asamen (Eds.), *Children & television: Images in a changing socio-cultural world* (pp. 38–52). Newbury Park, CA: Sage Publications.

Fogiel-Bijaoui, S. (2003). Familism, post-modernity and the State. In H. Naveh (Ed.), *Israeli family and community: Women's time* (pp. 38–62). London: Vallentine Mitchell.

Fornäs, J., & Bolin, G. (Eds.). (1995). *Youth culture in late modernity*. London: Routledge.

Fraiberg, S. H. (1959). *The magic years: Understanding and handling the problems of early childhood*. New York: C. Scribner's Sons.

Freud, S. (1995). Creative writers and day-dreaming. In E. Spector Person, P. Fongy, & S. A. Figueira (Eds.), *On Freud's "creative writers and day-dreaming"* (pp. 3–13, 143–153). New Haven: Yale University Press. (Original work published 1908)

Freud, S. (1958). *On creativity and the unconscious: Paper on the psychology of art, literature, love, religion.* New York: Harper & Row.

Gilligan, C. (1982). *In a different voice: Psychological theory and women's development.* Cambridge: Harvard University Press.

Glaser, B. G., & Strauss, A. L. (1967). *The discovery of grounded theory: Strategies for qualitative research.* Chicago: Aldine.

Golomb, C. (1992). *The child's creating of pictorial world.* Berkley, CA: University of California Press.

Götz, M. (1999). *Mädchen und Fernsehen. Facetten der Medienaneignung in der weiblichen Adoleszenz* [Girls and Television. Facets of media appropriation in female adolescence]. München: KoPäd.

Götz, M. (Ed.). (2002). *Alles Seifenblasen? Die Bedeutung von Daily Soaps im Alltag von Kindern und Jugendlichen* [Only soap bubbles? The significance of daily soaps for the everday life of children and adolescents]. München: KoPäd.

Götz, M. (2003). Fantasies of fighting and fighters. *TelevIZIon, 16,* 18–22.

Greenfield, P., & Beagles-Roos, J. (1988). Radio vs. television: Their cognitive impact on children of different socio-economic and ethnic groups. *Journal of Communication, 38(2),* 71–72.

Greenfield, P., Farrer, D., & Beagles-Roos, J. (1986). Is the medium the message? An experimental comparison of the effects of radio and television on imagination. *Journal of Applied Developmental Psychology, 7(4),* 237–255.

Greening, T. (Ed.). (1984). *American political humanistic psychology.* San Francisco, CA: Saybrook Publications.

Gunter, B., & McAleer, J. (1997). *Children & television.* Routledge: London.

Gupta, S. (2003). *Re-reading Harry Potter.* New York: Palgrave Macmillan.

Hanke, R. (1998). Theorizing masculinity with/in the media. *Communication Theory, 8,* 193–203.

Hawkins, R. (1977). The dimensional structure of children's perceptions of TV reality. *Communication Research, 4(3),* 299–320.

Herzog, H., & Ben Rafael, E. (2001) *Language and communication in Israel.* New Brunswick, NJ: Transaction Publishers.

Himmelweit, H. T., Oppenheim, A. N., & Vince, P. (1958). *Television and the child.* London: Oxford University Press.

Hipfel, B. (1997). Inszenienierungen des begerherns: Zur rolle der phantasien im umgang mit medien [Staging desires: The role of fantasies in exposure to media]. In A. Hepp & R. Winter (Eds.), *Kultur-medien-macht* [Culture-media-power] (pp. 143–159). Opladen: Westdeutscher Verlag.

Hodge, B., & Tripp, D. (1986). *Children and television: A semiotic analysis.* Cambridge, MA: Polity Press.

Hoffner, C. (1996). Children's wishful identification and para-social interaction with favorite television characters. *Journal of Broadcasting and Electronic Media, 40,* 289–402.

Hoffner, C., & Cantor, J. (1991). Perceiving and responding to mass media characters. In J. Bryant & D. Zillman (Eds.), *Responding to the screen: Reception and reaction processes* (pp. 63–101). Hillsdale, NJ: Lawrence Erlbaum Associates.

Horn, R., & Horn, W. (1997). *Einmal himmel und zurück: 13 Phantasiereisen für kinder im alter von 4-11 jahre* [Once to heaven and back: 13 fantasy flights of children between the ages of 4-11 years]. Lippstadt: Kontakte-Musikverlag.

Horton, D., & Wohl, R. R. (1956). Mass communication and para-social interaction: Observations on intimacy at a distance. *Psychiatry, 3,* 215–229.

Huesmann, L. R., & Eron, L. D. (Eds.). (1986). *Television and the aggressive child: A cross-national comparison.* Hillsdale, NJ: Lawrence Erlbaum Associates.

Huston, A. C., Donnerstein, E., Fairchild, H., Feshback, N. D., Katz, P. A., Murray, J. P., Rubinstein, E. A., Wilcox, B. L., & Zuckerman, D. (1992). *Big world, small screen: The role of television in American society.* Lincoln, NE: University of Nebraska Press.

Information Culture Center of Korea. (2000). Available at www.icc.pr.kr (in Korean).

James, A., Jenks, C., & Prout, A. (1998). *Theorizing childhood.* Cambridge: Polity.

James, A., & Prout, A. (Eds.). (1990). *Constructing and reconstructing childhood: Contemporary issues in the sociological study of childhood.* London: Falmer Press.

Jenks, C. (1996). *Childhood.* London: Routledge.

Jones, G. (2002). *Killing monsters: Why children need fantasy, superheroes, and make-believe violence.* New York: Basic Books.

Jones, G. (2003). Battle-Zord Nu-Nu meets Power Ranger Po. *TelevIZIon, 16,* 15–17.

Katsumo, H., & Maret, J. (2004). Localizing the Pokémon TV series for the American market. In J. Tobin (Ed.), *Pikachu's global adventure: The rise and fall of Pokémon* (pp. 80–107). Durham, NC: Duke University.

Kästner, E. (1970). *The 35th of May.* Berlin: Dressler Verlag.

Kinder, M. (Ed.). (1999). *Kids' media culture.* Durham, NC: Duke University Press.

Kline, S. (1993). *Out of the garden: Toys and children's culture in the age of TV marketing.* London: Verso.

Klinger, E. (1971). *Structure and functions of fantasy.* New York: Wiley-Interscience.

Kohn, M. L. (1989). *Cross-national research in sociology.* Newbury Park, CA: Sage.

Korea Education Development Institute. (2002). Available at www.kedi.re.kr (in Korean).

Korea Network Information Center (2002). Available at www.nic.or.kr (in Korean).

Korzenny, F., & Ting-Toomey, S. (Eds.). (1992). *Mass media effects across cultures.* Newbury Park, CA: Sage.

Lealand, G., & Zanker, R. (2003). *You'd have to change the world. Children and media in New Zealand in the new millennium.* Available at http://www.netsafe.org.nz/downloads/conference/netsafepaperslealndzankermillennium.pdf

Lemish, D. (1997a). Kindergartners' understandings of television: A cross cultural comparison. *Communication Studies, 48*(2), 109–126.

Lemish, D. (1997b). The school as a wrestling arena: The modeling of a television series. *Communication: European Journal of Communication Research, 22*(4), 395–418.

Lemish, D. (1998). Spice Girls' talk: A case study in the development of gendered identity. In S. A. Inness (Ed.), *Millennium girls: Today's girls around the world* (pp. 145–167). New York: Rowman & Littlefield.

Lemish, D. (2002). Between here and there: Israeli children living cultural globalization. In C. V. Feilitzen & U. Carlsson (Eds.), *Children, young people and media globalisation* (pp. 125–134). Göteborg: Nordicom, Göteborg University.

Lemish, D., & Barzel, I. (2000). 'Four mothers': The womb in the public sphere. *European Journal of Communication, 15*(2), 147–169.

Lemish, D., & Bloch, L.-R. (2004). *Pokémon in Israel.* In J. Tobin (Ed.), *Pikachu's global adventure: Making sense of the rise and fall of Pokémon* (pp. 165–186). Durham, NC: Duke University Press.

Lemish, D., & Cohen, A. A. (in press). Tell me about your mobile and I'll tell you who you are: Israelis talk about themselves. In R. Ling (Ed.), *Mobile communications: Re-negotiation of the public sphere.* London: Springer-Verlag.

Lemish, D., Drotner, K., Liebes, T., Maigret, E., & Stald, G. (1998). Global culture in practice: A look at children and adolescents in Denmark, France and Israel. *European Journal of Communication, 13*(4), 539–556.

Lemish, D., Liebes, T., & Seidmann, V. (2001). Gendered media meanings and uses. In S. Livingstone & M. Bovill (Eds.), *Children and their changing media environment: A European comparative study* (pp. 263–282). Mahwah, NJ: Lawrence Erlbaum Associates.

Liebes, T. (2003). *American dreams, Hebrew subtitles: Globalization from the receiving end.* Cresskill, NJ: Hampton Press.

Liebes, T., & Katz, E. (1990). *The export of meaning.* New York: Oxford University Press.

Lindlof, T. R., & Taylor, B. C. (2002). *Qualitative communication research methods.* Thousand Oaks, CA: Sage Publications.

Livingstone, S. (2002). *Young people and new media: Childhood and the changing media environment.* London: Sage Publications.

Livingstone, S. (2003). On the challenges of cross-national comparative media research. *European Journal of Communication, 18*(4), 477–500.

Livingstone, S., & Bovill, M. (Eds.). (2001). *Children and their changing media environment: A European comparative study.* Mahwah, NJ: Lawrence Erlbaum Associates.

MacBeth, T. M. (Ed.). (1996). *Tuning in to young viewers: Social science perspectives on television.* Thousand Oaks, CA: Sage Publications.

Machover, K. (1949). *Personality projection in the drawing of the human figure.* Springfield, IL: Thomas.

Maeda, M. (2000). The effect of a video produced by young African people on perceptions of Japanese pupils about Africa. *Journal of Educational Media, 25*(2), 87–106.

Mander, J. (1978). *Four arguments for the elimination of television.* New York: Quill.

Mazzarella, S. R. (1999). The 'Superbowl of all dates': Teenage girl magazines and the commodification of the perfect prom. In S. R. Mazzarella & N. O. Pecora (Eds.), *Growing up girls: Popular culture and the construction of identity* (pp. 97–112). New York: Peter Lang.

Mazzarella, S. R., & Pecora, N. O. (Eds.). (1999). *Growing up girls: Popular culture and the construction of identity.* New York: Peter Lang.

McNeal, J. U. (1999). *The kids market: Myths and realties.* New York: Paramount Market Publishing.

McRobbie, A. (1993). Shut up and dance: Youth culture and changing modes of femininity. *Cultural Studies, 7,* 406–426.

Messenger Davies, M. (1989). *Television is good for your kids.* London: Hilary Shipman.

Messenger Davies, M. (1997). *Form, fake and fantasy.* Hillsdale, NJ: Lawrence Erlbaum Associates.

Meyers, M. (Ed.). (1999). *Mediated women.* Cresskill, NJ: Hampton Press.

Montasser, A., Cole, C. F., & Fuld, J. (2002). The tower in red and yellow: Using children's drawings in formative research for *Alm Simsim,* an educational television series for Egyptian children. *Early Education and Development, 13*(4), 395–408.

Neuman, S. B. (1991). *Literacy in the television age.* Norwood, NJ: Ablex.

Neuss, N. (1999). Batman, Michael Jordan und, the different Mexico: Wesen und Bedeutung von Phantasiegefährten und Phantasieländern [Batman, Michael Jordon, and the different Mexico: Nature and the importance of imaginary companions and fantasylands]. In N. Neuß. (Ed.), *Ästhetik der Kinder—Interdisziplinäre Beiträge zur ästhetischen Erfahrung von Kindern* [The aesthetics of children—interdisciplinary contribution to the aesthetic experience of children] (pp. 47–62). Frankfurt a.M.: Beiträge zur Medienpädagogik.

Neuss, N. (in press). Understanding children's drawings—structural moments in an international comparison. In M. Götz, (Ed.), *Mit Laserschwert und Sissikleid: Kinderfantasien und Fernsehen* [With a laser sword and a Sissi costume: Children's fantasies and television]. Munich: KoPäd.

Peirce, K. (1990). A feminist theoretical perspective on the socialization of teenage girls through *Seventeen* magazine. *Sex Roles, 23,* 491–500.

Piaget, J. (1951). *Play, dreams and imitation in childhood.* London: Routledge.

Piaget, J. (1969). *The origins of intelligence in the child.* New York: International University Press.

Piaget, J., & Inhelder, B. (1969). *The psychology of the child.* New York: Basic Books.

Pipher, M. (1995). *Reviving Ophelia*. New York: Ballantine.

Pollack, W. (1998). *Real boys: Rescuing our sons from the myths of boyhood*. New York: Henry Holt & Co.

Potter, J. W. (2001). *Media literacy* (2nd ed.). Thousand Oaks, CA: Sage.

Price, M. E., & Verhulst, S. G. (Eds.). (2002). *Parental control of television broadcasting*. Mahwah, NJ: Lawrence Erlbaum Associates.

Pruyser, P. W. (1983). *The play of the imagination: Toward a psychoanalysis of culture*. New York: International Universities Press.

Radway J. (1984). *Reading the romance: Women, patriarchy and popular literature*. London: Verso.

Ränsch-Trill, B. (1996). *Faszination und entsetzen: Die kunst und das böse* [Fascination and anxiety: Art and bad things]. Braunschweig, Germany: Technical University.

Raviv, A., Bar-Tal, D., Raviv, A., & Ben-Horin, A. (1996). Adolescent idolization of pop singers: Causes, expressions, and reliance. *Journal of Youth and Adolescence, 25*(5), 631–750.

Reeves, B. (1979). Children's understanding of television people. In E. Wartella (Ed.), *Children communicating: Media and development of thought, speech, understanding* (pp. 115–155). Beverly Hills, CA: Sage.

Renckstorf, K. (1996). Media use as social action: A theoretical perspective. In K. Renckstorf, D. McQuail, & N. Jankowski (Eds.), *Media use as social action. A European approach to audience studies* (pp. 18–31). London: Libbey.

Roberts, D. F., & Foehr, U. C. (2004). *Kids & media in America*. Cambridge, MA: Cambridge University Press.

Robertson, R. (1994). Globalization or globalization? *The Journal of International Communication, 1*(1), 33–52.

Rogers, C. R. (1961). *On becoming a person: A therapist's view of psychotherapy*. Boston: Houghton Mifflin.

Rogers, C. R. (1969a). *Freedom to learn*. Columbus, OH: Charles E. Merrill Publishers.

Rogers, C. R. (1969b). *A view of what education might become*. Columbus, OH: C.E. Merrill Books.

Rogers, C. R., & Stevens, B. (1967). *Person to person: The problem of being human—a new trend in psychology*. Lafayette, CA: Real People Press.

Rolandelli, D. R. (1989). Children and television: The visual superiority effect reconsidered. *Journal of Broadcasting and Electronic Media, 33*(1), 69–81.

Ross, K., & Byerly, C. M. (2004). *Women and media: International perspectives*. Oxford, Ebgland: Blackwell.

Schramm, W., Lyle, J. & Parker, D. E. (1961). *Television in the lives of our children*. Stanford, CA: Stanford University Press.

Schroder, K. C. (1994). Audience semiotics, interpretive communities and the 'ethnographic turn' in media research. *Media, Culture and Society, 16*(2), 337–343.

Schütz, A. (1967). *The phenomenology of the social world*. Evanston, IL: Northwestern University Press.

Seidler, V. J. (1997). *Man enough: Embodying masculinities*. London: Sage.

Seiter, E. (1999). Power rangers at preschool: Negotiating media in child care settings. In M. Kinder (Ed.), *Kids' media culture* (pp. 239–262). Durham, NC: Duke University Press.

Signorielli, N. (2001). Television's gender role images and contribution to stereotyping. Past, present, future. In D. Singer & J. L. Singer (Eds.), *Handbook of children and the media* (pp. 341–358). Thousand Oaks, CA: Sage Publications.

Singer, D. G. (1993). Creativity of children in a television world. In G. L. Berry & J. K. Asamen (Eds.), *Children & television: Images in a changing sociocultural world* (pp. 73–86). Newbury Park, CA: Sage Publications.

Singer, D. G., & Singer, J. L. (Eds.). (2001). *Handbook of children and the media*. Thousand Oaks, CA: Sage Publications.

Singer, J. L. (1975). *The inner world of daydreaming*. New York: Harper & Row.

Singer, J. L. (1980). The power and limitation of television: A cognitive-affective analysis. In P. H. Tannenbaum (Ed.), *The entertainment functions of television* (pp. 31–65). Hillsdale, NJ: Lawrence Erlbaum Associates.

Singer, D. G., & Singer, J. L. (1990). *The house of make-believe*. Cambridge, MA: Harvard University Press.

Singer, J. L., & Singer, D. G. (1976). Can TV stimulate imaginative play? *Journal of Communication, 26*, 74–80.

Singer, J. L., & Singer, D. G. (1981). *Television, imagination, and aggression: A study of preschoolers*. Hillsdale, NJ: Lawrence. Erlbaum Associates.

Singer, J. L., & Singer, D. G. (1983). Implications of childhood television viewing for cognition, imagination and emotion. In J. Bryant and D. R. Anderson (Eds.), *Children's understanding of television: Research on attention and comprehension*. New York: Academic Press.

Singer, J. L., Singer, D. G., & Rapaczynski, W. S. (1984). Children's imagination as predicted by family patterns and television viewing: A longitudinal study. *Genetic Psychology Monographs, 110*, 43–69.

Singer, J. L., & Switzer, E. (1980). *Mindplay: The creative uses of fantasy*. Englewood Cliffs, NJ: Prentice Hall.

Stein, A. H., & Friedrich, L. K. (1972). Television content and younger children's beavior. In J. P. Murray, E. A. Rubinstein & G. A. Comstock (Eds.), *Television and social behavior, Vol. 2: Television and social learning, Surgeon General's Report* (pp. 203–317). Washington, DC: US Government Printing Office.

Strauch, I. (2004). *Träume im übergang von der kindheit ins jugendalter* [Dreams on the way from childhood to adolescence]. Bern: Verlag Hans Huber.

Strauss, A., & Corbin, J.(1994). Grounded theory methodology: An overview. In N. Denzin & Y. Lincoln (Eds.), *Handbook of qualitative research* (pp. 273–285). Thousand Oaks, CA: Sage Publications.

Taylor, M. (1999). *Imaginary companions and the children who create them*. Oxford: Oxford University Press.

Teichman, Y. (2001). The development of Israeli children's images of Jews and Arabs and their expression in human figure drawings. *Developmental Psychology, 37*(6), 749–761.

Teichman, Y., & Zafrir, H. (2003). Images held by Jewish and Arab children in Israel of people representing their own and the other groups. *Journal of Cross-Cultural Psychology, 34*(6), 658–676.

Thorne, B. (1993). *Gender play: Girls and boys in school*. Buckingham, England: Open University Press.

Tobin, J. (2000). *"Good guys don't wear hats": Children's talk about the media*. New York: Teachers College, Columbia University.

Tobin, J. (2004). *Pikachu's global adventure: The rise and fall of Pokémon*. Durham, NC: Duke University Press.

Tseelon, E. (1995). *The masque of femininity: The presentation of woman in everyday life*. London: Sage.

Tufte, B., Lavender, T., & Lemish, D. (Eds.). (2003). *Media education around the globe: Policies and practices*. Newark, NJ: Hampton Press.

United States General Accounting Office. (2000, September) *"Commercial Activities in Schools," Report to Requesters*. (Report No. GAO/HEHS-00-156).

Valkenburg, P. M. (2001). Television and the child's developing imagination. In D. G. Singer & J. L. Singer, (Eds.), *Handbook of children and the media* (pp. 121–134) Thousand Oaks, CA: Sage Publications.

Valkenberg, P. M., & van der Voort, T. H. A (1994). Influence of TV on daydreaming and creative imagination: A review of research. *Psychological Bulletin, 116*, 316–339.

Vande Berg, L. R., & Wenner, L. A. (Eds.). (1991). *Television criticism: Approaches and applications*. New York: Longman.

Van der Voort, T. H. A., & Valkenburg, P. M. (1994). Television's impact on fantasy play: A review of research. *Developmental Review, 14*, 27–51.

Van der Voort, T. H. A. (1986). *Television violence: A child's-eye view*. Amsterdam: North-Holland.

Van Evra, J. (1990). *Television and child development*. Hillsdale, NJ: Lawrence Erlbaum Associates.

Van Zoonen, L. (1994). *Feminist media studies*. Thousand Oaks, CA: Sage.

Wartella, E. (2002). New directions in media reseach and media effects on children. *Australian Symposium on "The Eyes of the Child: The World They'll See in the 21ˢᵗ Century."* Available at Dramaticonline.com

Wartella, E., & Reeves, B. (1985). Historical trends in research on children and the media: 1900–1960. *Journal of Communication, 35*(2), 6–21.

Wasko, J. (2001). *Understanding Disney*. Cambridge, England: Polity Press.

Wasko, J., Phillips, M., & Meehan, E. R. (Eds.). (2001). *Dazzled by Disney?: A global Disney audiences project*. London: Leicester University Press.

Williams, T. M. (Ed.). (1986). *The impact of television: A natural experiment in three communities*. New York: Academic Press.

Winn, M. (1977). *The plug-in drug*. New York: Viking Press.

Winn, M. (2002). *The plug-in drug: Television, computer, and family life*. New York: Penguin Press.

Winter, R., & Neubauer, G. (1998). *Kompetent, authentisch und normal? Aufklärungsrelevante Gesundheitsprobleme, Sexualaufklärung und Beratung von Jungen. Eine qualitative Studie im Auftrag der BZgA* [Competent, authentic, and normal? Health problems connected with education, sex education and counseling of boys. A qualitative Study commissioned by the German Federal Center for Health Education BZgA]. Bundeszentrale für gesundheitliche Aufklärung (BZgA)—Abteilung Sexualaufklärung, Verhütung und Familienplanung [Ed. BZgA-Fachheftreihe. 14]. Köln: BZgA.

Winter, R., & Neubauer, G. (2001). *Dies und Das. Das Variablenmodell "balanciertes Junge-und Mannsein" als Grundlage für die pädagogische Arbeit mit Jungen und Männern* [This and that. The model of variables "balanced being a boy and a man" as the basis for pedagogical work with boys and men]. Tübingen: Neuling.

Witt, S. (2000). The influence of television on children's gender role socialisation. *Childhood Education, 76*(5), 322–324.

Wolf, N. (1991). *The beauty myth*. New York: Doubleday.

Wolf, N. (1997). *Promiscuities: The secret struggle of womanhood*. New York: Random House.

Child Index

Media Texts Index

Author Index

Subject Index

A

Accommodation, 7–8
Action-adventure, 90, 152–153
Aesthetics, 83, 98–99, 119, 138, 184
Aggression, 7, 37, 124, 135, 138, 149, 200
American Dream, 182
Americanization,193
Amusement, 43–44, 50–51, 60, 65, 67–68,
      78, 85, 114–115, 122, 139, 143,
      147, 197
   park, 50–51, 68, 78, 122, 139
Antecedent variables, 28
Appearance, 21, 27, 72, 88–90, 93,
      117–119, 128, 130, 132, 148,
      201
Assimilation, 7–8
Audience, 152–153, 201
   child, 56, 63, 73, 84, 92, 118, 129, 182

B

Beautification, 117, 147
Book, 23, 38, 79, 81–82, 100, 102–104,
      121, 131, 152, 173, 179,
      186–187, 190–191, 200
   see also Media-Texts Index
Boy Code, 135
Boyhood, 137, 148

C

Categorization, 39–40, 83
Catharsis, 7
Childhood, xi, 5, 7, 16, 20, 100, 113,
      178–179
Christian, 30, 32, 60, 68, 77, 119, 123,
      133, 137, 165, 167
Christianity, 31
Class (school), 73, 82, 91, 105, 107
Class (status), 32, 73, 151–152
Cognition, 5
Cognitive development, 7, 20
Community, 47, 71, 93, 121, 140, 183
   European, 30
   imagined, 192
Comprehension, 12
Computer(s), 23, 29, 134, 176–178, 187,
      189, 191, 198
   game, 4, 38, 68, 81–82, 88, 96, 99–100,
      144–145, 152, 173, 175–177,
      186, 188–189, 200
Concrete operations, 20
Conflict, 38–39, 43–44, 48–49, 51, 60, 65,
      67, 79, 106, 113–115, 122–123,
      135, 137, 139, 142–143, 147,
      149, 153, 163, 166, 168, 176,
      197, 201–203
   Israeli-Palestinian, 31, 192
Confucian, 31, 172–173, 179